# Best Hikes Seattle

Simple Strolls, Day Hikes, and Longer Adventures

Third Edition

## Peter Stekel

**FALCON**GUIDES

GUILFORD, CONNECTICUT

*This edition is dedicated to my dear friend from
Sequoia National Park, Annie Esperanza.*

# FALCONGUIDES®

An imprint of The Rowman & Littlefield Publishing Group, Inc.
4501 Forbes Blvd., Ste. 200
Lanham, MD 20706
www.rowman.com
Falcon and FalconGuides are registered trademarks and Make Adventure Your Story is a trademark of The Rowman & Littlefield Publishing Group, Inc.

Distributed by NATIONAL BOOK NETWORK

Photos by Peter Stekel, Carl Gronquist (pg. 173), Parker Lee Torres (pg. 210), and Jennie Goldberg (pg. 262)
Maps by Tim Kissel; map corrections by Melissa Baker

British Library Cataloguing in Publication Information available

**Library of Congress Cataloging-in-Publication Data**
Names: Stekel, Peter, author.
Title: Best hikes Seattle : simple strolls, day hikes, and longer
   adventures / Peter Stekel.
Description: Third edition. | Guilford, Connecticut : Falcon Guides, [2021]
   | Includes index.
Identifiers: LCCN 2021011893 (print) | LCCN 2021011894 (ebook) | ISBN
   9781493043262 (trade paperback) | ISBN 9781493043279 (epub)
Subjects: LCSH: Hiking–Washington (State)–Seattle Metropolitan
   Area–Guidebooks. | Seattle Metropolitan Area (Wash.)–Guidebooks.
Classification: LCC GV199.42.W22 S4274 2021  (print) | LCC GV199.42.W22
   (ebook) | DDC 796.5109797/772–dc23
LC record available at https://lccn.loc.gov/2021011893
LC ebook record available at https://lccn.loc.gov/2021011894

# Contents

**Overview**

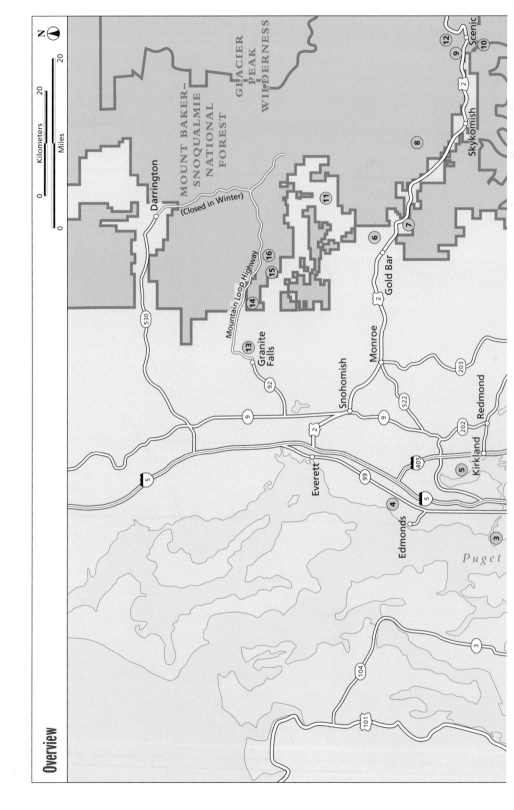

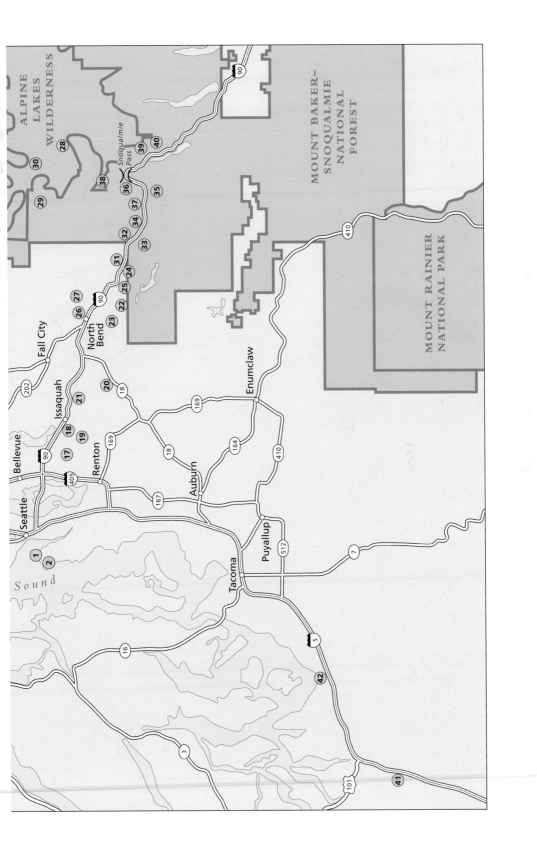

# Acknowledgments

*"In wildness is the preservation of the world."*

—Henry David Thoreau

I walked every one of these trails. No doubt about it. Dawn Meekhof and/or Michele Hinatsu walked nearly every one of them with me. So did Peter Hesslein during many of the hikes made for the third-edition revisions. My thanks to these friends for helping make the miles pass with good company, good humor, and good conversation. Jennie Goldberg, Laurel Hansen, Victor Kress, Elizabeth "Boo" Turner, Neil Gitkind, and Karen George also accompanied me on some of the trails for this book.

The best part about hiking is hiking with a companion. Thanks also to all of my hiking partners over the years, especially Rich Stowell, Gregg Fauth, Tommy James, Alice Goldberg, Bill Tweed, Scott Atkinson, Katie O'Hara, Susan Buis, Jim and Bronwyn Buntine plus replicates Dougal and Kate, Ken Corathers, Steven Jacobs, Margaret Hill Stowell, Bob Specht, Ronnee Helzner, Garrett Munger, Les Chow, Peggy Moore, Sylvia Haultain, Nate Stephenson, Janet and Ken Cermak, Elizabeth Hurley, Lois Charles, Susan McGrath, Stan Bluhm, Sheri Margolis, Rich Christian, Dan Rucci, Dixon Davis, Sylvia and Peter Jones, Jim Meadowcroft, Elana Lombard, Sandy Borg, and everybody at Camp Wolverton BSA and Post 90–Pacific Palisades, along with scientists and naturalists at Sequoia & Kings Canyon National Parks. You have made thousands of trail miles fun, exciting, and educational.

Every writer stands on the backs of giants. Therefore, I want to acknowledge those writers of previous guidebooks. They came first and did most of the hard work: Ron Adkinson, Joan Burton, Bob Dreisbach, Harvey Manning, Mike McQuaide, Marge and Ted Mueller, Craig Romano, Jeff Smoot, Bob and Ira Spring, Bryce Stevens, Karen Sykes, Andrew Weber, Robert L. Wood, and John Zilly. Forgive me if I have forgotten anyone.

Without the people who pushed to create the parks colloquially known as the Issaquah Alps or the US Congress to create the Wild Sky and Alpine Lakes Wilderness Areas, many of the trails in this book would not be very attractive for hiking. Thank you, all of you, for your time, effort, and vision. Also, thanks to American Whitewater for their work in helping to extend protection to the Wild Sky Wilderness and for keeping our rivers free and flowing. Thank you to my editor at FalconGuides, John Burbidge, for shepherding yet another version of *Best Hikes Seattle* to fruition. I appreciate the fine work done by Tim Kissel and Melissa Baker on the maps you see in this third edition of *Best Hikes Seattle*. Melissa Hayes did an excellent job of copyediting. I'm especially grateful for the flexibility of Emily Chiarelli, associate production editor with The Rowman & Littlefield Publishing Group.

Thank you to Tom O'Keefe and Scott Silver for your past contributions to earlier editions of this book. I also want to thank Kevin Callahan for everything he has

*A hiker rests along the Robe Canyon Trail (#14).*

taught me about music because it's the same thing as art, which is the same thing as writing. And you would be amazed to know how much hiking is like art.

This book, like all my others, would never have happened without the love and support of Jennie Goldberg.

# Preface to the Second Edition

The grace of a second edition is that it allows an author the opportunity to recognize and correct any errors occurring in the first. In this edition of *Best Hikes Near Seattle*, I was able to correct typos and misspellings, and update trail parking pass requirements (for the Northwest Forest Pass and Discover Pass), phone numbers, e-mail addresses, and website addresses. Some factual errors have been repaired as well, and the resource list in Appendix A has been updated, as has the Further Reading list in Appendix B. Important information about the Middle Fork Snoqualmie Road project and the new Wild Sky Wilderness has also been added.

Owners of the previous edition of *Best Hikes Near Seattle* should consider upgrading to this one. The text of the entire book has been reviewed and updated as well as rewritten in many places. The introductory text has been enlarged, and the section on wilderness restrictions and regulations has been updated. A new section covering the Northwest Forest Pass and Discover Pass has been added. Though trails are unlikely to change in any significant way, trail access, trailheads, and roads *are* frequently modified. Therefore, trail access, trailhead descriptions, and driving directions have been checked and updated where necessary. There are many new photos.

The purpose of *Best Hikes Near Seattle* remains unchanged—introducing both new and long-term hikers of the region to trails that are approximately 60 minutes or 60 miles from downtown Seattle. But the author believes there is more to hiking than shuffling your boots down the trail. That's why there are so many sidebars describing the natural history of our area and that's why the introduction is so descriptive. It should never be enough to simply be on a trail; hikers should know something about the landscapes through which they traverse.

Happy trails to you!

Peter Stekel
Seattle, WA
May 2015

# Preface to the Third Edition: A New Title, Some New Hikes, and Still Lots of Great Information!

Time waits for no one, time marches on, and time takes time to be time. Time, time, time . . . See what's become of us! No matter how you think of time, it's always messing around with us and changing our world. So it is with hiking guides as well.

Since the second edition of this book appeared in 2015, three of its trails have disappeared fully or in part, and another is in similar danger. Because of this, those four trails have been removed from this edition of *Best Hikes Seattle* (new title!) and have been replaced with other trails. In addition, introductory information has been updated, new and fresh photos have been added, and errors have been corrected.

The completion of the Middle Fork Snoqualmie Road project opened up new recreation possibilities in that area, followed by a heavy winter storm that promptly closed the road long-term 7.2 miles east of the Mailbox Peak trailhead. More on this later!

Trailhead data for every hike has been checked and revised where necessary. This usually involves documenting the addition of paved parking lots and the installation of vault toilets where no pavement or toilets previously existed. Some trails have rerouted sections or name changes. Trail resources and permitting data, along with contact info, have been checked and updated.

As 2020 kicked into gear, the COVID-19 pandemic had a serious and significant impact on land management agencies and, hence, access to our trails and public lands. As of press time, we are still sifting through the ramifications of COVID-19. When you read these words in *Best Hikes Seattle*, you will know more about the impacts of COVID-19 than I did when they were written.

Nevertheless, I hope to see you all on these trails!

Peter Stekel
Seattle, WA
December 2020

# Introduction

In spite of many things—homes and highways, factories and farms, an expanding population—the Pacific Northwest retains the same allure that first pulled people here from all over the world during the nineteenth century: the impression of limitless space from the shores of Puget Sound and on into deep green forests and beyond; a feeling that anything is possible here—fame, success, wealth, a life of accomplishment and purpose.

To all this, add the attraction of vast outdoor recreational opportunities available to people of all skill levels or experience. Places to hike, bike, climb, ski, kayak, and canoe can be found in every direction. Because of their proximity, the Cascade Mountains, Alpine Lakes Wilderness, and the Wild Sky Wilderness can feel like one extended backyard playground. From the greater Seattle area, it's possible to find yourself on many wonderful hiking trails within 60 minutes or 60 miles of leaving the

*Many of Seattle's best hikes are within the Mount Baker–Snoqualmie National Forest.*

city. Welcome to the heavenly Pacific Northwest! When all superlatives are exhausted, it's nice to realize that, even for a city, Seattle is a beautiful place situated within a gorgeous setting. Now, if somebody could only do something about solving Seattle's traffic and transit problems!

With all the possible outdoor sports and activities to divert a person's attention, hiking remains the easiest and least expensive. Of course, it's possible to spend hundreds of dollars on boots, and another few hundred dollars on the latest, greatest rain jacket, clothing, and day pack, but you can get by just fine with less. Really. No special equipment is necessary, and, as long as the weather and terrain are not extreme, a simple backpack, sturdy shoes with ankle support, comfortable pants or shorts, and some warm clothing are all you need to get started. This makes hiking a fantastic way for people to jump into outdoor recreation. Today, as in the past, hiking is an egalitarian activity—which is why it continues to have such broad support and interest among all ages and backgrounds of people.

▶ **Seattle is a beautiful city in a gorgeous setting, with opportunities available in every direction to hike, bike, climb, ski, kayak, and canoe.**

## Weather

Seattle is a great place to live. Some think we live in a perpetual hazy shade of winter. That isn't anywhere close to true. Our climate is perfect. With mild winter temperatures, cool summers, and summer drought, it's possible to play outside nearly every day of the year. Sure, it rains here once in a while, but 36 inches a year (measured at SeaTac International Airport) isn't that much! Nobody ever talks about how much it rains annually in Mobile, Alabama (60 inches); Miami, Florida (49 inches); or Houston, Texas (44 inches). Even Boston (40 inches) and New York City (39 inches) get more rain than Seattle. Of course, there's the Hoh Rain Forest in Olympic National Park (145 inches), but let's face it, that's why it's called a rain forest!

Though our climate may be perfect, the same can't be said for our weather. Our average number of rainy days (158), cloudy days (226), and days of sun (58) are what people really care about when they moan and groan about how much it rains in Seattle. October to March is the wet season in the Northwest; 67 percent of our rain falls between those months. July and August are the driest; November to February, the wettest. Seasonal Affective Disorder (SAD) is a big worry for people who require more sunlight than the sun is able to provide during the short days of winter. Some people even take vitamin D supplements and use SAD lights.

Because of topography, where all this rain and cloud measuring is done becomes very important. Precipitation and sky cover increase from west to east. And with elevation, all that rain turns to snow. So places like North Bend (along I-90) with 60 inches and Monroe (along US 2) with 47 inches of precipitation are wetter and cloudier than Seattle. It behooves hikers to pay attention to what is going on in these two towns, since they are central to many hikes in this book. Referring to the

*Seattle's mild climate means hiking can be done year-round—even in the rain.*

Washington State Department of Transportation website for road conditions is a good way to check on the weather. To get started, point your browser to www.wsdot .com/traffic.

All the latest weather conditions and forecasts for the Seattle area are available at www.wrh.noaa.gov and www.accuweather.com. National Oceanic and Atmospheric Administration (NOAA) weather radio is also available for conditions and forecasts. Radios that pick up only the NOAA broadcast can be purchased at any consumer electronics store or online (do a search for "NOAA Weather Radio").

Hikers in our area should be aware of a phenomenon called the "Puget Sound Convergence Zone." Weather coming in from the Pacific Ocean is split by the Olympic Mountains. Some weather flows south, through Chehalis Gap, where the Chehalis River runs into the ocean. Some more weather flows north, through the Strait of Juan de Fuca. The Cascades create an eastward barrier, redirecting the two weather flows through Puget Sound. When the two opposing currents collide (from Everett to Tacoma), the air rises, cools, and produces locally heavy rain or snow.

There's a saying that climate is what you want and weather is what you get. Ah, for those mild winters and cool, dry summers! And that's why everybody keeps talking about our "liquid sunshine" and "sun breaks." As all Seattle dwellers joke, it only rains twice a year here: August to April and May to July. And the significance of daylight saving time can't be ignored—it gives us an extra hour of rain. Optimistic hikers can always be recognized by the sun visor on their rain hat. We don't live in the Pacific Northwest—we live in the Pacific *Northwet*. People here develop an orange cast during the winter; some call it rust!

Everybody talks about the weather, but nobody does anything about it. Still, skiers don't let little things like snowstorms get in the way of having a good time, and hikers don't see any reason to stay at home when it's raining. The hiking season in Seattle never ends. It's that topographical thing again—there is always some place to go that will be warmer or drier than somewhere else, even in winter. Sure, the sweltering months of July and August (average high temperature of 75 degrees Fahrenheit) bring the evil yellow sky orb bearing down on us. The orb creates an occasional heat wave that drives temperatures into the barely survivable upper 80s or lower 90s—Fahrenheit, that is. Temperatures like that propel the less-serious hikers out of their homes and into the hills. But the real fun is had when the "bad" weather arrives.

Embrace the rain and inclement weather because it's always going to be a factor when hiking in the Pacific Northwest. There are advantages. Popular places see fewer people on rainy days—though plenty of folk aren't hesitant about going then. Rainy days present great opportunities for leaving stuffy houses. A wet autumn hike means not having to share any huckleberries on the trail—except with the usual tooth-and-claw forest dwellers. All the fall colors are yours and yours alone to enjoy. And at the end of the day, no matter how wet you are, you can always go home and take a hot shower and drink a hot toddy. The Boy Scout adage of "Be Prepared" is a wise admonishment for wet weather. Bring along the best rain gear you can afford, and carry additional warm (and dry) clothes along with plenty of food and energy snacks. Wrap them all up in a plastic garbage bag, shove it into your pack, and be on your way! Keep a dry change of clothes in your car—just in case.

## Trail Etiquette

In any kind of weather, it's considered rude to pass fellow hikers without some friendly greeting. We're all on this blue orb together, so let's make the best of it and acknowledge one another's presence with a "Hello." Maybe even stop to chat. If the person you encounter is plugged into their music machine and can't hear you, eye contact and a nod of the head go a long way in lieu of a verbal greeting.

When proceeding down the trail, it's considered polite to yield to the poor souls huffing and puffing up. Sometimes hikers laboring against gravity will graciously

# GOING TO THE BATHROOM IN THE WOODS

After you leave the parking lot, the likelihood of finding a toilet diminishes. So what happens if you're halfway up the trail and hear the call of nature?

Some believe in digging a hole. Others disagree, believing that critters come by and dig it up, and claim that it's better to scatter some forest duff over the pile. No matter what your philosophy, an important question is, what happens to the toilet paper? How often have you looked behind a boulder or large tree and found a sodden wad of toilet paper poking out from beneath a rock? Somebody evidently had some business back there before walking off, contented. Now here you are a few hours or a day or a week later, and the paper is still there.

There is a better way. Put the used TP in a plastic bag inside a paper lunch sack and take it home with you. At home, flush the TP down the toilet to the side sewer—to the trunk line, to the main line to the sewage treatment plant at West Point in Magnolia. Let Metro take over from there. Your bags can go into the trash.

Something else to keep in mind: Locate your personal toilet at least 100 feet from lakes, rivers, and creeks. Try to stay that far away from trails, viewpoints, and obviously desirable rest or lunch spots, too. And remember what your mother taught you: Afterward, wash your hands. If no water is available (and, of course, you would *never* use soap in a stream or lake, would you?), hand sanitizer works. Look in the travel section of your local pharmacy, and you'll be able to purchase a 1-ounce bottle of hand sanitizer that you can carry in your day pack.

(even gratefully) take the initiative and stop, permitting speedy downhillers to zoom by. This brief respite also allows an opportunity for breath catching, pack strap adjusting, weary bone resting, and snack ingesting. Particularly at these times, a cheery greeting or smile is always appreciated from passing hikers.

Trails are designed and built to high standards, and cutting switchbacks is not only impolite but expensive to repair. Erosion is encouraged when many feet follow the initial insult. All this hastens the demise of that section of trail, which will then require somebody to return with rakes and shovels and other implements of construction to repair what has been so inconsiderately wrought.

If you must hike while plugged in to music, keep the volume down. You may not care much for your eardrums, but there are others on the trail who appreciate either conversing with their friends or being alone within the silence of their thoughts. Some trails are popular with runners; make way for them and marvel at how they always seem to avoid falling or breaking an ankle.

We all need rest from time to time. Try to find a place off the trail. If this isn't possible and you must sit on the trail, keep your feet, legs, and backpacks from dangling in the path where they might encumber other hikers or cause them to trip, stumble, and fall.

When catching up to other hikers, whether you are going up or down the hill, if they do not hear the tramp-tramp-tramp of your feet, a slight clearing of the throat or an "Excuse me" is usually enough to get them to step aside and allow you to pass.

The arrival of COVID-19 protocols has made these sorts of behaviors challenging. Seeing hikers approach from up the trail, people begin stepping out of the way to maintain their 6 feet of physical distance while drawing up face masks. It is challenging, but not impossible. Hikers still find ways to be friendly and polite and engage in conversation.

## Dogs

The USDA Forest Service requires that all dogs on trails be kept on a 6-foot leash at all times. A tight leash will not present a trip wire to other hikers. A leashed dog will eliminate the need to pull fighting dogs apart and also is a kindness extended to your fellow travelers who are walking without a pet. Controlling your dog also keeps your pet from chasing or harassing wildlife or running off, maybe never to be seen again. There is a pretty stiff fine if you are

*Woman's best friend needs conditioning hikes, too.*

caught failing to follow the leash rule. During the summer it is common to find rangers patrolling the popular trails as well as checking cars for Northwest Forest Passes.

The Forest Service asks that you be kind to your pet. Familiarize yourself with trail situations that can be hazardous for a dog. Update all vaccinations, and provide flea and tick control. If you and your dog should become separated, make sure your pet has identification. Dogs, like people, need to build up their endurance before attempting a long hike. People wear shoes; dogs obviously don't. Trails contain sharp rocks that can tear a dog's feet. When you stop to eat or drink, share your bounty with Rover.

*Be kind to other hikers and clean up after your dog.*

Dog lovers should check out *Best Hikes with Dogs in Western Washington* by Dan Nelson. It's a bit outdated but remains the best local resource for places to hike with your dog.

Be kind to other hikers. Keep Fido or Fifi under control—and pick up after your pet.

## What to Bring

It is popular to list the "Ten Essentials" of what hikers must carry in their pack. Of course, one person's essential is another's not-so-essential. Birdwatchers (in the UK they're called "twitchers," which sounds so much more amusing!) won't leave home without binoculars and a bird book. You can't botanize without a field guide for our flora. Can't angle without a pole and lures (does anyone use bait anymore?). Can't take photographs without a camera (bring extra batteries and memory cards for digital cameras).

As far as what survival gear to carry, a day hiker may need less than a backpacker. Shorter, simpler trails might require a shorter list of essentials. A walk to Weeks Falls (#24) requires significantly less of everything than a hike to nearby Twin Falls (#25), which in turn demands less than an overnight backpacking trip to Snoqualmie Lake (#30), which needs less than a multiday trip, and ... you get the point. Even the "hard-core" survival list of essentials is debatable. The "Ten Essentials," like Hemingway's *Moveable Feast*, is a moving target.

For instance, a compass and topographic map are always listed as an essential. But how useful are they when the person carrying the map and compass doesn't know how to use them? At their worst, many people can find north using a compass but have no idea what declination is (and how to correct for it) or how to place themselves onto a map. Making the leap from three dimensions (the real world) to two dimensions (a topo map) takes knowledge, training, and experience. And if you don't know where you are, a map and compass aren't going to help. For them to work, you need to have a starting point—a datum.

The uninitiated might think that hauling around a GPS eliminates the need for map and compass skills, since it will provide a datum—your location—at all times. Ignoring the technological weaknesses of GPS (interference, issues with accuracy, need for batteries, must be kept out of water), it's important to note that having a datum doesn't mean you know how to get from where you are to where you want to be. That still takes, at least, a map. A GPS can provide the map as well as waypoints, a route, or a track, but the user still must know how to read it.

And what about apps? There are several that will provide you with trails, routes, and descriptive text. If you use any of them, make sure you download all the data at home before hitting the trail because Internet access is not guaranteed once you leave town.

The most essential of essentials is intangible. It's what you heard from your mother your whole life: "Use your head!" Many problems in the outdoors can be obviated by paying attention, being prepared for weather, being familiar with the route, and knowing the time needed to complete it in plenty of daylight. Staying found is better than trying to find your way home when lost.

With all of this in mind, here is an extensive list of essentials. Select the ones that are best for a particular experience or situation. Leave behind the ones you feel are extraneous, can't afford, or don't know how to use.

Carry a liter of water (more on hot days), and don't forget to drink it. If your urine is not clear, frequent, and copious, you're not drinking enough. Bring food. Energy bars are good for snacks, but bring real food, too. Remember, hiking up McClellan Butte (#33) is not part of a diet plan. As mentioned earlier, if you are hiking with a dog, bring food and water for your pet as well.

Some sort of navigating device (see above) is preferable to hiking blind. *Best Hikes Seattle* contains trail descriptions and an area map along with GPS waypoints for trailheads. Consider this navigation guide as the barest of the barest and not the only guide.

A first-aid kit is nice to have but introduces its own set of essentials. People prone to blisters will want lots of moleskin and/or molefoam, and antiseptic. Hikers who regularly take medication should carry that with them, plus an extra dose or two in case they are late in getting home. Asthmatics will want to have inhalers with them.

*Happy hikers on Lake Dorothy Trail (#29 and #30)*

Allergic to bees and wasps? Don't forget your EpiPen (although EpiPens should be considered a last resort). Consult your physician or allergist about a regimen of desensitizing shots. Begin with the Northwest Asthma & Allergy Center (www.nwasthma .com).

Other first-aid kit items might include gauze pads (many purposes and functions), waterproof tape, scissors (for cutting gauze pads, tape, or bandages), Band-Aids (many sizes and shapes), antibacterial ointment (check expiration date), pencil and paper (for recording health data in case of serious injuries), fire starter, and oral thermometer. Over-the-counter medications to forestall the negative effects of hiking (stiff muscles and sore joints) are helpful. So is a pocketknife (leave the Bowie knife at home). This list is by no means exhaustive. Add or delete items according to what personal experience has taught you.

Though many hikes in this book are in deep forest, and it seems the sun never shines in the Pacific Northwest, sunglasses and sunscreen are excellent items to carry. So is a cap (with a bill), a hat (to keep your head warm), gloves, wool or fleece sweater, rain jacket (doubles as a windbreaker), small flashlight or headlamp (check the batteries), extra dry socks, a clean shirt for the drive home, toilet paper and extra plastic bags for waste, and a whistle. Add spare batteries for your GPS unit, too.

Put it all into a backpack and off you go!

As for what to wear when hiking, it's up to you. Some prefer shorts to long pants (shorts wearers should carry wind pants in case the temperature drops) and T-shirts

## GREEN TIP:

**Keep in mind that bear hunting starts in early August. Deer season opens mid-October across much of the state, and elk season opens at the end of the month. If you hear shooting, stop. Raise your voice to let hunters know you're near. While moving through the landscape, wear bright clothing. Talk while you walk to alert hunters of your presence. Or, turn around and find another place to walk.**

to long-sleeved sport shirts (to protect sun-sensitive bodies). Sun-protective shirts are easy to find these days; their protection is measured at "UPF" (ultraviolet protection factor) vs. SPF for sunblock. Sports bras give support and comfort for women. Single or double walking sticks help with steep or uneven stretches and serve to steady you on snow, talus, or stream crossings.

As for nonessentials, cell phones top the list—unless you're using the map function or reading an e-book version of *Best Hikes Seattle*! Few things are more annoying to the rest of us than hearing someone deep in a telephone conversation while hiking. Besides, unless you're hiking at Tiger, Cougar, or Rattlesnake Mountains or around Mount Si and North Bend, cell phones aren't likely to work. Go ahead and carry one if you feel you need to, but please turn it off, or put it in airplane mode, and save the battery just in case you really do need it for the drive home.

Another nonessential, as far as I'm concerned, is any sort of music player. If your need for being plugged in to your own private soundtrack is that important, there isn't much need to be outdoors. Hiking is more than just exercise—it involves using all your senses. Don't close off your ears. And certainly don't shut down your brain.

## More on Maps

Every responsible hiker carries topographic maps whether they understand how to read the contour lines or not. For the Snoqualmie Pass area, Tiger, Cougar, and Rattlesnake Mountain and Mount Si, the large-detail Green Trails maps can't be beat. For other areas, US Geological Survey (USGS) 7.5-minute quadrangle maps are great for topographic detail. Regular Green Trails maps work well for geographic and cultural details and trail delineation and mileage; their major weakness is being larger-scale than USGS maps. Whichever you use, and a case can be made for carrying both, they are superior to sketch maps such as the ones appearing in this book. This guide's maps are intended solely to give hikers an overview of the area covered in the text and for trip planning.

The Alpine Lakes Protection Society (ALPS) publishes a shaded-relief topographic map that covers most of the hikes in this book. Its larger scale means it isn't as detailed as a USGS or Green Trails map, but it does have the distinct advantage of covering a huge amount of territory. For that reason alone, it's a map well worth carrying. You'll certainly want to keep a copy at home for planning purposes.

## The "Art" of Mileage

Without pushing a wheel equipped with an odometer, computing trail mileage is an art, not a science—and a tricky art at that. There is what you see on trail signs, what you see written on maps, what you read in guidebooks, what your GPS unit says, and what your own internal odometer tells you is the distance between points. Sometimes the numbers jibe. More often, they don't. Occasionally the numbers can be disturbingly, even amusingly, different.

It's best to take all published mileages with a grain of salt, or maybe even a pinch. Plan hikes by consulting maps and by relying on past experience of what you can (and can't) do for a given type of distance and terrain. Five miles on the Iron Goat Trail (#12), which is mostly flat, will expend less time and effort and be kinder to your body than an equal distance that also gains 4,000 vertical feet, such as the hike up Mount Si (#27)!

Mileages in this book are based on GPS readings taken during each hike using a Garmin GPSmap 76CSx and WGS 84 map data. In some cases this information varied greatly from trail markers, Green Trails maps, and the bulk of other published sources. In those instances, the GPS data were tossed out in favor of majority rule.

Most of the base maps for the first edition of *Best Hikes Seattle* were generated by the Garmin GPSmap 76CSx and downloaded to a Dell 8250 PC with 1.5 GB of RAM, running Windows XP and Garmin base map software. This third edition of *Best Hikes Seattle* made use of a Dell XPS PC with 16 GB of RAM and updated or new maps were rendered using the online mapping tool GPS Visualizer. The maps were then provided in hard copy or PDF to a graphic artist who drew the final maps, including roads and place names determined to be essential in helping the reader make decisions or identify important landmarks.

## Getting More Information on Where to Hike

You'll find that the trails in *Best Hikes Seattle* are generally either within 60 miles or 60 minutes of downtown Seattle. With the Internet, it's hard to find any hike in the Seattle area that isn't mentioned at least once on a website like www.wta .org or somewhere else, including the US Forest Service Mount Baker–Snoqualmie National Forest website.

So why publish a book when everything is potentially available online?

Getting a group of hikes together in a compendium that facilitates decision-making is the best reason for a hiking guide. Searching the web by hike name and sorting through thousands of hits is a tedious and sometimes unrewarding process. The Internet works best if you already know the name or location of a hike. For people new to an area and with no geographical knowledge, nothing beats a book— and you can take it along with you (either in traditional print form or as an e-book).

Is another hiking book for the Seattle area really needed? Does it make sense to revise a hiking book? Aren't there already dozens of hiking guides for the region?

Have the trails changed that much since the last book was published? Have the access points moved? The answers are yes, yes, yes, no, and no—at least, not a lot of them.

It's true. There are lots of hiking guides. You may already own several of them. I sure do! Hiking guides are highly individualized, and each reader finds something different to explore or discover based on each author's approach. Some writers prefer a historical approach; others feel the need to attack motorized recreation and resource extraction, while many prefer to focus on plants and animals.

*Best Hikes Seattle* has a different approach. Not only will you find the usual trail information and descriptions, but you will also find sections describing plants, animals, birds, and invertebrates. Unlike the typical trail guide, there is a lot to *read* in this book that has very little to do *specifically* with any particular trail. But reading these extra sidebars will help you understand what makes the hiking around Seattle so special and desirable. There are also some inspirational words about hiking scattered about to help, well, inspire you.

Most trails don't change much over the years, although they sometimes disappear due to logging activity, lack of use, poor maintenance, or from being washed away. The biggest changes over the years have to do with rules and regulations, access roads, toilets, and trailhead parking. Roads have been paved and vault toilets have been built. If you encounter other recent changes, please e-mail them to: editorial@falcon.com. We'd love to hear from you!

## Flora and Fauna

All but a few of the trails in *Best Hikes Seattle* stay below the mountain vegetation zones of Pacific silver fir and mountain hemlock and remain in the lowland Douglas fir and western hemlock forest. For the former, climb the high mountains and ridgetops to where trees refuse to grow. The latter zone is most familiar to hikers in the Seattle area, since it's the vegetation that surrounds where they live and work. Left to the land's own devices, from the shores of Puget Sound to a few hundred feet below Snoqualmie or Stevens Pass, the dominant trees would be Douglas fir, western hemlock, and western red cedar. Common shrubs in all zones include huckleberry, blackberry, Himalayan berry, blueberry, devil's club, stinging nettle, mahonia, sword fern, and salal. The most common tree associated with our conifer forests is the red alder.

Old-growth forest is not a type of vegetation but refers to the maturity level of a stand of trees. For instance, lowland forests begin assuming old-growth characteristics after 175

*Canada jays are inquisitive and will steal your lunch if you have left it unattended.*

# LITTLE BIRD, BIG MOUTH: THE PACIFIC WREN

When breeding season is done, most birds either fly the coop to sunnier climes or hunker down locally to quietly await the following spring. Not the Pacific wren (*Troglodytes pacificus*). Though rarely seen, this secretive little bird energetically sings year-round. It sounds like a squeaking monster gone haywire from too much coffee—producing a continuous stream of melodious notes and trills that lasts 5 to 10 seconds.

The Pacific wren is the only wren found outside the New World, occurring also in Europe, Asia, and North Africa. Males are polygynous (they have more than one mate) and often build "dummy" nests to draw away predators. Preferred nesting sites include natural cavities like old woodpecker holes, rocky crevices, under tree stumps, and within the roots of an upturned tree. They prefer dense coniferous forests. Persons lucky enough to see this 3- to 5-inch-tall bird will spot it teetering and bobbing, flitting about in low tangles of vegetation and around logs where it is searching for a meal of insects. The Pacific wren is reddish-brown with pink legs. The bill is short and thin.

Pacific wrens bring a spot of musical joy into our winter hikes.

to 250 years of growth and reach their prime between 350 and 750 years. Younger stands of trees lack the traits indicative of old-growth forests: large size, trees occurring in a mix of different ages and sizes, greater spacing between individuals, much woody debris on the ground and in the creeks, many snags (standing dead trees), and a shrub layer that can thrive in filtered sunlight.

Birds like the goshawk, northern spotted owl, and pileated woodpecker are more common in old-growth forests. So are northern flying squirrels, martens, and red tree voles.

Animals that hikers are likely to see, hear, or feel in the Seattle area include the American black bear, mule deer, elk, American robin, Pacific wren, raven, frog, deerfly, and mosquito.

## Restrictions and Regulations

Fires are prohibited above 4,000 feet on the west side of the Cascades and above 5,000 feet on the east side in the Mount Baker–Snoqualmie National Forest. Other forest areas may have fire restrictions due to high use and/or no fuel. Check for specific regulations pertaining to the area you plan to visit. Fires are highly restricted in city or county parks to supplied barbecue grates in picnic areas. No fires are allowed on any Washington State Department of Natural Resources land covered in this book.

Motorized and mechanized equipment are not allowed in the Mount Baker–Snoqualmie National Forest wilderness areas. This includes bicycles, carts, wagons, chain saws, hang gliders, drones, off-road vehicles and other wheeled vehicles, or landing

*Hiking appeals to all ages.*

aircraft. Air-dropping or picking up supplies, materials, or people are prohibited. There is a limit of twelve for a group, in any combination of people and pack and saddle animals. Groups exceeding twelve must divide into physically and logistically separate parties and maintain a minimum distance of 1-mile separation.

Hikers entering the Mount Baker–Snoqualmie National Forest Alpine Lakes Wilderness will need a Northwest Forest Pass in order to leave cars at trailheads. You are asked to self-register at trailheads and dangle a permit from your pack. Although many hikers are inclined to allow Rover to rove, dogs must be kept on a short leash. Regulations for the Wild Sky Wilderness are the same as for the Alpine Lakes Wilderness.

Camping with pack and saddle animals is allowed only at designated sites in the national forest and is prohibited in many other areas. Pack and saddle animals are not allowed within 200 feet of lakes except to get a drink or pass on a trail. Forage is poor throughout the region. It pays to check and confirm regulations and restrictions as it is your responsibility as a citizen of this great nation to know the law and reduce your personal impact on our public lands.

The most controversial restriction in the national forest is the Northwest Forest Pass. It's required by the Federal Lands Recreation Enhancement Act (FLREA). An outgrowth of the older Fee-Demo program, FLREA requires user fees from people who want to park their cars and recreate on federal land. For all the Mount Baker–Snoqualmie National Forest hikes described in this book, you will need a Northwest Forest Pass or risk an expensive citation.

In 1958, following the post–World War II popularity of spending time in the outdoors, the Outdoor Recreation Resource Review Commission proposed that recreation could be managed like any other industry. Prior to this, public-land visitors weren't viewed as representing an important, commercial market. Also, recreation on public lands wasn't seen as having exploitable commodity value. Later, during the Reagan administration, government began to see the outdoors not as a place where citizens ventured for the quiet contemplation of nature, but as a profit center for private enterprise catering to a consumer base. This philosophy culminated in the 1996 Recreation Fee–Demonstration Program.

During the Clinton administration there was a move away from logging, mining, and grazing on public lands and a move toward selling recreation instead. The trend since then has been to commercialize, motorize, and package fee-based experiences on America's public lands. For the working poor—whose weekly entertainment budget is stretched thin enough—these user fees can be profound. Once upon a time, our public lands were supported by our tax dollars and were free for all to use. This has become less and less the case.

Privatization has its proponents, and they all make a good case for it. Free-market capitalists think there should be no public lands at all since they compete with private landowners who could be providing the same services. Libertarians say public lands should be self-funded via user fees and from profits created by selling natural resources. The recreation industry expects privatization to benefit the products and services they manufacture, distribute, or provide.

Some suspect this move toward privatization has been encouraged by creative budgeting. Between 1994 and 1996 the Forest Service saw a slashing of its recreation budget. The agency was finally forced to admit that it had no money for recreation, and Congress agreed to implement temporary fees. Since then the Forest Service budget has increased but hasn't kept pace with inflation, deferred maintenance, and regional expenses. This leads many to believe that the fees are here to stay. Current experience justifies this belief.

Understandably finding itself in a perpetual funding crunch, the Forest Service has been forced to make recreation decisions based on what provides much-needed revenue. Hence, more emphasis has been placed on activities like RV camping, since those activities require more amenities and generate more money. Lost in the shuffle are those activities like hiking that cannot be managed to enhance revenue. As a result, many trails are not being maintained except by volunteers. If no volunteers exist, trails fall into disarray, disuse, and then disappear. The Washington Trails Association (WTA) and The Mountaineers run regular volunteer trail maintenance projects. Consider helping them out.

Fee-Demo and FLREA have never grossed more than $50 million in a year. On top of this, the Government Accountability Office (GAO) estimates that fee collection and enforcement of FLREA consumes 50 percent of the funds it generates. When private interests are allowed to control public land and turn it into a private, moneymaking operation, the inevitable result is that people who can't afford to pay are excluded from resources and the heritage that belongs to all of us.

Perhaps the answer to this quandary can be found in the original study done by the Outdoor Recreation Resource Review Commission in the 1950s. They suggested it was appropriate to charge a fee for some services on public lands (e.g., admission to national parks, use of campgrounds), while other uses should be free (access to national forests, hiking, primitive car camping, etc.). That seems like a more reasonable balance doesn't it?

## A Plethora of Trail Passes: Which One Do You Need?

Beginning in 2011 the State of Washington saw the wisdom of "pay-to-play" and began requiring a Discover Pass to use state park, Washington Department of Fish & Wildlife (WDFW), and Department of Natural Resources (DNR) land. The pass is a vehicle parking pass. If you park on private property and then walk onto state park, WDFW, or DNR land, the pass is not necessary. The Discover Pass is not valid at national forest trailheads, where you will need a Northwest Forest Pass. If you are caught using state lands without a Discover Pass, the penalty is $99. This penalty is reduced to $59 if an individual provides proof of purchase of the Discover Pass to the court within fifteen days after the notice of violation. Penalties are subject to change.

The Discover Pass can be used with two vehicles; there is space on the pass to write each vehicle's license plate number or phrase. You will need your Discover Pass for places like Tiger Mountain, Wallace Falls State Park, Mount Si and Little Si,

and Dirty Harry's Peak. The Discover Pass will set you back $30 for an annual pass or $10 for a one-day pass. Discover Passes can be purchased at many outdoor stores, other retailers, online, or when you renew your license tabs. Annoyingly, retailers add a "transaction fee" to the cost. There are plenty of user exemptions to the pass, such as being able to use a handicap placard at some sites. Lots more fine print to study can be found at www.discoverpass.wa.gov/faq/#buying.

If you already have a WDFW Pass, it can sometimes be used at certain sites requiring a Discover Pass. Check any reader board at the trailhead to be sure. These passes can be purchased online or at many outdoor retailers, especially those that specialize in hunting and fishing. A WDFW pass will set you back $32, and you can read all about it at https://fishhunt.dfw.wa.gov.

*To avoid a nasty fine, make sure you have the correct trail pass displayed in your vehicle before hitting the trail.*

Anywhere you go in the Mount Baker–Snoqualmie National Forest, you will need to pay $30 for an annual Northwest Forest Pass. Day passes are "generally" $5 according to the USFS Region 6 website. The Northwest Forest Pass is also valid in all Washington and Oregon national forests. The pass can be purchased at some trailheads and most outdoor stores. The fine for not using this pass is $75. Trailheads operated by the Forest Service will also accept other passes in lieu of a Northwest Forest Pass. If you are 62 or older, consider purchasing a lifetime "America the Beautiful, National Parks and Federal Recreational Lands Pass" (also called Interagency Pass) for $80 ($20 for an annual pass). It's valid on all federal public lands, nationwide. If under 62, the same pass (now called an Interagency Annual Pass) will cost you $80 yearly. Some places, like Mount St. Helens National Volcanic Monument, have their own pass. Read more about all of these different passes, including the free Interagency Annual Military Pass and the free Interagency Access Pass (for the disabled), as well as requirements and possible exemptions, at https://www.nps.gov/planyourvisit/passes.htm#CP_JUMP_5088574.

The reason given for needing a permit for all of these public lands is "budgetary." This is where one of the many tax-cutting / reduce-government-spending chickens has come home to roost. With the exception of gaining access to national parks (but not national monuments or historic or battlefield sites), it was only a generation ago when the public did not have to pay to use their public lands.

Some of the aggravation in having to buy the Northwest Forest Pass is the lack of physical improvement seen on any of the trails. If not for volunteers from the Washington Trails Association, The Mountaineers, and other groups who perform trail repair and construction, there would be no improvements visible at all. It appears that Northwest Forest Pass monies are either eaten up by administration, enforcement, and adjudication or the paving of trailhead parking lots and construction of vault toilets.

Nevertheless, the Forest Service maintains that "the majority—80–95 percent—of proceeds from recreation fees goes right back into maintaining and improving the trails, land and facilities you use most." They also say that "Most of this work is not, and should not be, noticeable." This might strike some as an odd way to tout your accomplishments to a doubting public. Wouldn't you want the public to see all the good work you've done?

For those hikers without a lot of ready cash at hand, as of 2020 King and Snohomish Counties and the City of Seattle have not instituted a parking permit fee to hike or use their parks. So, you're covered for places like Rattlesnake Mountain, Fort Lawton–Discovery Park, Robe Canyon, Sky Country History Circuit, O. O. Denny Park, and a few other places.

On the other hand, government budgets are continually under attack and subject to cuts or reapportionments. Before beginning any hike, check the reader boards (if provided) at trailheads for any up-to-date data on whether you must pay to play. Or whether you're displaying the correct pass. The Forest Service is very good about

*So many passes, so little time*

posting signs informing the public if a Northwest Forest Pass is required. Most, but not all, DNR lands are posted as well. In some areas it is still possible to park some distance away from the trailhead and escape the requirement to pay. If you are a registered guest at a Forest Service campground and there is a trailhead adjacent, you need not have a Northwest Forest Pass as long as your car remains at your campsite.

Some would argue that a hiking guide is not the proper place to lobby citizens of the United States. On the other hand, what's the alternative? If hikers, anglers, paddlers, equestrians, hunters, picnickers, birdwatchers, boaters, botanizers, and everyone else who uses our public lands don't tell our elected representatives that we expect those public lands to be fully funded and cared for, who else is going to do it? As some politicians like to say when discussing taxes, it's our money. It's time to remind those politicians that we want it spent wisely. Did you know there are over 5.4 million annual visitors to Mount Baker–Snoqualmie National Forest and millions more using state parks and Department of Natural Resources lands? Make your voice heard.

# THE EFFECT OF THE 2020 COVID-19 PANDEMIC ON PUBLIC LANDS

The COVID-19 pandemic in 2020 underscored the years of challenges faced by land management agencies and Washington citizens concerned with our public spaces. One great issue to emerge was the realization that our national parks and forests, state and county and city parklands, were not sufficient outdoor spaces to absorb the sudden influx of people, many of whom for the first time recognized the existence and value of their public lands.

King County and the greater Seattle area were hit hard by COVID-19 beginning in late January 2020. Following the direction of Washington governor Jay Inslee, we practiced "social distancing" (maintaining a minimum distance of 6 feet from other people), remained at home with shelter-in-place voluntary "lockdown," and reduced unnecessary travel. These actions helped flatten the curve of infection so that hospitals and medical workers weren't flooded with sick and/or dying people that could have overwhelmed our medical system and resources. The governor encouraged us to work from home, curtail gathering in large crowds, and recreate out-of-doors. And so we did.

In terms of the latter, the response to using our public lands was so overwhelmingly successful that social distancing became problematic. This led to parking areas and trails at these public lands being closed. All the hikes in this book were affected by these closures, and the author experienced difficulty checking every trailhead and every trail for on-the-ground changes. Some popular trails in *Best Hikes Seattle*, like Rattlesnake Mountain (#23), where physical and social distancing could not be maintained, were closed and remained closed well past the book's submission deadline.

By midsummer of 2020, many public lands in the Seattle area were again available for recreation, as Washington State political leaders began a science-reasoned and incremental "opening up." Attending events at venues like stadiums, gyms, theaters, concert halls, bars, restaurants, and movie theaters was restricted. This resulted in even more people turning to their open spaces. Predictably, this resulted in a surge in the use of parks, camping areas, waterways, hiking trails, and rails-to-trails routes.

With a mixture of happiness, surprise, and (for some!) horror, it became normal to see once rarely used trails with lots of people on them. Popular trails became even more popular. Passage of the bipartisan-approved Great American Outdoors Act, signed into law on August 4, 2020, came just in time. Up to $1.9 billion became available between 2021 and 2025 to address deferred maintenance on federal lands.

As 2020 came to a close, we saw an influx of people flocking to public lands. And it was COVID-19 changes in behavior that demonstrated we do not have enough parks, open spaces, or outdoor places in the Seattle area to meet the demands of the many people in our region.

As we go to press with this third edition of *Best Hikes Seattle*, there are many political, social, cultural, ethical, and medical questions still unanswered about COVID-19. How will it affect our parks and forests? Our country? Our economy? Our health and well-being? How will it affect each of us, individually and collectively? The future is, as always, predictably unpredictable. At least we have a vaccine! Two, even, and maybe more!

However, there is one predictable question for hikers and nature lovers. As more of us head to the outdoors to find solace and inspiration during our difficult and troubling times, what can we do to ensure there will always be enough parks and other outdoor places for recreation? And what of quiet contemplation? Or science? Understanding our own place in this complex web of life? In our hour of darkness, in our time of need, as our parks and forests increasingly become a place of refuge from what bears down deeply upon us, where will we go to find the quiet and solitude and joy and rejuvenation that have become the tradition of outdoor recreation? Only the future—and wise guidance from citizens and political decision-makers alike—will tell. Grant us the vision to pursue this answer. And again, make your voice heard.

*All recreation sites were closed during the COVID-19 pandemic to reinforce social and physical distancing.*

# How to Use This Book

Each region begins with an introduction that provides a general overview for the hike chapters featured within that region. To aid in quick decision-making, each hike begins with a summary. Next come the hike "specs," including where the hike starts; hike distance and type of hike; approximate hiking time; difficulty rating; trail surface; best hiking season; other trail users; status on dogs; what agency manages the land; town nearest the trailhead; information about fuel and other services available in the area, along with availability (and type) of toilet at the trailhead; whether a Northwest Forest Pass or Washington State Discover Pass are necessary; useful maps; whom to contact for updated trail information; and any special hazards you might encounter on the trail. Contact data such as addresses, phone numbers, email, and web addresses of land management agencies and interested groups will be found in Appendix A. Note: When it comes to hiking time and difficulty . . . at publication time the author

*Some of Seattle's best hikes are near the South Fork Snoqualmie River.*

was 68 years old and in good health, with no physical limitations though he has slowed down since this book's first edition over a decade ago! He hikes the book's trails weekly and spends the rest of the week on 3-5 mile walks on the neighborhood streets of Seattle. This should help you interpret his opinions on this topic.

"Finding the Trailhead" gives you directions from downtown Seattle to where the hike begins.

"The Hike" presents this author's impressions of the trail. It isn't possible to cover everything you will see—and who would want that anyway? Taking a hike is not just about exercise or getting outdoors. It's also about exploring a place and learning about it on your own. The hike description is meant to serve as a guide. You are encouraged to make, and record, your own impressions.

"Miles and Directions" includes specific mileages to identify the trailhead, turns, trail junctions, and points of interest. "Options" suggests hike extensions or interesting detours. Where it appears, "Hike Information" lists other data such as historical facts, miscellaneous local information resources, recommendations for places to eat, and anything else that didn't fit elsewhere in the trail description.

Appendixes at the end of this guide not only list clubs and organizations that advocate for trails, contact information for land management agencies, but also suggested books to read for more information about where you have been, or are going to be, hiking.

Hiking involves a certain degree of appreciation of nature and love of the outdoors. Don't ever forget the reason you are out here.

# Trail Finder

| Hike No. | Hike Name | Hikes for Children | Hikes for Backpackers | Training Hikes | Wildflower Hikes | Weekday Hikes (to avoid crowds) | Historical Hikes | View Hikes |
|---|---|---|---|---|---|---|---|---|
| 1 | Alki Beach Trail | • | | • | | | | • |
| 2 | Alki Stair Climb and College Street Ravine | | | • | | | | • |
| 3 | Fort Lawton–Discovery Park | • | | • | | | • | • |
| 4 | Meadowdale Beach Park | • | | • | | | | • |
| 5 | O. O. Denny Park | • | | • | | | | |
| 6 | Wallace Falls State Park | | | | | • | | • |
| 7 | Lake Serene | | • | • | • | • | | • |
| 8 | Barclay and Eagle Lakes | | • | | • | • | | • |
| 9 | Deception Falls | • | | | • | | | |
| 10 | Surprise Lake | | • | | • | | | • |
| 11 | Boulder Lake | | • | | • | | | |
| 12 | Iron Goat Trail–Martin Creek to Wellington | • | | • | • | | • | • |
| 13 | Robe Canyon Historic Park–Lime Kiln Trail | • | | • | • | | • | |

| Hike No. | Hike Name | Hikes for Children | Hikes for Backpackers | Training Hikes | Wildflower Hikes | Weekday Hikes (to avoid crowds) | Historical Hikes | View Hikes |
|---|---|---|---|---|---|---|---|---|
| 14 | Robe Canyon | | | | • | | | • |
| 15 | Heather Lake | | • | | • | | • | • |
| 16 | Lake Twenty-two | • | • | | • | • | | • |
| 17 | Sky Country History Circuit | | | • | | • | • | • |
| 18 | Cougar Mountain | | | • | | • | | |
| 19 | Jim Whittaker Wilderness Peak | | | • | | • | | |
| 20 | Tiger Mountain–East Summit | | | • | | | | • |
| 21 | Tiger Mountain–High Point Trail | | | • | | • | | |
| 22 | Cedar Butte | • | | • | | • | | • |
| 23 | Rattlesnake Mountain–East Peak | | | • | | | | • |
| 24 | Weeks Falls | • | | • | | • | | |
| 25 | Twin Falls | | | • | | • | | |
| 26 | Little Si | | | • | | • | | • |
| 27 | Mount Si | | | • | | • | | • |
| 28 | Myrtle Lake | | • | | • | • | | |

| Hike No. | Hike Name | Hikes for Children | Hikes for Back-packers | Training Hikes | Wildflower Hikes | Weekday Hikes (to avoid crowds) | Historical Hikes | View Hikes |
|---|---|---|---|---|---|---|---|---|
| 29 | Taylor River | • | • |  | • | • |  |  |
| 30 | Snoqualmie Lake–Lake Dorothy |  | • |  | • | • |  | • |
| 31 | Dirty Harry's Peak |  |  | • | • |  |  | • |
| 32 | Bandera Mountain |  |  | • | • |  |  | • |
| 33 | McClellan Butte |  |  | • | • |  |  | • |
| 34 | Mason Lake and Mount Defiance |  | • |  | • | • |  | • |
| 35 | Annette Lake |  | • |  | • | • |  |  |
| 36 | Melakwa Lakes |  | • |  | • | • |  |  |
| 37 | Olallie Lake |  | • |  |  | • |  |  |
| 38 | Snow Lake |  | • |  |  | • |  |  |
| 39 | Lake Lillian |  | • |  | • | • |  | • |
| 40 | Margaret Lake |  | • |  | • |  |  | • |
| 41 | Mima Mounds | • |  |  | • | • | • | • |
| 42 | Billy Frank Jr. Nisqually National Wildlife Refuge | • |  |  | • | • | • | • |

# Map Legend

### Municipal

≡⟨90⟩≡ Interstate Highway

≡⟨101⟩≡ US Highway

≡⟨7⟩≡ State Highway

───── Local Road

= = = = Unpaved Road

├──┼──┤ Railroad

•–•–•–• Power line

### Trails

------ Featured Trail

------ Trail

### Water Features

Lake/Reservoir

Marsh

River/Creek

Waterfall

### Land Management

National Forest

Wilderness

State/Regional Park

Preserve/Watershed

### Symbols

▭ Bench

⊃⊂ Bridge

▲ Campground

⟩⟨ Gap/Saddle

•–• Gate

⌁ Lighthouse

🅿 Parking

▲ Peak

⊞ Picnic Area

■ Point of Interest/Structure

🎣 Ranger Station

🚻 Restrooms

○ Town

① Trailhead

◈ Viewpoint/Overlook

❓ Visitor Center

# Urban Walks

Some days, it just doesn't pay to leave town. Traffic is horrendous and I-5 is a barely moving parking lot. The bridges across Lake Washington may resemble barges transporting automobiles to Alaska up the Inside Passage. It could be snowing in the mountains. Or there isn't enough time to spend on getting to a trailhead.

When your legs are dying to stretch and your heart and lungs demand aerobic exercise, the Seattle area is fortunate to have many large city and county parks that take the sting out of having to remain close to home. Those listed here all have access or views of Puget Sound or Lake Washington. With only slight variations, all are family-friendly. Since about four million people live along the shores of Puget Sound, don't expect to have these urban parks to yourself, although they can be amazingly empty on weekdays or rainy winter afternoons.

Puget Sound is an estuary—a place where salt and fresh water coalesce before the mix reaches the ocean. It's connected to the Pacific Ocean (and the Strait of Georgia to the north) by the Strait of Juan de Fuca. The Sound is actually a

*Denny Party Monument—Alki Beach*

*Trail's end at Puget Sound*

system of flooded glacial valleys carved by a million years of continental glaciation. At one time, a lobe of ice reached as far south as Olympia and at least as far east as Grouse Ridge (near exit 38 on I-90). The beaches and bluffs around the edge of Puget Sound represent the accumulated sediments from this glaciation. About 20,000 years ago Seattle was buried by 3,400 feet of glacial ice—the height of five Space Needles.

Lake Washington is the second-largest lake in the state (Lake Chelan is the largest) and was created by glaciation. The lake is primarily fed by the Sammamish and Cedar Rivers.

# 1 Alki Beach Trail

Sometimes it's impossible to be rid of Seattle—those days when I-5 is a barely moving parking lot and you don't get anywhere until the news on NPR recycles a second time. Or the weather is terrible and the thought of driving to go hiking is anathema. Those days it's best to remain home reading a good book or exploring Seattle's urban walks.

The Alki Beach Trail draws people year-round and is one of the most popular walks anywhere in Seattle. Summer crowds are definitely a hindrance, but Alki is a great place for leg-stretching the rest of the year. Views are just as good—even better when winter snow covers the Olympics. Walk, jog, or bring your bike. Bring a picnic basket! Exercise the dog, or come down for a cuppa joe and some fish and chips.

**Start:** Trailhead at Harbor Avenue SW and West Seattle Bridge off-ramp; alternative start at 63rd and Alki Avenues SW
**Distance:** 7.0 miles out and back; 3.5 miles one-way with car shuttle return
**Approximate hiking time:** 3 to 4 hours
**Difficulty:** Easy
**Trail surface:** Sidewalk, dirt, grass
**Seasons:** Year-round
**Other trail users:** Bikes, horses (police in summer months), runners, skateboarders, in-line skaters, baby strollers
**Canine compatibility:** Leashed dogs permitted on trail but no dogs allowed on beach
**Land status:** City of Seattle Department of Parks and Recreation; Port of Seattle; Metro-King County; Seattle City Light

**Nearest town:** Seattle (Alki neighborhood)
**Services:** Restaurants, bars, coffee—lots of coffee; no toilet at trailhead; flush toilets at Jack Block Park (with outdoor cold showers—seasonally operative), Seacrest Park on Harbor Avenue, on Alki Avenue at 57th (with outdoor cold shower), and Alki at 63rd
**Northwest Forest Pass:** No
**Discover Pass:** No
**Map:** USGS Duwamish Head
**Trail contacts:** Seattle Department of Parks and Recreation, Seattle City Light, Port of Seattle, and King County Parks and Recreation
**Special hazards:** Bikes, in-line skaters, dogs, cars, inattentive people; no potable water at trailhead

**Finding the trailhead:** From I-5 north or south, take exit 163 and drive west on the West Seattle Bridge (older maps might refer to it as the West Seattle Freeway). Or from WA 99 south, exit to the West Seattle Bridge (aka the "High Bridge" versus the "Low Bridge" that spans Duwamish Waterway and swings open for ship traffic). Take the Harbor Avenue exit, turning right at the traffic signal at the end of the ramp. Drive 0.2 mile, pass Westside Bicycles (best place for all your bicycling needs), the Active Space building, and park. As of press time the High Bridge is closed due to structural issues and a detour is in place for the foreseeable future—at least to late 2022. Follow the detour signs or your phone app. Access to the Low Bridge is limited to transit, freight, and emergency vehicles except between 9 p.m. and 5 a.m. Break the rules and suffer a huge fine. Alternatively, take the bus. Alki is serviced by the #56. GPS: N47 34.456' / W122 22.240'

## The Hike

Walk north beside Harbor Avenue SW under a lovely, wide, tree-lined asphalt multiuse trail. Pass Jack Block Park on the right. Pass in succession the *Luna Girls* statue (200 feet north of Salty's Restaurant—great food but pricey for those on a budget), then Seacrest and Don Armeni Parks. Both parks afford fantastic views of Elliott Bay and the downtown Seattle skyline. Views only get better as you round Duwamish Head to Luna (aka Anchor) Park. A stairway provides access to a small sandy beach. From 1907 to 1913 Luna Park was the site of a large amusement park. The stairs are closed seasonally to provide sanctuary to marine mammals.

From here the multiuse trail splits. Walkers should take the water side of the trail, leaving the wider, paved part for bikes and other self-propelled wheeled vehicles. This portion of the trail was formerly a railroad trestle. A seawall was constructed to protect the tracks, and the area between Puget Sound and the cliffs to the left (south) was

*Alki Point lighthouse and the Bainbridge Island ferry*

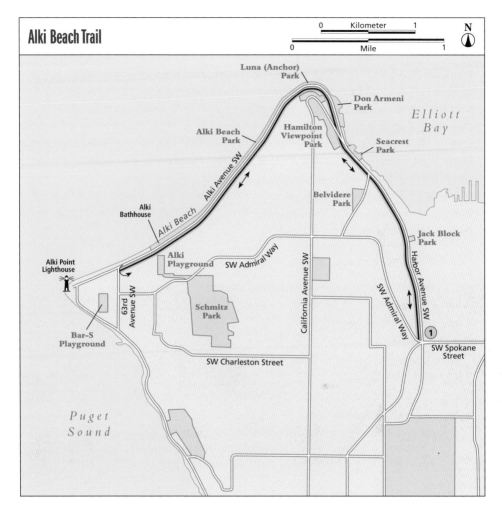

## Alki Beach Trail

0 Kilometer 1

0 Mile 1

N

Luna (Anchor) Park

Don Armeni Park

*Elliott Bay*

Alki Beach Park

Hamilton Viewpoint Park

Seacrest Park

Alki Bathhouse

Alki Avenue SW

Alki Beach

Belvidere Park

Jack Block Park

Harbor Avenue SW

Alki Point Lighthouse

Alki Playground

SW Admiral Way

63rd Avenue SW

Schmitz Park

California Avenue SW

SW Admiral Way

Bar-S Playground

SW Charleston Street

SW Spokane Street

1

*Puget Sound*

filled in, eventually becoming Alki Avenue. The condos are more recent and began arriving on the scene during the 1980s when they replaced single-family homes.

The trail remains atop the bulkhead until the beach is reached at 57th Avenue SW. Notice the embedded plaques, which illustrate the history of Seattle with words and pictures. Designed by an artistic team led by Donald Fels, the project was funded with money from Seattle's 1% for Art Program during the 1990s reconstruction of the Alki Beach Trail.

Beginning at 57th Avenue SW is Alki's small "business district" of restaurants, some of which convert themselves into bars after 10 p.m. A sandy beach begins here, as well as the crowds. In summer stop and enjoy the volleyball games, or simply take a load off your feet and savor some people-watching.

When ready, get back on the path and keep walking until you reach the end of the trail. Numerous places afford access to the water. The colorful building on the right (north) is the Alki Bathhouse. Rebuilt and opened in 2005, the bathhouse serves as a meeting room and neighborhood art studio. Classes, sponsored by the Parks Department, are taught throughout the year.

Beside the bathhouse is a small replica of the Statue of Liberty, originally a gift in 1952 from Reginald H. Parsons and the Seattle Council of the Boy Scouts of America. In 2007 the statue was recast and in September 2008 installed on the same site. Community involvement and fund-raising were crucial to this project. Spend some time reading the commemorative bricks in the plaza surrounding the statue. Just before the end of the trail, at Alki Avenue and 63rd Avenue SW, is a concrete column commemorating the 1852 founding of Seattle by the Denny Party.

From here, one-way walkers can wait for the free shuttle bus that picks up and delivers passengers to the Elliott Bay Water Taxi. Round-trip walkers can turn around here and retrace their steps.

## Miles and Directions

**0.0**  Harbor Avenue SW and West Seattle Bridge trailhead

**0.6**  Jack Block Park

**0.9**  *Luna Girls* sculpture

**1.4**  Don Armeni Park

**2.4**  Luna (Anchor) Park at Duwamish Head, 213'

**3.2**  Alki Bathhouse

**3.5**  63rd Avenue SW and Alki Avenue SW (**Option:** One-way hikers, head for your bus.)

**7.0**  Arrive back at trailhead

**Options:** Railroad aficionados can extend the walk 1 mile east with an excursion from the Harbor Avenue trailhead to Chelan Cafe for lunch. There are numerous places along the way to observe the rail yard used by the nearby steel plant and container ship facility.

## Hike Information

The *Luna Girls* sculpture recalls the elaborate 12-acre amusement park called Luna Park, built over the waters of Elliott Bay at Duwamish Head. It operated from 1907 to 1913 with a carousel, Ferris wheel, roller coaster, dance hall, movie theater, and swimming pool. *Luna Girls* was financed by 150 individual subscribers, designed by Lezlie Jane, and donated in 2014 to the City of Seattle. Thank you, Lezlie. We love you.

Don Armeni Park has a boat launch. Luna (aka Anchor) Park has views of Puget Sound and downtown Seattle. Both are administered by the Seattle Department of Parks and Recreation. Don Armeni Park is also home to scores of resident Canada geese. Please don't feed the birds—it only encourages them to stay, and they need to learn how to migrate.

The Elliott Bay Water Taxi runs between Seacrest Dock (this will supposedly change when, or if, a permanent dock is built) and Pier 50, downtown (check the water taxi schedule at kingcounty.gov/depts/transportation/water-taxi/west-seattle

Luna Girls *along Alki Beach Trail*

.aspx). A free shuttle bus runs from the water taxi dock to Alki and West Seattle Junction.

Jack Block Park, administered by the Port of Seattle, provides a nice detour, and features parking, flush toilets, a drinking fountain, and a picnic area. Elliott Bay, Harbor Island, Duwamish Waterway, and the container facility can be seen from numerous observation platforms and viewpoints. The sculpture over the entrance, designed by Donald Fels, is supposed to represent the keel and ribs of a sailing ship.

Alki Point Lighthouse (3201 Alki Ave. SW) offers free public tours conducted by volunteers from the US Coast Guard Auxiliary on Saturday and Sunday from June through August (1:30 to 4 p.m.). Tours are 30 minutes long and cover lighthouse history and operations, artifacts, and US Coast Guard roles and missions. Tours can be arranged by e-mail at alkilighthouse@cgauxseattle.org. Please respect the privacy of the people living in the two residences adjacent to the lighthouse. The last human beings to staff the lighthouse before it became automated retired in 1970. It's possible to walk the gravelly beach around Alki Point and the lighthouse during low tides.

> *"The walker's companions are the stones in his boot, the rain in his face, the unreadable map . . . but a wide open space."*
>
> —Anonymous

# 2 Alki Stair Climb and College Street Ravine

Getting prepared for the hiking season can involve time in the gym though our 2020 COVID experience certainly changed that! But time spent on a treadmill or stair-climbing machine isn't very interesting. Fortunately Seattle is blessed in having some steep hills. Though the hills stymied road building, our city fathers saw to it that pedestrians were provided with stairs. Such wisdom! And what better way to get in shape than to utilize those stairs? Adjacent to Alki Beach are two tall sets of nearly 200 stairs to climb. Combine them with a pleasant walk in a quiet neighborhood. Afterward try a delightful amble through the wild College Street Ravine and a possible detour though Schmitz Park. Surrounded by a dense urban neighborhood, the College Street Ravine and Schmitz Park are home to resident and migratory birds plus small mammals like foxes, coyotes, opossums, squirrels, and many pesky raccoons.

**Start:** Alki and 53rd Avenues SW

**Distance:** 2.5-mile loop (does not include repeated stair climbs)

**Approximate hiking time:** 1.5-plus hours (depending on how many times you climb the stairs before starting up College Street Ravine)

**Difficulty:** Easy

**Trail surface:** Sidewalk, forest path

**Seasons:** Year-round

**Other trail users:** Runners

**Canine compatibility:** Leashed dogs permitted

**Land status:** Seattle Department of Parks and Recreation; private property

**Nearest town:** Seattle (Alki neighborhood)

**Services:** Restaurants, bars, coffee—lots of coffee; no toilet at trailhead; flush toilets at Jack Block Park (with outdoor cold showers—seasonally operative), Seacrest Park, on Alki Avenue at 57th (with outdoor cold shower), and Alki at 63rd

**Northwest Forest Pass:** No

**Discover Pass:** No

**Map:** USGS Seattle

**Trail contact:** Seattle Department of Parks and Recreation

**Special hazards:** Stinging nettle, Himalayan berry, off-leash dogs, possible automobile traffic

**Finding the trailhead:** From I-5 north or south, take exit 163 and drive west on the West Seattle Bridge (older maps might refer to it as the West Seattle Freeway). Or from WA 99 south, exit to the West Seattle Bridge (aka the "High Bridge" versus the "Low Bridge," which spans Duwamish Waterway and swings open for ship traffic). Take the Harbor Avenue exit, turning right at the traffic signal at the end of the ramp. Follow Harbor Avenue to the north and then around Duwamish Head as it turns west and becomes Alki Avenue SW. Park your car between 53rd and 57th Avenues SW. As of press time the High Bridge is closed due to structural issues and a detour is in place for the foreseeable future—perhaps as late as 2022! Follow the detour signs or your phone app. Access to the Low Bridge is limited to transit, freight, and emergency vehicles except between 9 p.m. and 5 a.m. Breaking the rules will lead to a steep fine. Consider taking the bus; the #56 services Alki. GPS: N47 34.907' / W122 24.232'

# The Hike

Begin at Alki and 53rd Avenues SW. Approach the concrete steps and climb, crossing Hobart Avenue SW to the remaining fifty-one stairs, which take you to Hughes Avenue SW.

Turn around, descend the stairs, and start all over again. This time, mix it up a bit. Try doing intervals. Run, then walk. Take two steps at a time, then three, then four. This is a popular place for fitness walkers, but you will have it all to yourself during the dark mornings of winter. Most dogs in the neighborhood are friendly and accustomed to people.

At the top of the stairs, try something different. Turn left (east) onto Hughes Avenue SW and walk downhill to Halleck Avenue SW. Turn right (east), enjoying the view of Puget Sound. Spot the stairway and descend 140 steps, through an overgrown forest straight out of the Enchanted Tiki Room, to Bonair Drive and Alki Avenue SW.

Turn left and walk back 0.1 mile to 53rd and start all over again. Total distance for this loop is 0.9 mile.

Had enough of stairs? Then instead of dropping down to Alki Avenue at the Halleck Avenue stairs, continue uphill on Hughes. Curve onto SW College Street, hoof it steeply uphill some more, and turn right (southwest) on 52nd Avenue SW, then jog

*The entrance to College Street Ravine*

*Welcome to College Street Ravine*

back onto SW College Street. Head directly to a Parks and Recreation sign identifying the start of the College Street Ravine as the Duwamish Head Greenbelt next door to 2302 51st Avenue SW. Please don't disturb the residents.

Community activist and former Seattle city council member Charlie Chong was instrumental in organizing neighbors in the late 1980s to save this green space from development. The ravine was acquired with funding through the 1989 King County open space and trails bond. We should all be thankful to Charlie Chong, who died in 2007. The wild critters certainly must be.

Walk up the ravine, being careful of stinging nettle alongside the path. During the wet seasons the ground can be awfully moist, so be prepared or be willing to get your feet wet and muddy. Locals tend to bring boards down to the ravine to cover the most egregiously moist zones.

College Street Ravine has shade aplenty, provided by mature red alder trees. The developing understory of native plants includes sword fern, buttercup, geranium, and young western red cedar. There are many exotics such as Himalaya berry and holly. English ivy is particularly common but volunteers are working on getting rid of it by pulling the plants out by hand. In the ravine's lower reaches, various spots are given over to poison hemlock (remember Socrates?), which resembles 6-foot-tall parsley. Note the red streaks, or striations, on the stem. All parts of the plant are poisonous.

## TRAIL HAZARDS 1

Few plants strike as much horror in people's hearts in the Pacific Northwest as stinging nettle (*Urtica dioica*) and devil's club (*Oplopanax horridus*). The worry is in the name!

A weedy herbaceous perennial from Europe, stinging nettle grows to 6 feet tall and has soft green leaves with strongly toothed margins. The plant is covered with brittle hairs that inject a combination of histamine, acetylcholine, and serotonin into anyone unfortunate enough to brush against it. But the plant is also edible early in the spring, and the ancient Greeks used it as a medicine!

*Stinging nettle is covered with brittle, stinging hairs that you will not want to brush against!*

Devil's club is an unusual native plant that often forms impenetrable thickets. Woe the poor hiker who cuts a switchback and stumbles into devil's club. The plant is covered with sharp hairs—even on its large, maple-like leaves—and causes contact dermatitis.

Far too soon, pop out of the ravine onto 48th Avenue SW and SW Niesz Court, in a quiet residential neighborhood. If you've had enough, turn around and retrace your steps down College Street Ravine to the Alki Stair Climb. Otherwise follow 48th to SW Waite. Turn left (east), soon turning right (west) onto SW Admiral Way. The large white building on the corner is an assisted-living home called Aegis Living. If so inclined, there are many bus stops for the #56 to carry you back down to Alki Avenue. Otherwise saunter down to SW Lander Street and turn right (west). Turn right (north) on 56th Avenue SW and walk to Alki Avenue. Turn right (east) to return to your car or the trailhead.

To extend your walk, continue one block further down Admiral Way to SW Stevens Street and enter the 53-acre Schmitz Preserve Park. Before the Schmitz Park Bridge was built in 1936, spanning the preserve, the road entered the park and the creek was covered in asphalt. Walk 0.2 mile along this old road until reaching a side path which drops to, and crosses, the now day-lighted creek. Then, turn right (north) and continue walking 0.5 mile on the old road, passing beneath the Schmitz Park Bridge. Exit Schmitz Preserve Park at 58th Avenue SW and the Alki Playground and Alki Elementary School. Follow 58th Avenue SW to Alki Avenue and the beach. Turn right (east) to return to your car and the trailhead.

## Miles and Directions

**0.0**  Alki and 53rd Avenues SW trailhead

**0.1**  Begin stair climb

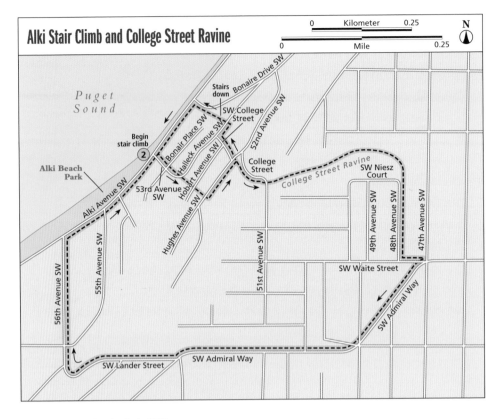

**0.3** Top of stair climb, 971'

**0.4** 52nd and Hughes Avenues SW (stairs down)

**0.5** Bonair Drive SW and Alki Avenue SW

**0.7** Alki and 53rd Avenues SW

**1.1** 52nd and Hughes Avenues SW

**1.2** College Street Ravine

**1.5** End of College Street Ravine (48th Avenue SW and SW Niesz Court)

**1.7** SW Admiral Way

**2.1** SW Lander Street and SW Admiral Way

**2.5** Arrive back at trailhead

## Hike Information

A broken water main beneath these stairs washed away the lower section below Hobart Avenue SW during the winter of 2009. This section was slowly rebuilt between 2009 and 2010 by SDOT's Roadway Structures crew and was funded by Bridging the Gap, a $365 million nine-year transportation maintenance and improvements levy approved by Seattle voters in 2006.

Interested in more stair climbs? Seattle Stairway Walks (www.seattlestairwaywalks .com) has twenty-five urban walks, including Alki, involving stair climbing. An inventory of stair walks in Seattle can be found at www.communitywalk.com/seattle/wa/ seattle_stairs/map/388644. You can find a Google map of all 650 public stairs—short, medium, and long—in Seattle at http://seattlestairs.home.comcast.net/~seattlestairs. Since 1995, Feet First has inspired, connected, and informed wide-ranging discussions with government agencies, developers, and community groups to promote walkable communities. Find them at www.feetfirst.org.

*"If you are attuned to look for beauty you can find it almost anywhere."*
—Waldo Ruess

# 3 Fort Lawton–Discovery Park

Discovery Park is a 534-acre natural area operated by Seattle Parks and Recreation. At one time it was all part of Fort Lawton, a US Army base. Something curious happened there late one moonless night on August 14, 1944: Private Guglielmo Olivotto, an Italian prisoner of war quartered at Fort Lawton, was found lynched in a ravine above the beach. For African Americans in that era, a lynching was not unusual. What made this case so peculiar was that three African-American soldiers were charged with the first-degree murder / lynching of Private Olivotto. Another forty black soldiers were accused of rioting on that hot August night and attacking the barracks of Italian POWs.

**Start:** East parking lot at entrance to Discovery Park Environmental Learning Center

**Distance:** 6.0-mile lollipop (longer or shorter, depending on your interest and time)

**Approximate hiking time:** 2 hours to all day

**Difficulty:** Easy

**Trail surface:** Dirt path, paved and gravel road

**Seasons:** Year-round

**Other trail users:** Bikes, runners, motorcycles, cars

**Canine compatibility:** Leashed dogs permitted

**Land status:** Seattle Parks and Recreation; US Army; some property possibly private in the future

**Nearest town:** Seattle (Magnolia neighborhood)

**Services:** Gas, restaurants, groceries; flush toilets and drinking fountain inside Environmental Learning Center; porta-potties throughout the park

**Northwest Forest Pass:** No

**Discover Pass:** No

**Map:** USGS North Seattle

**Trail contacts:** Seattle Department of Parks and Recreation Daybreak Star Cultural Center, United Indians of All Tribes Foundation

**Special hazards:** Stinging nettle

**Finding the trailhead:** From anywhere in Seattle, navigate to the Fisherman's Terminal on W Emerson Street and travel west. Turn right (north) onto Gilman Avenue W, which wends its way through the Magnolia neighborhood, eventually becoming W Government Way and entering Discovery Park. Once inside the park, turn left (east) into the Discovery Park Environmental Learning Center (east) parking lot. GPS: N47 39.467' / W122 24.367'

## The Hike

After visiting the Discovery Park Environmental Learning Center (open Tuesday through Sunday 8:30 a.m. to 5 p.m.; closed holidays), walk through the parking lot to W Government Way. Find the sidewalk, turn left (northwest), and walk up the street for 0.2 mile. Turn right (northeast), pass through a cyclone fence gate, and enter the small Fort Lawton Cemetery (closes at dusk) marked with a sign stating, "We honor those who have made the supreme sacrifice." Private Guglielmo Olivotto's grave is in the extreme northeast corner of the cemetery.

*The old light keepers' houses at West Point, Discovery Park*

As a POW, Private Olivotto wasn't buried within the quadrangle of the cemetery where US servicemen and their families were interred. For more than ten years, a simple wooden board marked his grave. Then members of Seattle-area Italian-American groups arranged for the current broken-column headstone. Note that Olivotto's given name is incorrectly spelled on the headstone.

Several feet south of the grave is the final resting place of a German POW, thirty-eight-year-old Captain Albert Marquardt, who died October 1, 1945, after drinking lacquer thinner. Though the war in Europe had ended May 8, 1945, with Germany's unconditional surrender, Captain Marquardt and many of his countrymen remained in the United States as POWs while awaiting repatriation. The captain's death certificate says "accidental death," though some people believe it was suicide because Marquardt preferred to remain in the USA and was despondent about returning to Germany. The autumn display of big leaf maples throughout the cemetery is truly stupendous.

Returning to W Government Way and the sidewalk, turn right (northwest) and reach the hilltop after 0.2 mile. Bear left onto Washington Avenue and enter Fort Lawton's historic district, passing a restricted vehicle access sign. Between 1899 and 1908, twenty-eight buildings were constructed on Fort Lawton's parade ground. Currently the residences of army and navy brass, the row of duplexes along Washington Avenue, along with three other buildings below the parade ground, are all that remain of the fort's former architectural glory. These houses on "Officers' Row" as well as the other residences within Discovery Park are owned by a private developer who rents them to military families. As of 2020 there are plans to pull down many of the military structures and construct affordable housing units.

Walk the length of Washington Avenue beneath century-old London plane trees. At a barbed wire–topped cyclone fence, the big golf ball–looking thing is part of NORAD—a North American aerospace warning system established in 1958. Today satellites have supplanted most of its functions. Turn around and retrace your steps, making for a flagpole. Stop and read the interpretive sign, admire the many images by nineteenth-century photographer Asahel Curtis, and enjoy the Olympic Mountain view. A plaque here memorializes Henry M. Jackson, US senator from Washington.

North of the flagpole is a two-story yellow building fronting Utah Avenue that served as Fort Lawton military headquarters in 1944. Situated in the wye created by Utah and Illinois Avenues and immediately east of headquarters is a field given over to straggling alders, Scot's broom, and other ruderal plant life. This is where the court-martial of the forty-three African-American soldiers was held between November and December 1944. After a five-week trial, twenty-eight men were found guilty (including two convicted of manslaughter in the death of Private Olivotto) in the largest and longest army court-martial of World War II.

Walk downhill (west) from the flagpole to Oregon Avenue. The building with raised clusters of pillars supporting a cupola served Fort Lawton as a PX / post gymnasium. Band barracks occupied the two-story house at one time. A brickyard surrounded the single-storied guardhouse. Chuckanut sandstone was used for building foundations. From the guardhouse front porch, it's possible to see jail cells through the windows. At the back is a massive iron door. After examining the buildings, walk north, beyond the bus waiting shelter. Turn left (west) onto a sidewalk beside Utah Avenue.

Pass Montana Circle and a cluster of junior officer homes constructed of brick or clapboard. Less ostentatious than Officers' Row, these homes also lack Olympic views. A row of seven giant sequoia trees towers over a playground. Continue west.

Two long buildings on one side of the street originally served as horse stables. When automobiles replaced horses, the stables became the motor pool. Across the street, a two-story house (notice the foundation is brick, not sandstone) served as a residence for nonmilitary personnel. A beautiful London plane tree graces the front walkway of this house along with an iron light standard.

Utah Avenue continues west. Cross the street (north) at the intersection of Utah Avenue and Hawaii Circle and walk northwest on an old two-lane asphalt road, formerly Illinois Avenue. Though this area is now field and dense forest, barracks for POWs and African-American soldiers were located here during the 1940s. In 0.1

**GREEN TIP:**
Keep your dog on a leash. Do not let it approach other people and their pets unless invited to do so.

*The lighthouse at West Point, Discovery Park*

mile, where the Loop Trail crosses Illinois Avenue, take a moment to look around. This is approximately where the riot began when three American soldiers attacked some POWs. It quickly got out of hand, eventually involving several hundred American soldiers, although only forty-three were ever charged. All traces of the barracks are long gone.

Turn left (west) at this intersection and walk 0.2 mile to the North Beach Trail, turning right (northwest) at a paved road. There is a bench and a portable toilet (seasonally) here. Where the paved road ends, bear left (west) and find a trail signed for North Beach. Drop down the bluff on 200 steps and an assortment of bridges and boardwalks, arriving on the shores of Puget Sound. There is good tide-pooling here. At low tide it's possible to walk along the beach to West Point.

Should the tide not be cooperating, double back to a wide dirt path and walk above the beach, eventually reaching West Point Lighthouse (access closed to visitors) and a King County sewage treatment plant. The North Beach profile has changed significantly since 1944 due to construction, landslides, and beach erosion. Looking northeast beyond the extensive facility development, two clumps of tall trees at the top of the bluff mark the approximate location of POW and African-American barracks in 1944. Private Olivotto was found at the bottom of the bluff below that point, where a road once existed. The actual lynching location was destroyed during construction of the West Point facility.

# RUSH TO JUDGMENT?

There was a substantial lack of evidence to support the army prosecutor's case against any of the black soldiers other than acceptance that a riot had occurred and Private Olivotto, an Italian POW, had been lynched. That didn't stop the lead prosecutor, Leon Jaworski, from pushing ahead—and also denying defense counsel from seeing crucial documents. Jaworski would later become famous as the man who got the goods on Richard M. Nixon. As Jack Hamann, a veteran reporter for PBS, CNN, NBC, and local Seattle television, documents in his book *On American Soil*, without this successful prosecution, Jaworski's advancement never would have occurred.

In late 2007 the US Army Board for Correction of Military Records ruled that Jaworski committed an "egregious error" by withholding crucial evidence in the soldiers' murder and rioting trial. Declaring the trial "fundamentally unfair," the board overturned the forty-three convictions.

It's interesting to speculate why the US government felt such a need to court-martial American soldiers for the death of one man during an incident where little evidence existed (even the murder weapon—a rope—was missing) and eyewitnesses were unreliable. After all, more than four years of world conflict was resulting in the death of tens of millions.

One reason may have to do with racism. Another reason could be our country's feelings of obligation to treat prisoners of war in a responsible and humane manner. The United States saw victory on the battlefield as a way to free Europe and Asia from totalitarian governments while remaining convinced that the people of those countries were not our enemies. Indeed, our opponents from that war are now some of our strongest allies.

Read a full account of the event in *On American Soil* by Jack Hamann (Algonquin Books, 2005), or visit www.nolittlethings.com/on-american-soil.html for more information on this fascinating story.

*Gravesite for World War II Italian POW Pvt. Guglielmo Olivotto at the Discovery Park military cemetery*

# Fort Lawton–Discovery Park

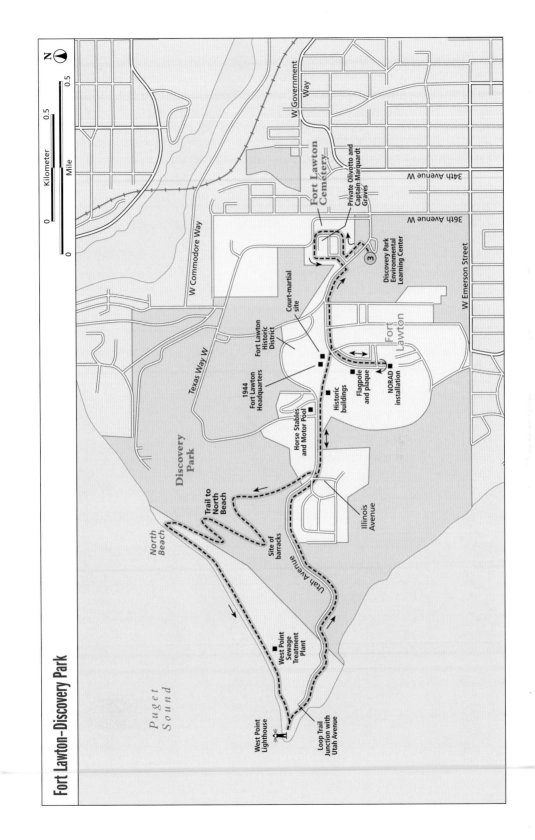

North

0    Kilometer    0.5

0    Mile    0.5

Puget Sound

North Beach

West Point Lighthouse

West Point Sewage Treatment Plant

Loop Trail Junction with Utah Avenue

Utah Avenue

Trail to North Beach

Site of barracks

Discovery Park

Texas Way W

W Commodore Way

Horse Stables and Motor Pool

1944 Fort Lawton Headquarters

Fort Lawton Historic District

Court-martial site

Fort Lawton Cemetery

Private Olivotto and Captain Marquardt Graves

W Government Way

Historic buildings

Flagpole and plaque

NORAD installation

Illinois Avenue

Fort Lawton

Discovery Park Environmental Learning Center

③

W Emerson Street

36th Avenue W

34th Avenue W

The path changes to asphalt and passes restricted parking and the wastewater treatment facility before ascending Utah Avenue. In 0.2 mile pass a trail junction; continue up for another 0.2 mile and a junction with the Loop Trail. Your choice is to return to the Environmental Learning Center by trail (1.3 miles) or by sidewalk along Utah Avenue (1 mile). Or take this opportunity to explore many of the other trails in Discovery Park. An interesting detour is to pass through the North Parking Lot—site of Fort Lawton's rifle range.

## Miles and Directions

**0.0** Discovery Park Environmental Learning Center trailhead

**0.4** Grave of Private Guglielmo Olivotto

**1.4** Flagpole and plaque

**1.7** Riot began here on August 14, 1944

**1.9** Site of Italian POW barracks

**3.0** Approximate site where Private Olivotto was murdered

**3.5** West Point Lighthouse

**5.0** Flagpole and plaque

**6.0** Arrive back at trailhead

## Hike Information

Discovery Park is a 534-acre natural area operated by Seattle Parks and Recreation. It is the largest city park in Seattle, and occupies most of the former Fort Lawton site. Discovery Park (open daily 4 a.m. to 11:30 p.m.) is one of the darkest places in Seattle, making it ideal for observing owls and nighttime celestial events like meteor showers, planets, and the aurora borealis during the occasional times it comes to town.

Discovery Park is home to the Daybreak Star Cultural Center, a Native American cultural center operated by a parent organization called United Indians of All Tribes. Daybreak Star functions as a conference center, a location for powwows and a Head Start school program, and an art gallery.

There are nearly 12 miles of walking/running/biking trails at Discovery Park, including a well-marked loop trail that winds around the park's historic attractions, fields, and forests. Remember, all housing in the park is private and not open to the public.

# 4 Meadowdale Beach Park

Even the tramp, tramp, tramp of many feet along this popular route won't prevent amblers and walkers from enjoying this fine urban trail. The rewards and pleasures are many—not the least of which are a deep, cool forest and arrival at trail's end on the shores of Puget Sound. Then there is the subtle beauty of a rare (for our area) forest tree and the autumnal arrival of chum salmon (*Oncorhynchus keta*) in Lunds Creek. All things considered, Meadowdale Beach Park, open from 7 a.m. to dusk, is a marvelous treasure.

**Start:** Parking area in Meadowdale Beach Park, Lynnwood
**Distance:** 2.5 miles out and back
**Approximate hiking time:** 3 hours
**Difficulty:** Easy, with one short, steep pitch
**Trail surface:** Old road
**Seasons:** Year-round
**Other trail users:** Runners
**Canine compatibility:** Leashed dogs permitted
**Land status:** Snohomish County Parks
**Nearest town:** Lynnwood

**Services:** Gas, restaurants, lodging, groceries; unisex portable toilet at trailhead
**Northwest Forest Pass:** No
**Discover Pass:** No
**Map:** USGS Edmonds East, Seattle
**Trail contacts:** Snohomish County Parks Department, Meadowdale Beach Park, Washington Water Trails Association
**Special hazards:** No potable water in winter at trailhead or on trail; active railroad line (mostly fenced) parallel to the beach

**Finding the trailhead:** From Seattle, drive north on I-5 to exit 182, WA 525. Proceed 2.8 miles to WA 99S. Follow WA 99S 1.8 miles to 168th Street SW and turn right (west). In 0.4 mile turn right (north) onto 52nd Avenue W at Beverly Elementary School. In 0.5 mile turn left (west) onto 160th Avenue W, following signs to Meadowdale Beach Park. Turn right in 0.2 mile onto 56th Avenue W, once again following signs to the park. In 0.2 mile turn left (west) onto 156th Street W at another park directional sign. In 0.3 mile 156th Street W passes through a gate and drops into the park.

Park hours: 7 a.m. until dusk; shelter hours: 7 a.m. until one hour prior to dusk. The paved parking lot fills quickly on weekends and sunny afternoons. No parking is allowed on 156th Street W. Meadowdale Beach Park closes at dusk. GPS: N47 51.437' / W122 18.971'

## The Hike

A couple of volunteer trails lead away from the parking lot and into the surrounding residential neighborhood. The actual trailhead is located on the east side of the parking lot. Loop downhill around the large grassy area on an asphalt path. Pass several picnic benches and enter the forest in 0.1 mile.

The wide, seasonally wet and muddy trail descends steeply through a forest of big leaf maple, Douglas fir, and western hemlock. Benches are placed periodically to aid short-breathed people as they huff and puff up the hill. Don't laugh! You'll be

*Some comfy logs, a gravelly beach, and a Puget Sound view at Meadowdale Beach Park*

returning this way soon enough. The steepest section is helped along by a staircase; the handrail was part of an Eagle Scout project in 1994 by Chris Simard of Troop 304.

Halfway down the 1.25-mile trail into Lunds Gulch, the pitch levels out and the trail begins to parallel the stream. Large tree stumps attest to the previous history of Meadowdale Beach Park.

The trail passes a large Sitka spruce and enters a copse of red alder. Sitka spruce is an important forest tree throughout its range from Kodiak Island to northern California. The clear-grained wood is highly desired in manufacturing musical instruments because of its high sound-conducting quality. The bark has the appearance of having large cornflakes glued to it; the needles are stiff and sharp and arise from a short peg (sterigma). The third-largest of North American conifers, Sitka spruce are beautifully shaped trees with boughs hanging almost all the way down to the ground.

In 1.0 mile reach a trail junction. Go left (southwest) and cross a bridge over Lunds Creek. Make your way by the ingeniously decorated ranger residence (private; please don't disturb), and proceed 0.3 mile toward the beach past a picnic shelter located on a large lawn. Or continue straight ahead (west) 0.3 mile, also toward the beach. Both trails meet at some portable toilets enclosed within an impressively designed rock shelter. Drinking water (not available in winter) can be found at both the picnic shelter and porta-potty shelter. There are picnic tables and trash cans located around the grassy area.

A short tunnel over Lunds Creek passes under the railroad track and onto a sandy beach. There are views northwest to Whidbey Island and west to Kingston on the Kitsap Peninsula. The beach can be walked, especially at low tide, for a short distance in either direction. Beware of passing trains, and keep off the railroad tracks.

This beach is part of the Cascadia Marine Trail, providing campsites to sea kayakers and other nonmotorized watercraft. After enjoying the view, retrace your steps back up the hill to the parking lot.

## Miles and Directions

- **0.0** Trailhead at east end of parking lot
- **0.3** Stairs
- **0.5** Sitka spruce
- **1.0** Trail junction
- **1.2** Beach
- **1.2** Tunnel
- **1.2** Toilets

## TREE STORIES 1

There are many things Douglas fir (*Pseudotsuga menziesii*, or false hemlock) is not: It's not a true fir because the cones are pendent. Also, the scales are not shed while the cone is still attached to the tree. It's not a hemlock because its leaves (needles) don't leave a persistent base when shed.

Conversely, there are many things the Douglas fir is: It's named in honor of David Douglas, the peripatetic early-nineteenth-century botanical collector for the Royal Horticultural Society in London. It is one of the most common forest trees in the Pacific Northwest. It is the most important source of lumber from southern Canada to northern California and from the Rocky Mountains to the Pacific Coast. It is a fairly recent arrival to the Northwest, having come on the scene little more than 7,000 years ago. The cones have protruding scales that resemble the hindquarters of little mice a tad too large to fit inside the cone. Trees reach heights of 250 feet with a diameter of 6 feet, and coastal trees attain ages between 200 and 800 years old. The tree is also known affectionately as the Doug fir.

*It looks like tiny mice are hiding between the cone scales on this Douglas fir cone.*

*Beautiful Lunds Creek slips, slides, and gurgles along the length of the Meadowdale Beach Park trail before entering Puget Sound at trail's end.*

**1.25** Ranger residence (private)

**2.5** Arrive back at trailhead

## Hike Information

Lunds Gulch was homesteaded by John Lund in 1878. The property was eventually acquired by the Meadowdale Country Club, which built a clubhouse, manicured lawns, an Olympic-size swimming pool, bathhouses, and a fish hatchery. Problems with road access contributed to the club's closure in the 1960s.

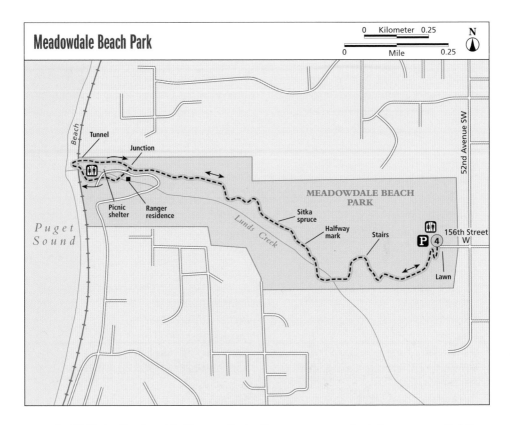

Meadowdale Beach Park

In 1968 the Snohomish County Parks Department acquired the property. Public access was denied from 1979 to 1988 due to the lack of emergency vehicle access. The park was closed again for a year in 1996 due to storm damage. Lunds Creek supports a small run of chum salmon. They can easily be seen in pools between the bridge and the beach. Meadowdale Beach Park was formerly known as Meadowdale County Park.

A gated access road leading down to the grassy lawn beside the ranger residence is provided for disabled persons. To apply for access, please download and mail/fax/e-mail the application form, or complete the online application (snohomishcountywa .gov/Facilities/Facility/Details/Meadowdale-Beach-Park-56).

> *"Walk and be happy, walk and be healthy. The best way to lengthen out our days is to walk steadily and with a purpose."*
> —Charles Dickens

# 5 O. O. Denny Park

During summer the popular beach at O. O. Denny Park is crowded with people over-dosing on sun while the sylvan trail up Denny Creek lies forlorn and ignored. That's too bad, because along with some good representatives of large standing wood is one Douglas fir with a 26.3-foot circumference, which previous writers have claimed to be 600 years old. But you don't have to be looking for big old trees to enjoy this hike. It's perfect for a jaunt after work when the only other option is cocktails with coworkers whose idea of the outdoors is either a tennis court or a municipal plunge. If you live or work on the east side, make a habit of taking a picnic dinner and walk this lovely trail every week during summer and fall. The path gets a bit too wet the remainder of the year, but it's still worth the effort.

**Start:** Trailhead in gravel overflow parking lot, across from the beach and picnic area along Holmes Point Drive

**Distance:** 1.6-mile lollipop with some out and back

**Approximate hiking time:** 2 to 3 hours

**Difficulty:** Easy, with several creek crossings and a muddy trail

**Trail surface:** Forested path, gravel, boards

**Seasons:** Year-round

**Other trail users:** Runners

**Canine compatibility:** Leashed dogs permitted

**Land status:** City of Kirkland Parks and Recreation

**Nearest town:** Kirkland

**Services:** Gas, restaurants, groceries, lodging; flush toilet at trailhead

**Northwest Forest Pass:** No

**Discover Pass:** No

**Map:** USGS Bellevue North

**Trail contact:** City of Kirkland Parks and Recreation

**Special hazards:** Devil's club, creek crossings, wet and slippery boardwalk. No sidewalks along Holmes Point Drive; while driving, keep a careful eye out for pedestrians walking along the road.

**Finding the trailhead:** From Seattle, cross Lake Washington on either I-90 or WA 520 to I-405 north. Reaching Kirkland, take exit 20A, NE 116th Street. Turn left (west) at the stoplight. NE 116th Street becomes NE Juanita Drive and then Juanita Drive NE. Turn left (north) onto Holmes Point Drive NE. Continue 1.1 miles and look for the trailhead parking lot on the left (west). A subsidiary gravel parking lot is located on the east side of Holmes Point Drive but may be locked. There is limited street parking on Holmes Point Drive. GPS: N47 42.584' / W122 14.994'

## The Hike

Begin by leaving the paved parking lot and carefully crossing Holmes Point Drive. Walk to the northern end of the gravel overflow parking lot, and find the trail behind a welcoming sign. Trails up the ravine were first constructed in 1926 by the City of Seattle when the park was chosen as a camping site for Seattle children in one of the

*A quiet and shady walk in the woods at O. O. Denny Park*

first outdoor education schools in the United States. The park was upgraded in 1934 by the Civilian Conservation Corps, which improved the trails.

The sometimes-muddy trail skirts a wet area on possibly slippery boards and enters a thick forest of Douglas fir and western red cedar. Denny Creek along with its anadromous fish population is below on the right (south). Cross more wet areas on a combination of bridges and boards, and in 0.2 mile reach a large Douglas fir.

The trail climbs on steps to avoid the creek, climbs through more wet areas on boardwalks and stairs, and emerges in a long, narrow copse of mature red alder. Light streams beautifully contrast with the dark, shady regions of the surrounding conifer forest on the upper slopes.

After 0.4 mile stop for a moment at an interpretive sign at the site of two homes built during the 1920s. This property was purchased in 1974 by King County for Big

### GREEN TIP:
Minimize the use and impact of fires. Use designated fire spots or existing fire rings (if permitted). When building fires, use small sticks that you find on the ground. Keep your fire small, burn it to ash, put it out completely, and scatter the cool ashes. If you can, it's best to avoid making a fire at all.

# HOW PLANTS WERE NAMED

**Blame it all on a guy, fixated on sex, born over 300 years ago in Sweden.**

The modern discipline of taxonomy—the art of naming and classifying living things—was invented by Carl Linnaeus, who once declared, "God creates, Linnaeus arranges." Albrecht von Haller, a contemporary of Linnaeus, called the master naturalist "the second Adam," since the biblical Adam had named everything on Earth the first time around. He just hadn't thought to use Latin!

The Linnaeus system relied on a binomial nomenclature—what we now refer to as genus + species. He also decided that organisms would be classified based upon their most conservative structures (i.e., those body parts less likely to be modified over time). This meant their sexual structures. In plants that meant flowers. Linnaeus wrote, "Every animal feels the sexual urge," and, "Yes, love comes even to the plants."

This did not endear him to some of his contemporaries during the late eighteenth century. They called the Linnaeus sexual system of plant classification indecent. One of his detractors, Johann Siegesbeck, called Linnaeus's work "loathsome harlotry," writing, "Who would have thought that bluebells, lilies, and onions could be up to such immorality?"

Indeed.

*Common bear grass is a popular and well-loved spring wildflower.*

Finn Hill Park. Turn right (south) and walk to a bridge over the creek and another interpretive sign that describes the fish ladder, which was conceived, designed, and built by volunteers in July 2002.

Behind you, the trail continues up the creek (northeast) for another 0.3 mile and involves splashing through the creek several times. Then, passing a bench that affords a nice place to sit and rest, the trail switchbacks steeply up the hill until it forms a wye. At this unmarked trail junction, a waytrail extends left (northeast), getting narrower and narrower until it disappears completely. A degree of bushwhacking brings adventurous hikers to the backyards of people living along Juanita Drive NE. This route is not recommended.

Turning right (south) at the wye brings you in 0.1 mile to trail access at the intersection of 76th Avenue NE and NE 125th Street.

Returning to the fish ladder and bridge, pass several more interpretive signs. The trail here is actually an old roadbed. Note the occasional decommissioned utility pole. Continue along this old road to another access point at 73rd Place NE. Turn right

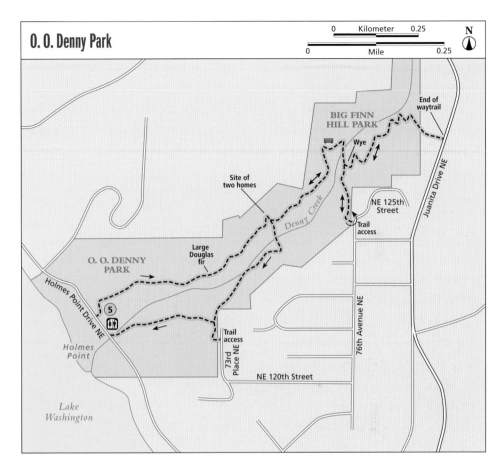

## O. O. Denny Park

BIG FINN HILL PARK

End of waytrail

Wye

Site of two homes

NE 125th Street

Trail access

Denny Creek

Large Douglas fir

O. O. DENNY PARK

Holmes Point Drive NE

5

Juanita Drive NE

76th Avenue NE

Trail access

73rd Place NE

NE 120th Street

Holmes Point

Lake Washington

(north), and descend toward Holmes Point Drive, crossing the street and reaching the paved parking lot.

## Miles and Directions

**0.0**   Holmes Point Drive NE trailhead

**0.2**   Large Douglas fir

**0.4**   Home site

**0.6**   Bench

**0.7**   Wye split in trail

**0.8**   Trail access at 76th Avenue NE

**1.4**   Trail access at 73rd Place NE

**1.6**   End of trail

**Options:** Bridle Trails State Park, Saint Edward State Park (includes 3,000 feet of shoreline and 316 acres representing the last large piece of intact forest on Lake Washington), Big Finn Hill County Park, and City of Kirkland's Juanita Bay Park are all within a few miles of O. O. Denny Park and offer a wide range of amenities from secluded wooded paths and horse-riding trails to baseball and soccer fields.

# Hike Information

O. O. Denny Park was once known as "Klahanie" and served as the country estate of Orion O. Denny (1853–1916), son of Seattle founder Arthur Denny. After the younger Denny died, his widow willed the property to Seattle. The park was formerly managed by King County. In 2013 the park was turned over to the City of Kirkland when that city annexed the Finn Hill area.

The lake side of the park has a grass lawn, picnic areas with benches, and a gravelly beach. O. O. Denny Park closes at dusk. Alcoholic beverages, fireworks, and weapons are not allowed. All fires must be in raised park grills only. There is a shelter available by reservation. No powered watercraft, including personal watercraft, are allowed within 300 feet of the park shoreline. Parking space is limited, so no trailer parking is allowed in either the parking lot or along Holmes Point Drive. Parking along Holmes Point Drive is limited and heavily enforced; read signs carefully.

# Skykomish River Valley

Rimmed by water and high mountains, the nineteenth-century city fathers of Seattle were hard-pressed to find a fast and reliable route for imports and exports. When ideas for a rail route were floated, the Great Northern Railroad preferred a route over Stevens Pass to Seattle's idea of Snoqualmie Pass. US 2 through the Skykomish Valley follows much of this pioneering railroad through mountains of stunning beauty and complexity. When hikers and motorists can take their eyes off the peaks, cliffs, and waterfalls, they gravitate toward the Skykomish River. Whitewater kayakers and anglers make "the Sky" an important recreational river.

*Bridging the creek below upper Deception Falls*

*Hikers enjoying the waterfall below Lake Serene*

Established and dedicated in May 2008, the Wild Sky Wilderness provides a valuable link between Alpine Lakes Wilderness, other Forest Service wilderness lands, and North Cascades National Park. The Wild Sky protects 106,000 acres of land under the jurisdiction of Mount Baker–Snoqualmie National Forest. The measure has always enjoyed the support of valley residents and businesses along with broad congressional support across party lines.

▶ **The Wild Sky Wilderness provides a valuable link between the Alpine Lakes Wilderness and North Cascades National Park.**

*Surprise Lake—calm and peaceful*

# 6 Wallace Falls State Park

Wallace Falls marks the entrance to the grand scenery of the Skykomish River Valley. The river is a popular whitewater run, and paddlers know it as "the Sky." Traveling eastward, every turn of the road reveals another character of the Sky's beauty. As for the falls, within 0.5 mile the Wallace River drops 800 feet, creating twelve distinct waterfalls. Like Bridal Veil Falls, some 8 road miles farther upstream, the main cascade of Wallace Falls can be seen from the highway as it gushes, foams, and leaps 265 feet. Walking the trail to the falls takes your breath away—and it isn't solely because it feels like you're heading straight up. This popular trail can be full of people in summer and nearly devoid of hikers in winter, which is a shame, since winter rains make Wallace Falls truly impressive.

**Start:** Wallace Falls State Park
**Distance:** 6.0 miles out and back
**Approximate hiking time:** 3 to 4 hours
**Difficulty:** Moderate, with many steep pitches
**Trail surface:** Forested path, old railroad bed
**Seasons:** Year-round
**Other trail users:** Mountain bike
**Canine compatibility:** Leashed dogs permitted
**Land status:** Washington State Parks
**Nearest town:** Gold Bar

**Services:** Gas, restaurants, groceries; flush toilets at trailhead; camping and cabins for rent at Wallace Falls State Park
**Northwest Forest Pass:** No
**Discover Pass:** Yes
**Maps:** Green Trails No. 142: Index; USGS Index; USDAFS Mount Baker–Snoqualmie National Forest
**Trail contact:** Wallace Falls State Park
**Special hazards:** Exposure, cliffs, steep and slippery trail

**Finding the trailhead:** From Seattle, drive north on I-405 and then northeast on WA 522 to Monroe, where the high school is strategically placed across the street from the state penitentiary. In Monroe drive 13 miles east on US 2 to the town of Gold Bar. Turn left (north) at First Avenue, following the signs to Wallace Falls State Park. In 0.4 mile turn right (east) onto May Creek Road. In 1.1 miles bear left (northwest) onto Ley Road. Enter the park and pass through a gate. The road ends in 0.2 mile at a large, paved parking lot. GPS: N47 52.008' / W121 40.684'

## The Hike

The Woody Trail begins beside the restroom. Pass an information kiosk explaining the history of Wallace Lake and Wallace Falls. Begin walking the wide way underneath power lines, sharing the route with mountain bikes. In 0.2 mile the way veers left (north), away from the humming electricity. Stop and enjoy views eastward up the Skykomish Valley.

In another 0.1 mile reach a trail junction. Left (northwest) is the Railroad Trail, which takes the long way (and the bicyclists) to the Wallace River's north fork. Hikers turn right (northeast) and continue on the Woody Trail. Drop to the river, passing

*Upper Wallace Falls—one of many distinctive falls of water in the Wallace Falls State Park*

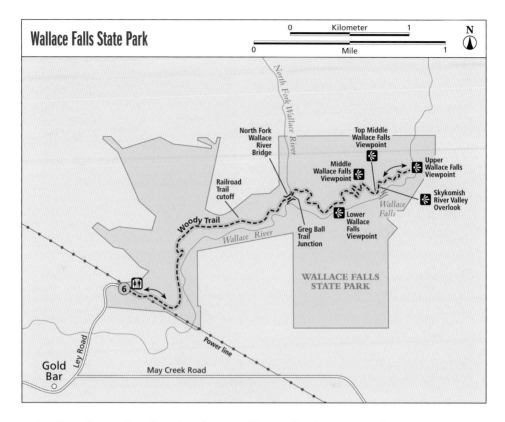

the first of many benches placed to provide rest for the weary and opportunities to appreciate the awesome beauty of nature. Periodic signposts tick off the mileage.

Abruptly the Woody Trail begins to climb steeply—first on switchbacks and then without. After 1 mile you reach a junction with a cutoff trail rising back to the Railroad Trail. Continue straight, upstream (north), on the Woody Trail. Another 0.5 mile brings you to the Greg Ball Trail to Wallace Lake. Bear right (east) and keep heading upstream, crossing the North Fork Wallace River on a stout bridge.

The Lower Wallace Falls Viewpoint is reached in 1.8 miles. There is a large picnic shelter with several big, heavy picnic tables. Tired? Hungry? Take a load off your feet and give thanks to the state park staff, who built the shelter and managed to haul the tables to this spot. Railings around the viewpoint help restrain the more inquisitive from risking their lives to obtain a better view. Look upstream for a faraway view to the middle falls.

The trail leaves the cliff and climbs as the river drops, but the din of rushing water never diminishes. In 0.5 mile come to the Middle Wallace Falls Viewpoint, followed by the Skykomish River Valley Overlook and trail's end at the Upper Wallace Falls Viewpoint 3 miles from the parking lot. From this point, although some maps show a trail leading another 3 miles to Wallace Lake, the route is difficult to follow, dangerous in many spots, and therefore not recommended. So, time to turn around and retrace your way back on the Woody Trail to the parking lot.

# THE BANANA SLUG

Our most common denizen of the forest must be the Pacific banana slug (*Ariolimax columbianus*). The slugs are often bright yellow, but green, brown, and white forms also exist. Growing up to 10 inches long, banana slugs are the second-largest species of land slug in the world. Only the European slug (*Limax cinereoniger*) gets longer.

*Banana slugs are common inhabitants of Pacific Northwest forests.*

Banana slugs make their living by crawling along the forest floor on their muscular foot, eating detritus. This makes them important decomposers as they process plant material and animal droppings into soil. They apparently also have a fondness for mushrooms. Movement is accomplished by waves of peristalsis—the same motion that delivers food from our mouths to our stomachs. Two pairs of tentacles sense light or movement and detect pheromones—chemical clues that help the slugs recognize one another. To avoid injury, the tentacles can be retracted.

A coating of slime protects the slug's skin and also provides a slick surface that aids in movement across the ground. The slime can also anesthetize any mucous membrane it comes in contact with, such as the lining of a predator's mouth, though not too many critters delight in eating banana slugs. Some of the slug's enemies include raccoons, geese, and ducks. It's possible to experience the numbing feeling caused by the slime by picking up a banana slug and letting it ooze across your fingertips.

## Miles and Directions

**0.0** Trailhead at restroom

**1.0** Woody Trail cutoff

**1.5** Woody Trail–Greg Ball Trail junction

**1.51** North Fork Wallace River Bridge

**1.8** Lower Wallace Falls Viewpoint, 319'

**2.0** Middle Wallace Falls Viewpoint

**2.5** Skykomish River Valley Overlook

**3.0** Upper Wallace Falls Viewpoint

**6.0** Arrive back at trailhead

# Hike Information

The lake, falls, river, and mount are named "Wallace" for Joe and Sarah Kwayaylsh, members of the Skykomish tribe, who were the first homesteaders in the area. The State of Washington acquired most of the land for the park in 1971 from the Weyerhaeuser Timber Company.

The Wallace Falls State Park Management Area is a 4,735-acre park with shoreline on the Wallace River, Wallace Lake, Jay Lake, Shaw Lake, and the Skykomish River. Park hours are 8 a.m. to dusk. There is a sign at the trailhead to tell you what time dusk is. The park has two walk-in tent sites and one restroom. There are two showers that campers can use, but a fee is required. The camping sites are 20 to 50 feet in from the parking area. Sites are very private, with picnic tables and campfire rings. Check-in time for camping (first come, first served) is 2:30 p.m.; quiet hours are 10 p.m. to 6:30 a.m.

There are five cabins adjacent to the trailhead parking area. Cabins feature a 6-foot covered front porch, picnic table, fire pit, electric heat and lights, and locking doors. They are furnished with bunk beds and a full-size futon. Two cabins have two rooms, providing privacy for the bunk beds, and two cabins have an ADA-compliant ramp. Cabin campers must bring their own linen and blankets. Reservations may be made year-round online at https://washington.goingto camp.com or by calling (888) CAMPOUT (888-226-7688).

Wallace Falls State Park is extremely busy on summer days, and the parking lot usually fills by 11 a.m. on weekends. Park personnel live on-site.

# 7 Lake Serene

Where the North and South Fork Skykomish Rivers come together, passengers in cars motoring along US 2 are treated to an amazing sight. To the south all eyes find it hard to miss the Yosemite-like visual delight of Bridal Veil Falls leaping a thousand feet into space with a series of foamy cataracts from its source in Lake Serene. Visiting the lake during the week or in the off-season, it's a serene experience as well, albeit a tough and exhausting one. But Lake Serene and Bridal Veil Falls are extremely popular places to visit, so hikers must be in a sharing mode on weekends. Once at the lake, be prepared for the jaw-dropping sight of Mount Index towering 3,500 feet above, dominating the scene.

**Start:** Trailhead for Lake Serene along US 2

**Distance:** 7.5 miles out and back

**Approximate hiking time:** 4 to 5 hours

**Trail number:** USDA Forest Service Trail 1068

**Difficulty:** Difficult; most steep sections surmounted by stairs

**Trail surface:** Sometimes rocky forested path, boardwalk, stairs

**Seasons:** Summer and fall

**Other trail users:** None

**Canine compatibility:** Leashed dogs permitted

**Land status:** USDAFS Skykomish Ranger District

**Nearest town:** Index

**Services:** Gas, restaurants, groceries, lodging; vault toilet at trailhead

**Northwest Forest Pass:** Yes

**Discover Pass:** No

**Maps:** Green Trails No. 142: Index; USGS Index; USDAFS Mount Baker-Snoqualmie National Forest, Alpine Lakes Wilderness

**Trail contacts:** Alpine Lakes Protection Society (ALPS), Mount Baker-Snoqualmie National Forest, Skykomish Ranger District

**Special hazards:** Loose rock, exposure (stay within guardrails near Bridal Veil Falls); no potable water at trailhead or on trail

**Finding the trailhead:** From Seattle, take WA 522 to Monroe, turning (left) east onto US 2. Drive US 2 through Gold Bar, passing signs to Wallace Falls State Park at First Avenue. Continue east for another 7.3 miles to Mount Index Road (FR 6020). Turn right (south) onto a wide, potholed, unpaved road. Drive 0.2 mile and bear right (south) at a fork onto FR 6020-109. Continue 0.1 mile to a parking area. GPS: N47 48.538' / W121 34.432'

## The Hike

The initial 1.5 miles of the Lake Serene Trail is on private property and follows an old logging road. The current trail to Lake Serene is not the trail that many old-time hikers in the region remember. That thing—hardly a trail at all—was an outrageously extraordinary up-and-down excursion into the fifth dimension across Utah-style slickrock and Jack-and-the-Beanstalk tree roots. Enough people were hauled down that old trail, blubbering in fear and on the verge of a nervous breakdown, that generations of guidebooks kept Lake Serene out of their pages.

*Beautifully serene Lake Serene*

No more. A new trail has changed it all. Not that some of the old trail features have disappeared completely!

The steep trail to Lake Serene seems unending—especially during the long, hot summer days that periodically sit over the Puget Sound region. Maybe that's why the trail, which feels as if it reaches from the depths of some bottomless hole and into the heavens, is so unbearable to so many people who come equipped for a walk in the park versus a strenuous hike.

From the parking area, walk around the gate on what is obviously an old road. After 0.1 mile note the hiker sign and bear right (south). Many of the old volunteer trails still exist—though the yearly renewable flagging is long, long gone. Keep your eyes sharp, and follow the main route to avoid getting off course.

Cross a small creek on a footbridge, and in another 0.3 mile cross it again. Believe it or not, cars used to come this far. After 1.2 miles from the trailhead, another sign directs hikers to the right (south) on a wide, obvious trail. Another fork and another trail sign

▶ **Edward Payson Weston made a bet that Abraham Lincoln would lose the 1860 presidential election. Weston's losing bet was to walk from Boston to Washington, DC, for the inauguration. He completed the 478-mile trip in ten days, ten hours—and received a congratulatory handshake from the new president.**

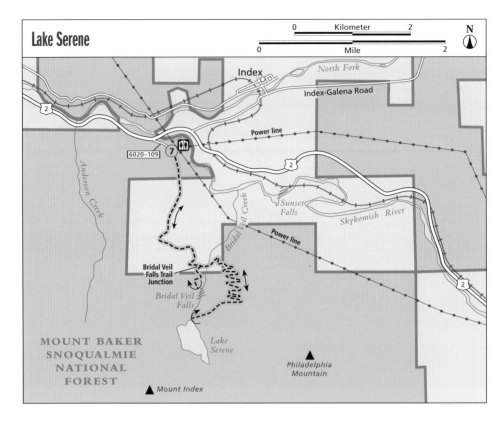

in 0.1 mile direct hikers left (southeast). In another 0.1 mile the trail bears left (southeast) at another fork. Turning the opposite direction leads to Bridal Veil Falls. It's worth the detour. On a hot day the spray of water is most refreshing. Stay within the guardrails, since the slope is wet and slippery. One false step could be embarrassing, and your friends and family will sorely miss you. Tired hikers stop at the falls, turn around, and head home.

Returning to the main trail, a series of stairs continues the trail down to a stream, crossing on a sturdy bridge with an even sturdier handrail. After that the trail climbs. And climbs. To infinity and beyond! Switchbacks take the trail west until it reaches a lip below the lake. All of a sudden, there it is! Lake Serene. It's difficult to know where to look first. The lake is certainly inviting—especially for hikers flushed in the face from the steep and direct climb. But Mount Index so dramatically overlords the view that it isn't easy to keep one's eyes from drifting toward the sky.

After reaching the lake, boardwalks head out in both directions. People like to swim in the lake on hot days, and it isn't hard to understand why—though the water is very cold. It's all snowmelt, you know.

To return, retrace your steps down the trail—and marvel at how almost vertical it was on the way up. Hopefully a walking stick will slow down the declivitous descent.

## Miles and Directions

**0.0** Trailhead on FR 6020-109

**1.8** Bridal Veil Falls trail junction

**3.7** Lake Serene

**7.5** Arrive back at trailhead

## Hike Information

Sunset, Canyon, and Eagle Falls are nearby, located on the South Fork Skykomish River. Wallace Falls State Park (Hike #6), with another very impressive drop of water, is located downstream near the town of Gold Bar.

The cabin, now in ruins, that lies off the Lake Serene Trail was built by miners during the early twentieth century. They were looking primarily for copper, though some gold and silver were also discovered. The Forest Service has decided to let the ruins deteriorate in place, and they are quickly returning to their elemental form.

# 8 Barclay and Eagle Lakes

This is actually two hikes. The first hike, to Barclay Lake, is an easy trail, suitable for young children. It has the added bonus of a lake with a shallow shoreline, large campsites, a designated day-use area, pit toilet, and the possibility of catching fish. The hike to Eagle Lake begins from Barclay Lake and gains nearly 1,500 feet in elevation on a trail that goes straight up. It is recommended only for hikers with experience in route-finding. Even in late spring the upper reaches of the trail in the vicinity of Stone and Eagle Lakes are snow-covered, and a 500-foot ascent through talus may be required.

**Start:** Trailhead along FR 6024
**Distance:** 4.6 miles out and back to upper Barclay Lake; 6.6 miles out and back to Eagle Lake (2.0 miles or more round-trip from Barclay Lake, depending on your route-finding skills)
**Approximate hiking time:** 3 hours round-trip to Barclay Lake; 6 to 8 hours round-trip to Eagle Lake
**Trail number:** USDA Forest Service Trail 1055
**Difficulty:** Easy to Barclay Lake; extremely difficult to Eagle Lake, which requires clambering over numerous fallen trees, a steep ascent while route-finding, a stream crossing, and climbing over talus
**Trail surface:** Forested path; rocky
**Seasons:** Summer and fall
**Other trail users:** None
**Canine compatibility:** Leashed dogs permitted
**Land status:** USDAFS Skykomish Ranger District

**Nearest town:** Index (limited services in Baring)
**Services:** Gas, restaurants, groceries, lodging; no toilet at trailhead
**Northwest Forest Pass:** Yes
**Discover Pass:** No
**Maps:** Green Trails No. 143: Monte Cristo; USGS Baring; USDAFS Mount Baker–Snoqualmie National Forest, Alpine Lakes Wilderness
**Trail contacts:** Alpine Lakes Protection Society (ALPS), Mount Baker–Snoqualmie National Forest, Skykomish Ranger District
**Special hazards:** Devil's club around lake outlet; snow in early season; muddy and/or water-covered trail to Barclay Lake. Trail to Eagle Lake from Barclay Lake is steep and requires route-finding and climbing over talus; snow in early season along with creek crossing.

**Finding the trailhead:** From Seattle, take WA 522 to Monroe, turning left (east) onto US 2. Drive US 2 through Gold Bar. Five miles east of Index on US 2 is the town of Baring—little more than a whistle-stop for the railroad. Look for a sign announcing "FR 6024–first left." The turn is directly opposite Der Baring Store. Cross the railroad tracks and drive north for 4.4 miles on a good gravel road. Pass FR 310 on the left in 1.5 miles and arrive at the trailhead parking. GPS: N47 47.545' / W121 27.549'

# The Hike

Leaving the parking lot, the trail undulates with very little elevation gain or loss until reaching Barclay Lake. The forest here is mature second-growth, with Douglas fir predominating. The canopy is thick enough to block all views of Baring Mountain and Barclay Creek. Stumps of many large trees line the trail until you reach the bridge crossing the creek.

At 0.7 mile from the trailhead, a split-log walkway helps hikers remain above the wet ground. Look around for flowers and the elephant-ear leaves of the musky-scented skunk cabbage (*Lysichiton americanus*). Similar in construction to calla lilies, the flower is actually the long yellow-green rod you see. It's surrounded by a yellow spathe (a large, showy, solitary bract).

After crossing Barclay Creek on a heavy-duty split-log bridge, the trail gently climbs to the lake. Pass the lake outlet to avoid devil's club and other physical obstructions and continue past the first campsite to the day-use area. If you have no plans to hike farther, this is a good place to stop for lunch or to splash in Barclay Lake. Take a look above you. That's Baring Mountain looming overhead, all but hidden from anywhere on the trail coming in. A sign directs hikers to an outdoor privy. Campsites are located lakeside and in the trees.

Hikers with experience in route-finding can continue on to Eagle Lake by walking over many fallen trees and passing more campsites to the head of Barclay Lake. Just past a small wooden bridge at the end of the lake, the Eagle Lake Trail branches off to the left. To the right is a small campsite under the trees.

The USGS topo map shows a trail to Eagle Lake. It's more like a game trail, occasionally flagged and ducked. It's not advisable to assume these markings will be there for you unless you leave them yourself for your descent. The difficult route goes straight up the deeply forested hillside, over big logs and through a well-developed shrub layer including devil's club. Ouch.

Keep climbing until you reach around the 3,200-foot elevation mark, and work your way to the stream on your right. Cross the creek below a rock wall, and continue traversing to the right. Signs of an old trail become more frequent; if you're lucky, you'll be able to see it. Ducks—another common term for cairns—are more frequent and helpful at this point.

Enter a wide gap in the hillside; follow it up to a snowfield (in early season) and ascend to the leftover large talus. In late summer move up the middle of the drainage between the trees and avoid the talus completely. Views across to Baring Mountain are particularly stunning from here—even more so than from the lake. At the top of the talus the route relents and flattens out. Stone Lake, not much more than a puddle, lies below to your right (east). Traverse above the drainage, around the shoulder of a hill to your left (west), through thin and spotty forest, and finally reach Eagle Lake, which is large and isolated in a beautiful cirque.

*The descent from Eagle Lake to Barclay Lake is long, steep, and intimidating. It requires bouldering skills.*

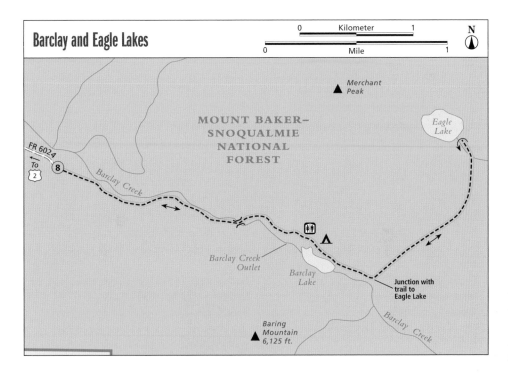

Retrace your steps to Barclay Lake; the return trip is easier since you now know the route. From Barclay Lake, retrace your route to the trailhead.

## Miles and Directions

- **0.0** Trailhead on FR 6024
- **1.3** Bridge over Barclay Creek
- **1.8** Barclay Lake campsite
- **2.3** Upper Barclay Lake and start of Eagle Lake Trail. **Option:** If not continuing to Eagle Lake, retrace your steps to the trailhead.
- **3.3** Eagle Lake
- **6.6** Arrive back at trailhead

## Hike Information

Don't forget to stop at the Reptile Zoo on your way home. It's located 1 mile east of Monroe at 22715 US 2, on the north side of the highway; (360) 805-5300; thereptile zoo.org.

# 9 Deception Falls

Rather than rushing across Stevens Pass to Leavenworth and points east, try a side trip to Deception Falls. This short, family-centric walk to some gorgeous waterfalls also provides an abundance of picnic places, a covered picnic area at the parking lot, and several vault toilets—all of which make Deception Falls a nice place for stopping while on a long drive. The waterfalls aren't too shabby either! The parking lot and toilets are closed during the winter.

**Start:** Trailhead at Deception Falls Nature Area
**Distance:** 0.5-mile loop
**Approximate hiking time:** 1 hour
**Difficulty:** Easy, with a few short uphill sections
**Trail surface:** Forested path, boardwalk, paved
**Seasons:** Year-round
**Other trail users:** None
**Canine compatibility:** Leashed dogs permitted
**Land status:** USDAFS Skykomish Ranger District
**Nearest town:** Skykomish
**Services:** Gas, restaurants, groceries, lodging; vault toilet at trailhead
**Northwest Forest Pass:** Yes

**Discover Pass:** No
**Maps:** Green Trails No. 176: Stevens Pass; USGS Scenic; USDAFS Mount Baker-Snoqualmie National Forest, Alpine Lakes Wilderness
**Trail contact:** Mount Baker-Snoqualmie National Forest, Skykomish Ranger District
**Special hazards:** The Tye River and both the upper and lower falls are at dangerous levels during spring runoff; keep a close eye on your children and don't go beyond any of the barriers. No potable water at trailhead or on trail; potable water available at the Skykomish Ranger Station.

**Finding the trailhead:** From Seattle, take WA 522 to Monroe, turning left (east) onto US 2. Drive US 2 to the Skykomish Ranger Station, and then go another 6.5 miles east on US 2 to Deception Falls Nature Area. Turn left (north) into the large paved parking lot. GPS: N47 42.929' / W121 11.725'

## The Hike

From the picnic area, drop down a paved trail for 100 feet to the first of two signed junctions. Go straight ahead, toward the lower falls. For the loop trail, turn left (northwest). In another 100 feet continue straight at a second signed trail junction, toward the upper falls. Turning left (north) is a shortcut to the lower falls and loop trail.

The trail crosses Deception Creek on a footbridge and then leads up stone stairs and under US 2 to a viewing platform. This is Upper Deception Falls. The water from Deception Creek tumbles over rocks and is impressive throughout the year—even in late summer during low flows. Take a moment to read the interpretive sign that briefly explains the geologic history of this area.

Retrace your steps under the highway bridge, down the stone steps, and across the footbridge to the second signed junction. Turn right (north) and continue down

*Upper Deception Falls*

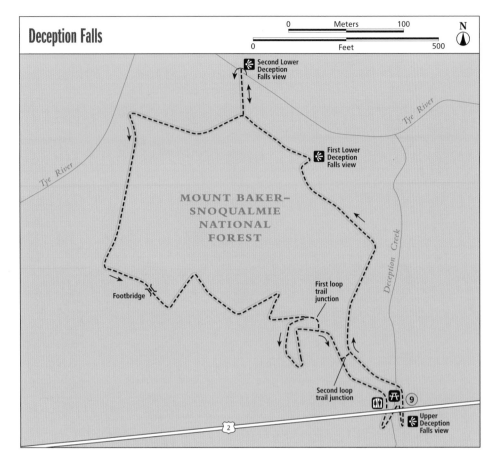

the loop trail toward Deception Creek, crossing a side channel of the creek that is a seasonally wet area. Don't forget to stop, not only to admire the creek and large trees, but also to read the many interpretive signs along the way that explain forest ecology.

Reach a spur trail and walk down twenty-two stairs to a large viewing platform overlooking the lower falls. Then return to the loop trail, turning right (north), and continue walking. Very soon find a different spur trail on the right (north), and follow it to another viewing platform. This one overlooks the Tye River as it makes an impressive 90-degree turn through bedrock, flowing through a rectangular notch and emerging into a pool below.

Continuing along the loop trail, curve southward, with the Tye River beside you for one last brief moment. Begin to climb up a hill toward the parking area. Cross a subsidiary creek on a nice footbridge—a great spot for a picnic lunch.

Some short, steep stretches of trail eventually lead to the first signed trail junction. Turn right (south) onto the asphalt path, and emerge at the parking lot 100 feet later.

# Miles and Directions

**0.0** Deception Falls trailhead

**0.1** Upper Deception Falls

**0.15** Cross creek

**0.2** First lower falls view

**0.3** Second lower falls view

**0.4** Footbridge

**0.5** Arrive back at trailhead

# Hike Information

About 4 miles east of Index on US 2 is Eagle Falls (N47 79.563' / W121 51.414') along the South Fork Skykomish River. At Milepost 39, keep your eyes peeled for a parking turnout on the south side of the highway. There are no signs. Volunteer paths lead to a rock formation and spots for viewing the falls, which drop 28 feet. River levels can be dangerously high, and rocks surrounding the falls can be wet and slippery, especially early in the season. Watch your step and keep an eye on yourself and your children.

To view Alpine Falls (N47 71.678' / W121 22.619'), continue 5.3 miles east of the Skykomish Ranger Station. West of the bridge crossing the Tye River is a turnout on the south side of the road. A short, obvious path leads to a lookout above the falls. Several steep waytrails lead down to the river below the falls, which drop 40 feet. River levels can be dangerously high, and rocks surrounding the falls can be wet and slippery, especially early in the season. The same admonishments to safety made about Deception and Eagle Falls apply here as well.

Stop by Der Baring Store for antiques shopping as well as good comfort food after your hike; 63501 Stevens Pass Hwy., Baring, WA 98224; (425) 524-8102.

# 10  Surprise Lake

For such an obscure trailhead, the way up to Surprise Lake (and beyond) gets a lot of foot traffic. This probably has to do with the trail's proximity to Surprise Creek (along with its many waterfalls) and the large number of campsites at the lake. Numerous avalanche chutes provide prime wildflower viewing in spring, and views up-canyon from the lake to cliffs and crags are very impressive. More adventurous hikers can hook up with the Pacific Crest Trail to points farther north or south, create a back-packing loop with Deception Creek (Forest Service Trail 1059), or utilize many other trails on a multiday excursion to reach Salmon La Sac (car shuttle needed).

**Start:** Surprise Creek Trail
**Distance:** 8.0 miles out and back
**Approximate hiking time:** 5 to 6 hours
**Trail number:** USDA Forest Service Trail 1060
**Difficulty:** Moderate, with many steep areas
**Trail surface:** Forested path, boardwalk; rocky
**Seasons:** Spring, summer, and fall
**Other trail users:** None
**Canine compatibility:** Leashed dogs permitted
**Land status:** USDAFS Skykomish Ranger District, Alpine Lakes Wilderness Area
**Nearest town:** Skykomish
**Services:** Gas, restaurants, groceries, lodging; camping at Forest Service Money Creek; pit privy with no walls at trailhead

**Northwest Forest Pass:** Yes
**Discover Pass:** No
**Maps:** Green Trails No. 176: Stevens Pass; USGS Scenic; USDAFS Mount Baker-Sno-qualmie National Forest, Alpine Lakes Wilderness
**Trail contacts:** Alpine Lakes Protection Society (ALPS), Mount Baker-Snoqualmie National Forest, Skykomish Ranger District
**Special hazards:** Devil's club, creek crossing on logs; no potable water at trailhead or on trail

**Finding the trailhead:** From Seattle, take WA 522 to Monroe, turning left (east) onto US 2. Drive US 2 to Der Baring Store in Baring. Drive 17.6 miles farther east to Milepost 58.7, passing the turnoff to Skykomish Ranger Station, Deception Falls, and Iron Goat Interpretive Center. Turn right (south) onto an unmarked road. This road crosses the Tye River and some railroad tracks and in 0.1 mile passes through a railroad service yard. Bear right (west) and continue 0.3 mile on a narrow, rough road (FR 840) to a small parking area and the trailhead. GPS: N47 42.479' / W121 09.397'

## The Hike

Self-register at the trailhead to enter the Alpine Lakes Wilderness. The trail starts along a power line road. In 0.2 mile reach the Surprise Creek Trail on the left (southwest). Begin climbing gently on a series of old steps and rough wooden bridges through deep second-growth forest alongside the creek. After 0.6 mile enter the Alpine Lakes Wilderness Area and delight in the much larger trees.

Meander through the old-growth forest, and at 1 mile cross Surprise Creek on a log. The trail steepens but climbs below an avalanche slope and talus field before climbing in earnest. The stream gradient changes as well, making Surprise Creek louder and louder with plenty of small waterfalls. The canyon narrows, and more avalanche slopes appear on both sides.

Devil's club (*Oplopanax horridus*) fills many of these avalanche slopes. This native plant is perfectly adapted to growing in disturbed areas. Spiny leaves discourage plant predators. Brittle stems easily break off the parent plant and take root. Many Northwest Indians included the fruit as part of their pharmacopoeia. Anglos have found the fruit to be poisonous and the remainder of the plant to cause contact dermatitis.

After 3 miles, and tired of pussyfooting around alongside the creek, the trail makes a couple of switchbacks to the northeast, getting higher up on the east canyon wall, and then resumes its steep climb. The trail crosses innumerable side channels, kisses the creek one last time, and turns away like a spurned lover. The following switchbacks are numerous, shorter and steeper than the previous ones, and continue for another 0.5 mile. Near the top of the switchbacks, a sign bolted to a tree announces that fires are prohibited past this point.

Sadly for those in hope of rest and respite, the end is not near. The trail continues its steep climb, utilizing a couple more switchbacks before finally flattening out

# HOW TO DEAL WITH BLISTERS

Blisters can feel just awful. How amazing it is that a little bubble of water on your toe can turn a fantastic hiking trip into disaster. Keeping in mind that blisters are caused by friction, the following hints may help to keep your hiking trips in the fun column.

It is said that "you don't break in boots, you break in feet." That's why it's wise to wear boots that fit. Ditto for socks. Padding is a good thing! Wear socks that aren't worn away in the heels and toes. It helps to keep your toenails trimmed, too, since this ensures that boots and socks fit properly. One last comment about socks: If your feet sweat a lot, bring an extra pair of socks and switch them out every hour or so. Dry socks won't rub as much.

Remove any pebbles, twigs, or other foreign objects from your shoe ASAP. Pay attention to any signals your feet send to your brain. A "hot spot" likely means rubbing has begun to build a new blister. It can happen fast. Real fast.

If a blister does form, add some padding. If you decide to pop the blister, be aware that infection could set in. Wash your hands and the affected foot, and sterilize a needle. After draining the blister, apply antiseptic. Hand sanitizer will do the trick. Wrap the blister to keep it clean. Check and change the bandage frequently, keeping it as dry as possible. Follow up at home with cleaning the area and changing the bandage.

*Beautiful, inviting, enticing Surprise Lake*

for its final approach to Surprise Lake. During this last 0.5 mile, gentle trail sections alternate with short spurts of steepness. Finally, after one last lung-buster, reach a trail junction with the Pacific Crest Trail (PCT) and a large camping area.

For the PCT, turn left (east). To continue on to the lake, bear right (southwest). Soon you will reach a trail junction with Trail 1060, a shortcut to the PCT. Continue straight for 1 mile to Glacier Lake and farther to Surprise Gap. Continue on waytrails past a privy to reach Surprise Lake in 0.1 mile. There are many camping areas alongside the eastern lakeshore as well as another privy. On a promontory, at what looks like the best camping site at Surprise Lake, is a great day-use-only area. The lakeside waytrail passes several other campsites before being lost in the rocks and boulders at the head of Surprise Lake. Remember, no campfires are allowed.

## Miles and Directions

**0.0** Trailhead on FR 840

**0.2** Junction of power line road and Surprise Creek Trail

**0.6** Boundary of Alpine Lakes Wilderness Area

**1.0** Cross Surprise Creek

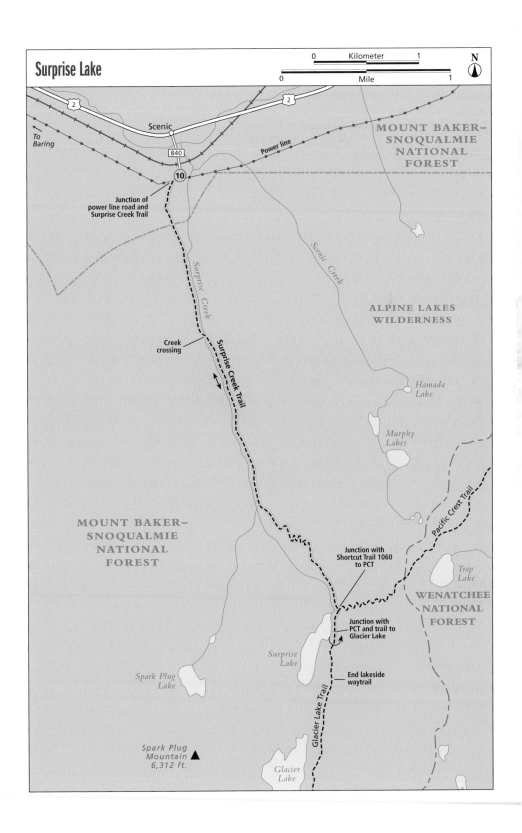

Surprise Lake

To Baring

Scenic

Power line

Junction of power line road and Surprise Creek Trail

MOUNT BAKER– SNOQUALMIE NATIONAL FOREST

Surprise Creek

Scenic Creek

ALPINE LAKES WILDERNESS

Creek crossing

Surprise Creek Trail

Hamada Lake

Murphy Lakes

Pacific Crest Trail

MOUNT BAKER– SNOQUALMIE NATIONAL FOREST

Junction with Shortcut Trail 1060 to PCT

Trap Lake

WENATCHEE NATIONAL FOREST

Junction with PCT and trail to Glacier Lake

Surprise Lake

Spark Plug Lake

End lakeside waytrail

Glacier Lake Trail

Spark Plug Mountain 6,312 ft.

Glacier Lake

**3.9** Junction with shortcut Trail 1060 to PCT

**4.0** Surprise Lake

**8.0** Arrive back at trailhead

## Hike Information

Stop at Zeke's Drive-In, a roadside diner located at Milepost 31.5 on US 2, 2 miles west of FR 62, for root beer floats and their famous big, fat, and juicy onion rings. Burgers and fries are equally as good, and the staff is very friendly. Zeke's isn't always open late, but when they're open, they're great; 44006 US 2, Gold Bar, WA 98251; (360) 793-2287.

# 11 Boulder Lake

The *Oxford English Dictionary* tells us there are at least a quarter of a million distinct English words, excluding words from technical and regional vocabularies. With that amazing richness, why are so many rocky bodies of water named Boulder River or Boulder Lake? No matter. All is not in a name, as you will discover from this lightly used trail. The rich understory, experienced only in old-growth forests—something you will see in abundance here—is delightfully refreshing. The nine designated camp-sites (closed from October 15 to June 15) at Boulder Lake have dynamite views of the lake basin and surrounding cirque.

**Start:** Trailhead along South Shore Road (marked first as Road SL4000 and then Road 61 on the Green Trails map)
**Distance:** 4.8 miles out and back
**Approximate hiking time:** 4 to 5 hours
**Difficulty:** Moderate, with some steep areas and possibility of downed trees
**Trail surface:** Forested path; rocky
**Seasons:** Summer and fall
**Other trail users:** None; lake is reported to be fishless with no appeal to anglers
**Canine compatibility:** Leashed dogs permitted
**Land status:** Department of Natural Resources—part of the 33,592-acre Morning Star Resource Conservation Area, which includes the former 6,700-acre Greider Ridge Natural Resources Conservation Area
**Nearest town:** Sultan
**Services:** Gas, restaurants, groceries; vault toilet at trailhead
**Northwest Forest Pass:** No
**Discover Pass:** Yes
**Maps:** Green Trails No. 142: Index; USGS Mount Stickney; USDAFS Mount Baker-Snoqualmie National Forest
**Trail contacts:** Commissioner of Public Lands, Department of Natural Resources, City of Everett, Public Works
**Special hazards:** No potable water at trailhead or on trail

**Finding the trailhead:** From Seattle, drive northeast on WA 522 to Monroe. Connect with US 2 and drive east to Sultan. Just past Milepost 23, turn left at the traffic signal onto Sultan Basin Road. Avoid diverting onto the many smaller side roads. The pavement ends at 10.5 miles, becoming wider and hard-packed, with occasional clusters of potholes. At 13.5 miles bear right at the fork onto South Shore Road. Stop at the self-registration station, marked prominently by a sign that reads "All Vehicles Must Check In." After registering, drive on, passing numerous fishing access points to Spada Reservoir. Stop at Bear Point and appreciate the reservoir view.

The road character now begins to change, becoming increasingly narrower and rockier. Pass the Greider Lakes trailhead at 20.7 miles, where the road continues to narrow. Although the road is rocky and the potholes are more frequent and deeper than before, the way is still passable for passenger cars. Drive another 1.3 miles and park at the Boulder Lake trailhead. GPS: N47 58.226' / W121 33.438'

# The Hike

Begin by the large sign announcing camping, driving, shooting, and dumping restrictions—and the lack of sanitary facilities at the lake. Ascend a rocky, abandoned road through an area clear-cut in the 1960s and replanted in 1970. Older guidebooks mention the open character of the country, but after fifty years the forest has experienced significant regeneration. See? It does come back. Early in the season it's possible to hear the roar of Boulder Creek, but it remains hidden and unknown behind green mansions until you reach a bridge over Boulder Creek in 0.1 mile.

Stopping on this bridge to admire the creek is *de rigueur* because the cascades, pools, and waterfalls are so impressive. Old-growth forest lovers will also want to take a peek at how this bridge was constructed.

The road is no longer much of a road and quickly devolves into a trail that makes a low traverse of Greider Ridge. It's amazing to contemplate that this small area receives 100 to 180 inches of annual precipitation. It's no wonder the city of Everett decided to build its domestic water supply along the Sultan River and collect some of the precious fluid.

After about a mile the traverse ends and—*boom!*—enter an old-growth forest and begin switchbacking up the hill. The nicely graded trail alternates with stairs reinforced with cedar planking. The steps are tall and deep and will have you panting for breath in no time. In 1.6 miles the trail crosses a sizable marsh along a boardwalk of split cedar rounds—designed both to keep your feet dry and to protect this sensitive area from trampling. Watch for skunk cabbage (*Lysichiton americanus*), marsh marigold (*Caltha* sp.), shooting star (*Dodecatheon* sp.), red columbine (*Aquilegia formosa*), and other wildflowers. Mosquitoes, too, in season. The marsh rim is covered with different kinds of huckleberries (*Vaccinium* spp.).

The boardwalk provides a swell place to stop and look around. The forest has become much more interesting. The trees are not all the same age and size. There are plenty of big openings in the canopy, and a highly developed understory of herbs and shrubs is evident. Observe the number of fallen trees and snags (standing, dead trees). This is what old-growth habitat looks like—so different from what we have become accustomed to by hiking in places with a history of human impact.

At 2.4 miles cross a bridge below the log-jammed outflow of Boulder Lake. There are nine numbered campsites either along the lakeshore or above it. Each has a fine view of the lake, a fire pit with a useless barbecue grill, and a roughly hewn bench. If you're here to camp (June 15 through October 15; the lake is closed to camping the remainder of the year), haul out all your trash. Behind Campsite 5 is a privy with

**GREEN TIP:**
Keep to established trails. If there aren't any, stay
on surfaces that will be least affected by your boots,
like rock, gravel, other hard surfaces, or snow.

*Boulder Lake in early season*

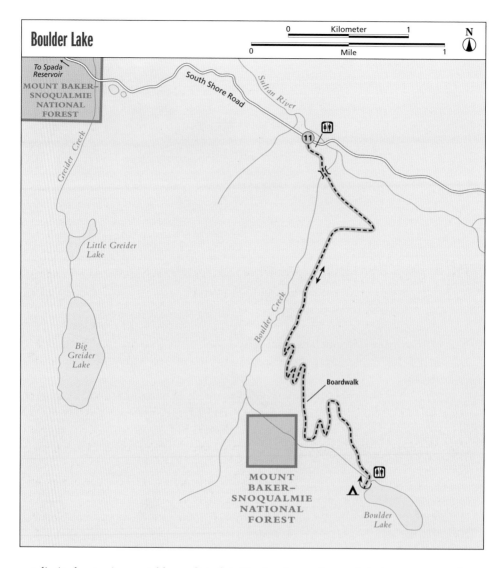

**Boulder Lake**

To Spada Reservoir

MOUNT BAKER–SNOQUALMIE NATIONAL FOREST

South Shore Road

Sultan River

Greider Creek

Little Greider Lake

Big Greider Lake

Boulder Creek

Boardwalk

MOUNT BAKER–SNOQUALMIE NATIONAL FOREST

Boulder Lake

a limited-capacity portable vault toilet. Don't rely on the vault being empty or the privy being operational.

Boulder Lake is situated in a narrow chasm with rocky crags high above. Directly across from the campsites is an immense talus slope, which no doubt gives the lake its descriptive name. The far end of the lake disappears around a forested corner, and adventurous souls will want to explore to see what there is to see.

The trail ends here. Had enough of azure waters, stark horizons, and a subalpine forest? Turn around and retrace your route back to the parking lot.

## Miles and Directions

**0.0**  Boulder Lake trailhead

**1.6**  Boardwalk

**2.4**  Boulder Lake

**4.8**  Arrive back at trailhead

> **Option:** The trail to Little and Big Greider Lakes provides a lower, shorter, easier, and more popular (i.e., more crowded) route.

## Hike Information

Spada Reservoir, operated by the City of Everett Public Works Department for domestic consumption, was formed in 1965 when Culmback Dam was built. The dam was raised in 1983 to increase water-storage capacity and to construct a hydropower project, which is operated by the Snohomish Public Utility District (PUD). Today the reservoir covers nearly 1,900 acres and has 17 miles of shoreline. The reservoir is named for John Spada, an original Snohomish County PUD commissioner and organizer of the Snohomish Soil Conservation District.

To maintain the water's high quality, recreational activities on the reservoir are limited. Gas-powered engines, swimming, and fishing with bait are prohibited. Both the watershed and the reservoir are patrolled daily, and access to the reservoir is restricted after sundown.

Kayakers consider the Sultan River, below Spada Reservoir, to be one of our region's premier whitewater runs. American Whitewater is working to improve flows and public access on the Sultan River for the benefit of fish, wildlife, and recreation as part of relicensing the Jackson Hydroelectric Project and Culmback Dam on this river.

A natural resource conservation area protects outstanding examples of native plant communities and other ecological features, such as subalpine meadows, wetlands, and lakes. In 2007 three natural resource conservation areas—Morning Star, Mount Pilchuck, and Greider Ridge—were unified under the name Morning Star NRCA. Public and private universities, other research institutions, and individual researchers conduct research in the Morning Star NRCA.

# 12 Iron Goat Trail–Martin Creek to Wellington

What today is a pleasant walk in a shady grove on a gentle grade was once the site of a terrible tragedy. In 1910 two stranded trains that had spent eight days trying to push through the snowy environment just west of Stevens Pass were swept away by a half-mile-wide avalanche. Ninety-six people died. That terrible route is now a mostly level walk through thick second-growth forest as it follows the old Great Northern Railroad route. This history is the prime reason for hiking the Iron Goat Trail. But there are also dazzling displays of wildflowers during spring, extensive views up and down the Skykomish River Valley, and a rich human history replete with this great tragedy. There are also many opportunities for loop hikes, but this particular hike makes a one-way trip from Martin Creek to the Wellington town site and trailhead, requiring a car or bicycle shuttle. Stopping at the Iron Goat Interpretive Site at Milepost 58.3 on US 2 is a requirement for understanding the trail, the railroad, and the people who made both happen.

**Start:** Trailhead at Martin Creek

**Distance:** 6.0 miles point-to-point with car or bicycle shuttle

**Approximate hiking time:** 4 to 5 hours

**Trail number:** USDA Forest Service Trail 1074

**Difficulty:** Easy, nearly level path

**Trail surface:** Forested path, boardwalk, old railroad bed; rocky

**Seasons:** Spring, summer, and fall

**Other trail users:** Runners, mountain bikes

**Canine compatibility:** No dogs allowed

**Land status:** USDAFS Skykomish Ranger District

**Nearest town:** Skykomish

**Services:** Gas, restaurants, groceries, lodging; camping at USDAFS Money Creek; vault toilet at trailhead

**Northwest Forest Pass:** Yes

**Discover Pass:** No

**Maps:** Green Trails No. 176: Stevens Pass; USGS Scenic; USDAFS Mount Baker-Snoqualmie National Forest, Alpine Lakes Wilderness

**Trail contacts:** Mount Baker-Snoqualmie National Forest, Skykomish Ranger District

**Special hazards:** Mountain bikes, stinging nettle, devil's club; no potable water at trailhead or on trail

**Finding the trailhead:** From Seattle, take WA 522 to Monroe, turning left (east) onto US 2. Drive US 2 through Gold Bar to Der Baring Store in the town of Baring. Continue east on US 2 for 14 miles. Pass the turnoff to Skykomish and the Skykomish Ranger Station, continuing east to Milepost 55 and Northwest Old Cascade Highway (FR 67). Turn left (north). Proceed 2.3 miles on a narrow, well-paved asphalt road to the junction with FR 6710, then turn left (northwest) and travel 1.4 miles on a narrow, well-graded gravel road to the small parking lot. A picnic bench and garbage can are beside the toilet. Passing the turnoff to Martin Creek trailhead, the Old Cascade Highway continues for another 2 miles to the Iron Goat Interpretive Site. GPS: N47 43.746' / W121 12.409'

To reach the Wellington trailhead and town site, continue east on US 2 toward Stevens Pass. At 23.6 miles from Der Baring Store (Milepost 64.4), continue past the Old Stevens Pass Highway on the left (north). It is unsafe to make the turn from this part of US 2, so drive on for 0.3 mile to Stevens Pass. Turn around at the pass and head west to the Old Stevens Pass Highway. Turn right (east, curving to north, then west) onto a rough and poorly paved asphalt road with plenty of Seattle-size potholes. After 2.9 miles turn right (northwest) at the junction with FR 050 onto a good gravel road to reach a large parking area in 0.3 mile. There are picnic tables, a garbage can, vault toilets, and a saddleback-style bicycle rack at Wellington. GPS: N47 44.830' / W121 07.658'

## The Hike

Cross FR 6710 at the Martin Creek trailhead to an information kiosk to find benches and a boardwalk. Follow the ADA-accessible boardwalk for 100 yards onto a wide gravel path. Soon you will reach an interpretive sign and self-registration station.

Continue east through a copse of mature red alder. These trees live not much longer than eighty to ninety years, so it's instructive to contemplate how this area appeared before World War II. Destructive logging practices during the late nineteenth and early twentieth centuries contributed to the avalanche problems encountered by the Great Northern Railroad.

*This retaining wall was built to protect the train tracks from landslides.*

*This snow shed was built after the 1910 Wellington winter disaster to protect trains and passengers from further harm.*

Immediately past these trees is a signed junction with the Martin Creek Crossover, which continues the ADA-accessible trail to the Iron Goat Interpretive Site along US 2. Bear left (north) and climb some switchbacks to the old railroad grade, passing the ruins of a collapsed snow shed. Snow sheds were built to protect trains and tracks from avalanches and rockslides.

In 0.5 mile reach the first of several tunnels. This tunnel and the ones that follow have not been maintained since the route was closed in 1929. Rockfalls, cave-ins, and other hazards make these tunnels unsafe for exploration. Keep out, but by all means look inside this one to see that the roof has collapsed and there is no way to get out the other side. Afterward make use of the bypass trail on the right (south).

Come to Milepost 1716; the marker was placed here by Iron Goat Trail workers to let walkers know how far it is to the end of the old Great Northern line in St. Paul, Minnesota. It also helps in ticking off the trail miles to the railroad's eastern terminus in Wellington. Steep grades, horrendous weather that routinely brought 35 feet of snow every winter, and avalanches made this stretch of track incredibly difficult to build and maintain. On occasion it could take up to twenty-four hours to make the trip from Wellington to Martin Creek.

A signed junction for the Corea Crossover (to the lower grade) lies just beyond, switchbacking downhill for 0.5 mile. It's possible to loop back to Martin Creek from here. Our trail continues straight ahead.

Ruins of a second snow shed are reached a mile later at Milepost 1715. All that can be seen is a pile of large, rough-cut lumber where the collapsed shed used to be. The trail now passes a long retaining wall, a good 25 feet tall. It, like the others that follow, was built to hold back the hillside from spilling out onto the tracks. In places, erosion of the concrete has revealed the massive amount of steel reinforcement used in its construction. On the far side of the wall, reach the Spillway Spur.

A short side trail leads hikers up fifty-five steps to the top of the wall and thence to a reservoir and timber spillway built across a branch of the Tye River in 1910 as part of the Great Northern's fire protection system. The spillway and reservoir were completely lost to history until discovered in 1991 by trail workers attempting to find a solution to drainage problems along the route.

After 1.8 miles reach the Embro Tunnel and skirt around on the pre-tunnel grade—the amount of fallen rock in the tunnel underscores how dangerous it is to enter. Beside Embro's west portal, stand atop a huge pile of rock excavated by tunnel construction. More than 100 feet long and 30 feet tall, the rock pile resembles the terminal moraine of a mountain glacier. The east portal is impressive when compared to the west since it retains its concrete archway, but rockfall has completely sealed the opening.

Leaving the east portal, come to several more sections of retaining wall, scenic vistas, and a forest of vine maple and red alder. The dense second growth that covers the hillsides and roadbed makes it difficult to comprehend the avalanche dangers encountered by the Great Northern. Most of the timber below Windy Mountain

*Boots on the trail beats boots in your closet!*

and beneath Delberts Ridge was logged off to provide railroad ties; fuel to feed the engines' boilers; and construction materials for bridges, trestles, and tunnel shoring. Lots of timber was shipped down to Puget Sound, where it was turned into houses. Historical photographs from a hundred years ago show that the heavily forested slopes of today were denuded of their cover. Without this clear-cutting there wouldn't have been issues with avalanches. The problem with sliding snow was solved—impermanently—by wall and tunnel construction.

Another long retaining wall begins around Milepost 1714 and continues to Windy Point. The concrete-lined tunnel here is in better shape than any of the preceding ones, but it's still unsafe to travel. Great Northern trains crossing Stevens Pass between 1892 and 1913 had to crawl around Windy Point because the curve was so sharp. Trains risked derailment if they traveled faster than 5 miles per hour. Passengers on one side faced a rock face; those on the other side looked into a deep abyss falling into the Tye River. The 0.25-mile Windy Point Tunnel reduced track curvature, allowed speedier travel, and shielded trains from avalanches.

Walk around the tunnel and come to a signed junction for the Windy Point Crossover Trail, dropping 1 mile south on switchbacks to the Iron Goat Interpretive Site. Then quickly arrive at a signed spur trail to a portable toilet. Whether you use the facilities or not, there is a nice view across the valley to Surprise Lake, US 2, and the Burlington Northern–Santa Fe train tracks leading through the 7.8-mile tunnel between Scenic and Berne. The same view, with an interpretive sign but without the privacy, can be had at a viewpoint 100 feet east of the spur trail.

Following the east portal is another long retaining wall. Leading up to Milepost 1713, start looking upslope; you'll notice many railroad spikes poking up out of the ground. The ties rotted away long ago. They're in clusters, resembling bunches of rust-colored toadstools. Pass another collapsed snow shed at Milepost 1712.57, constructed in 1910. It was 256 feet long and made with 12-by-12-inch roof timbers. It looks like a big wooden blanket draped over the hillside.

More retaining walls lead up to a concrete snow shed built after the 1910 Wellington disaster. A double row of pillars on 10-foot centers hold up the roof. Midway through is a viewpoint with interpretive signs explaining the March 1, 1910, Wellington avalanche disaster and memorializing the ninety-six people who were swept to their deaths.

# Iron Goat Trail–Martin Creek to Wellington

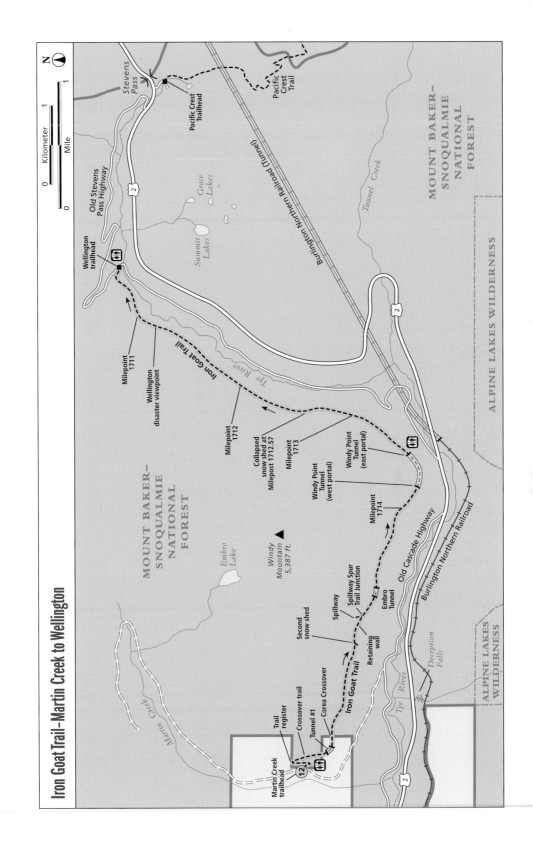

It is now possible to see rotted railway ties in small patches, the rails having been salvaged for scrap when the line was abandoned. At Milepost 1711 the east portal of the all-concrete snow shed is reached along with another hiker register. Cross a footbridge, pick up a wide gravel path, and follow it to the Wellington trailhead parking lot and your shuttle vehicle.

## Miles and Directions

**0.0**  Martin Creek trailhead

**0.5**  First railroad tunnel

**1.6**  Spillway junction

**1.8**  Embro Tunnel

**3.0**  Windy Point Tunnel (west portal)

**3.1**  Toilet/Windy Point Crossover

**3.2**  Windy Point Tunnel (east portal)

**5.5**  Concrete snow shed (west portal)

**5.7**  Wellington disaster viewpoint

**6.0**  Reach Wellington trailhead and your shuttle

**Options:** At the Iron Goat Interpretive Site (Milepost 58.3 on US 2, 17.3 miles east of Der Baring Store), there are vault toilets, a restored caboose, and interpretive displays. A 1-mile spur trail climbs steeply on several switchbacks to Windy Point. An ADA-accessible trail also leaves from here and leads to Martin Creek.

## Hike Information

For hikers interested in making a bike shuttle, leave your bicycle at Wellington (elevation 3,100 feet) and drive back to the Martin Creek trailhead. Once you've finished the hike at Wellington, pick up your bike and ride 0.2 mile to the Old Stevens Pass Highway. Turn right (west) and follow the old highway on alternating gravel and broken asphalt for 2 miles. This portion of the roadbed ends at a footbridge across the Tye River; cars can travel no farther. Cross the river and continue downhill to the Iron Goat Interpretive Site (elevation 2,100 feet) and the red caboose. Leave the interpretive site parking lot at Milepost 58.3 and pick up the old highway again. In about 2 miles find a gravel road on your right (northwest) and follow it another 2 miles to Martin Creek trailhead (elevation 2,450 feet).

# Mountain Loop Highway

The South Fork of the Stilly, as the Stillaguamish River is affectionately known, has always provided challenges to people. In the early days of Anglo settlement around Puget Sound, loggers and miners had a devil of a time getting the fruits of their labor

*Hiking the old railroad route through Robe Canyon (#14)*

*The mighty Stillaguamish River flows through Robe Canyon.*

to market. Road builders couldn't find any flat spots. Railroads, following the river through Robe Valley, were constantly washed away by floods. This historical lack of access continues to this day. The Mountain Loop Highway is closed by snow every winter; it's even occasionally washed away by winter storms.

▶ **The South Fork of the Stillaguamish River has a history of presenting severe challenges to the local inhabitants.**

# 13  Robe Canyon Historic Park–Lime Kiln Trail

The Lime Kiln Trail provides hiker access to a portion of the historic Everett–Monte Cristo Railroad. Built in 1892–93, it was abandoned in 1933. The rock-and-mortar limekiln was built in 1900 and produced anhydrous lime, used as a whitening agent at the Lowell paper mill and as a flux agent at the smelter in Everett.

Like many towns west of the Cascades, Granite Falls was once much larger than it is today, servicing smaller towns like Robe along the banks of the South Fork Stillaguamish River. In the boom days of mining, logging, and the railroads, Granite Falls was an economic engine. Transportation, construction, and service-industry jobs are the main employers today.

Though resource extraction doesn't register stronger than a blip these days, it does create historical interest for people walking along the Lime Kiln Trail. A tetanus booster is recommended for those who choose to wander off-trail; rusted artifacts from the region's logging and railroad past lie hidden in the forest duff. Relicts have been gathered by past hikers and placed on display along the trail and at the kiln. Leave them where they are for other people to enjoy.

---

**Start:** Trailhead along Waite Mill Road
**Distance:** 6.0 miles out and back
**Approximate hiking time:** 4 hours
**Difficulty:** Easy
**Trail surface:** Forested path, gravel road, historic railroad grade
**Seasons:** Spring, summer, and fall
**Other trail users:** Runners
**Canine compatibility:** Leashed dogs permitted
**Land status:** Snohomish County Parks; private property
**Nearest town:** Granite Falls

**Services:** Gas, restaurants, groceries, lodging; vault toilet at trailhead
**Northwest Forest Pass:** No
**Discover Pass:** No
**Maps:** Green Trails No. 109: Granite Falls; USGS Granite Falls; USDAFS Mount Baker–Snoqualmie National Forest
**Trail contacts:** Snohomish County Department of Parks and Recreation
**Special hazards:** Stinging nettle, devil's club; no potable water at trailhead or on trail; Stillaguamish River is deep, swift, and cold and not suitable for swimming.

---

**Finding the trailhead:** From Seattle, take I-5 north through Everett to US 2 exit 194 east. At the eastern end of the Hewlett Avenue trestle, follow signs directing you to WA 204 and Lake Stevens.

Where WA 204 meets WA 9, turn left (north). At WA 92 turn right (east) and proceed to Granite Falls. Pass through town and turn right onto S Alder Avenue. Turn left at a T intersection onto E Pioneer Street. Pioneer becomes Menzel Lake Road. In about 1 mile turn left onto Waite Mill Road. Follow this for a short distance; after passing a school bus turnaround, bear left at the wye and follow a gravel road uphill to the Robe Canyon Historic Park parking lot and trailhead. GPS: N48 04.641' / W121 55.957'

# The Hike

The wide, well-marked Lime Kiln Trail takes off from the Robe Canyon Historic Park parking lot and gently ascends a small hill through second- and third-growth Douglas fir forest. This first stretch is an easement through private property. Please

respect the property owners by not wandering off-trail, even though the depth of slash and dense undergrowth are serious impediments to travel.

At the T intersection, turn right (south). Leaving private property behind, the trail narrows into a forest path. The trees feel older and taller now as the canopy closes in. Stumps of moderate-size trees pop out of underbrush dominated by sword fern, thimbleberry, and salmonberry.

Cross a large, well-built bridge at Hubbard Creek. Appreciate the beauty of the scene by taking advantage of a rustic bench. Hubbard Lake lies upstream of the bridge. Shortly after the bridge, the trail drops onto a forest path on the

*A relict along the trail to the lime kiln*

left (north). Continuing straight ahead is a maze of logging roads capable of keeping any mountain biker occupied for years.

Stinging nettle loves this part of the trail. Early in the season, when the stinging hairs are still soft and pliable, it's possible to get by with only a warning while brushing the plant. By April this is no longer so, and even a gentle touch can lead to daylong self-recriminations.

The trail quickly drops onto the old Everett–Monte Cristo Railroad grade and starts paralleling the river. The overstory forest of Sitka spruce with moss- and fern-covered trunks is as beautiful as it is odd. Sitka spruce is highly uncommon so far inland. Early in spring, watch for the nodding pink flowers of bush gooseberry. Vine maples are also prevalent through here.

▶ **Ancient Egyptians, Greeks, and Babylonians used limekilns in the production of quicklime from limestone to make the mortar that held their building blocks together. This helped the Egyptians quite a bit in building the pyramids.**

The drainage ditch on the uphill side of the trail serves to keep water off the grade. Keep your eyes open for a spot where runoff is channeled beneath the grade to a V-shaped notch carved some 6 feet through the bank.

Around about this time you're probably wondering where the limekiln is that gives the trail its name. Old pieces of rusted iron have begun to appear, along with broken pieces from circular saw blades. Come around a slight bend in the trail and there it is—the limekiln. It's a tall, squat structure built of native rock. Ferns and other epiphytic plants cover the kiln. It's

*A hiker pauses beside the old limekiln used in the early twentieth century to produce anhydrous lime.*

possible to climb up the hill and around the kiln and see it from all angles. Take nothing but pictures—all artifacts are protected by law.

After another mile, a sign announces the end of the trail and also points to a short loop that plunges down to the river. Walk to the end of the trail first and look several hundred feet down to the water. Through shrubs and trees you can also look across to the opposite bank and see a concrete pillar—all that remains of a railroad bridge that once crossed the Stillaguamish here.

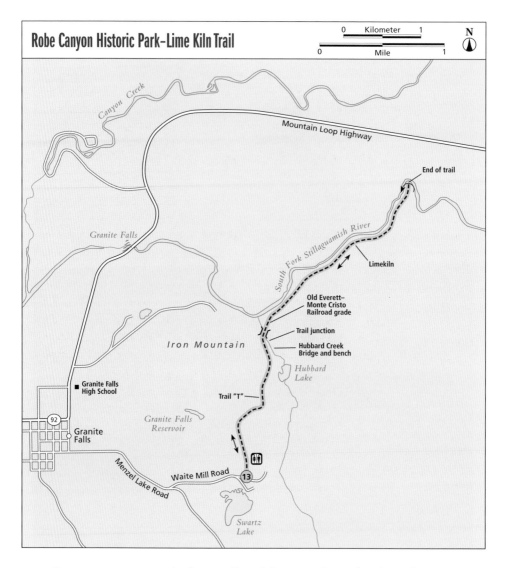

Retrace your steps to the loop trail, and drop steeply to the river. This is a nice place for lunch. Upstream and around the corner, the river is wide and placid, but a particularly nasty rapid is just downstream. Avoid the temptation to play or swim here.

For the return trip, retrace your steps to the parking lot.

## Miles and Directions

**0.0** Lime Kiln trailhead

**0.7** Trail "T"

**1.0** Hubbard Creek Bridge and bench

**2.0** Trail junction

**2.7** Limekiln

**2.8** End of trail

**3.0** Loop trail to South Fork Stillaguamish River

**6.0** Arrive back at trailhead

> **Option:** The town of Granite Falls is named for an amazing waterfall, and a trip there is *de rigueur*. On your return to town from the hike, from the intersection of South Alder and Stanley, drive north 1.5 miles past Granite Falls Middle School and High School. The road becomes Mountain Loop Highway. After passing a plant nursery on the left, the road bends right. Before the highway bridge, spot the parking lot on your left or the large turnout on the right. Walk down the stairs to the Granite Falls viewpoints and fish ladder.

## Hike Information

The entrance to Robe Canyon Historic Park is marked by a tasteful and colorful sign. Park in the large gravel lot. Use the portable toilet, and at the information kiosk read the extensive history of Robe Canyon and the story of acquiring the park property. Don't miss the many historic photos on the back of the kiosk.

Robe Canyon is one of Washington's most difficult whitewater kayak runs. During this hike you'll be able to see some of the "easier" rapids at the bottom end of the run. To the inexperienced eye, these rapids look scary—and they are—so just imagine the difficulty of rapids lying upstream! Whitewater kayakers refer to the Stillaguamish as "the Stilly," most likely facetiously because the water is anything but still.

# 14 Robe Canyon

Over a hundred years ago, some entrepreneurs with more cash than brains decided to build a railway through Robe Canyon. It never occurred to them that keeping a route open through several miles of vertical canyon prone to landslides and flooding would be impossible. It was a good try but they failed—miserably and monumentally. The railroad builders left us with a challenging and exciting walk that will have you stumbling over and slipping into and through history with nearly every step. This is the upper section of Robe Canyon Historic Park and part of the Monte Cristo Railroad grade built in 1893.

Hanging gardens above the trail are great places to look for wildflowers. Adventurous hikers will delight in passing through three defunct railroad tunnels. Many parts of the trail have either washed away or been carried off by slides, so one false step could send you careening down into life-threatening whitewater. It's worthwhile to make a detour to the Lime Kiln Trail (#13) in Robe Canyon Historic Park on the other side of the river to read the complete history of the Monte Cristo Railroad and its construction through Robe Canyon.

**Start:** Old Robe Canyon sign on south side of WA 92, the Mountain Loop Highway
**Distance:** 3.4 miles out and back
**Approximate hiking time:** 3 hours
**Difficulty:** Strenuous, with uneven surfaces and lots of downed trees; trail washed out in many places; not recommended for children or the faint of heart
**Trail surface:** Forested path, old railroad bed; rocky
**Seasons:** Year-round
**Other trail users:** None
**Canine compatibility:** Leashed dogs permitted. A sign at the trailhead states the area is hazardous to unleashed dogs.
**Land status:** Snohomish County Department of Parks and Recreation

**Nearest town:** Granite Falls
**Services:** Gas, restaurants, groceries; no toilet at trailhead
**Northwest Forest Pass:** No
**Discover Pass:** No
**Maps:** Green Trails No. 109: Granite Falls; USGS Granite Falls; USDAFS Mount Baker-Snoqualmie National Forest
**Trail contacts:** Snohomish County Department of Parks and Recreation, Mount Baker-Snoqualmie National Forest, Skykomish Ranger District
**Special hazards:** Loose and slippery rock, exposure and danger of falling, cliffs; trail washed out and missing; no potable water at trailhead or on trail; flashlight advised for those hikers attempting to pass through Tunnel 6

**Finding the trailhead:** From Seattle, take I-5 north through Everett to US 2 exit 194 east. At the eastern end of the Hewlett Avenue trestle, follow signs directing you to WA 204 and Lake Stevens.

Where WA 204 meets WA 9, turn left (north). At WA 92 turn right (east) and proceed to Granite Falls. Follow E Stanley Street through downtown Granite Falls to S Alder Avenue. Turn left (north). Pass Granite Falls Junior and Senior High Schools. At the stop sign, S Alder becomes the Mountain

Loop Highway. Drive 7 miles to the trailhead, passing Granite Falls (the waterfall) after 1.4 miles and crossing the South Fork Stillaguamish River. Continue on the Mountain Loop Highway until you spot the sign for Old Robe Canyon on the right (south) side of the highway. The wooden sign announcing the trailhead has been defaced and is barely readable. The brickwork surrounding the sign resembles a two-dimensional, old-fashioned, wood-burning bread oven. Like the sign, it appears to be perpetually vandalized. GPS: N48 06.587' / W121 51.378'

## The Hike

Keeping the railroad track open through this stretch of narrow canyon was an impossible task. Once you hike down from the trailhead and enter Robe Canyon, you'll wonder why anyone wanted to put a railroad through here in the first place. The hillsides move and slide so often, they may as well be alive.

From the trailhead along the Mountain Loop Highway, drop rapidly on switchbacks, passing a picnic area and warning signs, to the South Fork Stillaguamish River and the old railroad grade. Even in winter the Stilly is wide here, with large gravel banks. A quick gaze downstream reveals canyon walls rising precipitously.

You get your first hint that this trail is not a common route at the river when you stumble upon a slab of concrete embedded with railroad ties. In order to keep the roadbed from washing away during winter floods and spring runoff, the Monte Cristo Railroad was blasted out of the Stilly's rock walls and "stabilized" in this novel

*The route through Robe Canyon; note evidence of the concrete railroad bed.*

*Crossing above Hole-in-the-Wall*

manner. It didn't work. What landslides and fallen trees couldn't extinguish, the river carried away.

While you're admiring the ingenuity of the road builders, don't forget to admire the fierce beauty of the river. Where the canyon begins, the river looks dangerous. If this impresses you, then farther downstream the canyon will frighten you to death.

After 1.2 miles the official trail ends. At 1.4 miles, if the first indications of danger (wiped-out trails and steep detours ending in abrupt drops into the river) have you considering turning back, you should do so now at Tunnel 6. The route not only deteriorates from here, but it does so quickly. Before reaching Tunnel 5 downstream, the route stops resembling a trail altogether. Should you choose to extend your hike past this point, the highlight will be a spot the extreme kayakers who run this section of river know as Hole-in-the-Wall.

After years of watching the Stilly claim their road, the engineers came up with a solution. They built retaining walls to push the river back, paved the roadbed, and embedded railroad ties within thick slabs of concrete. The river didn't even notice. It not only claimed the roadbed, but also washed away a few of the sextuplet of tunnels carved through the canyon walls to allow trains to pass unencumbered by geology or hydrology.

As for Hole-in-the-Wall, the river undercut the retaining wall, and slides washed away the rest. What today appears like a Roman causeway or viaduct is actually a wall suspended like a glacial hanging valley. At 1.6 miles from the trailhead, it marks a perfect turnaround point. On the other hand, not a few folk have seized their courage by the throat and ventured across the causeway to be finally stymied by Tunnel 3 and the official end of the unofficial trail.

*"Of course there are people entirely indifferent to the sight of flowers or of meadows in spring, or, if not indifferent, at least preoccupied elsewhere. They devote them-selves to ball-games, to drinking, gambling, money-making, popularity-hunting."*
—John Ray, seventeenth-century English naturalist

## Miles and Directions

**0.0**   Robe Canyon trailhead on WA 92
**0.7**   South Fork Stillaguamish River
**1.2**   End of official trail

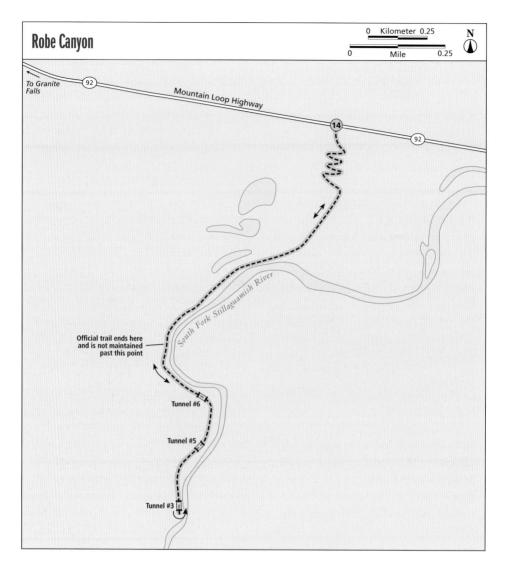

To Granite Falls

Mountain Loop Highway

South Fork Stillaguamish River

Official trail ends here and is not maintained past this point

Tunnel #6

Tunnel #5

Tunnel #3

**1.4** Tunnel 6

**1.5** Tunnel 5

**1.7** Tunnel 3

**3.4** Arrive back at trailhead

**Option:** The town of Granite Falls is named for an amazing waterfall, and a trip there is highly recommended. On your return to town from the hike, from the intersection of S Alder and Stanley, drive north 1.5 miles past Granite Falls Middle School and High School. The road becomes Mountain Loop Highway. After passing a nursery on the left, the road bends right. Before the highway bridge, spot the parking lot on your left or the large turnout on the right. Walk down the stairs to the Granite Falls viewpoints and fish ladder.

# 15 Heather Lake

The very popular walk to Heather Lake is short, but it's a classic: old-growth and mature second-growth forest, perennial creeks, peekaboo views, and a lake situated in a beautiful setting. Mount Pilchuck towers above, and long ribbons of water fall into the lake. Midsummer swimming is always a possibility, and anglers are known to frequent the lake. Wildflower displays along the rocky shoreline are usually pretty good, as is berry picking in the fall.

**Start:** Heather Lake trailhead alongside Pilchuck Road (FR 42)
**Distance:** 6.1-mile lollipop, including a circuit around the lake
**Approximate hiking time:** 3 to 4 hours
**Trail number:** USDA Forest Service Trail 701
**Difficulty:** Moderate
**Trail surface:** Forested path, boardwalk; rocky
**Seasons:** Spring, summer, and fall
**Other trail users:** Runners
**Canine compatibility:** Leashed dogs permitted
**Land status:** USDAFS Darrington Ranger District
**Nearest town:** Granite Falls

**Services:** Gas, restaurants, groceries, lodging; unisex vault toilet at trailhead
**Northwest Forest Pass:** Yes
**Discover Pass:** No
**Maps:** Green Trails No. 109: Granite Falls; USGS Verlot; USDAFS Mount Baker-Snoqualmie National Forest, Alpine Lakes Wilderness
**Trail contacts:** Alpine Lakes Protection Society (ALPS), Mount Baker-Snoqualmie National Forest, Darrington Ranger District, Verlot Public Service Center, Everett Mountaineers
**Special hazards:** Stinging nettle, devil's club, loose rock; no potable water at trailhead or on trail

**Finding the trailhead:** From Seattle, take I-5 north through Everett to US 2 exit 194 east. At the eastern end of the Hewlett Avenue trestle, follow signs directing you to WA 204 and Lake Stevens.

Where WA 204 meets WA 9, turn left (north). At WA 92 turn right (east) and proceed to Granite Falls. Follow E Stanley Street through downtown Granite Falls to S Alder Avenue. Turn left (north). Pass Granite Falls Junior and Senior High Schools. At the stop sign, S Alder becomes the Mountain Loop Highway (WA 92). Pass Granite Falls (the waterfall) in 1.4 miles; cross the South Fork Stillaguamish and continue upstream. In 11 miles east of the town of Granite Falls, reach the USDA Forest Service Verlot Public Service Center on the north side of WA 92. After another 1 mile, turn right (south) onto the Pilchuck Road (FR 42). In 0.2 mile the road turns to gravel. In 1.3 miles reach a wide spot in the road on the right (north) with parking for a dozen or so cars. GPS: N48 04.963' / W121 46.443'

## The Hike

Cross FR 42 (south) and find the trailhead marked by a sign and reader board. Walk a bit up the trail and self-register. The forest here is dense—a mix of old-growth and

*Heather Lake*

mature second-growth trees. Some of the tree stumps are outrageously huge. The notches seen on these giants allowed early loggers to work from platforms high above the ground, where the tree's circumference was less.

Amble up a rocky trail beside a creek; after 0.5 mile merge with an old road and descend a wide path crowded with young trees. The old road allows more light to penetrate the thick forest canopy and encourages more growth than directly under the trees. After 0.7 mile from the trailhead, leave the road and return to a rocky, root-strewn trail. Begin a constant, but not horribly steep, uphill climb through old growth forest.

In 1.4 miles cross a small creek; Heather Creek thunders unseen to the right (west). Start some steep, short switchbacks. The last 0.3 mile to Heather Lake is more or less a level ramble through the forest. Reach the lake after 2 miles. Pass a sign announcing the toilet on the left (east). A side trail leads to the right (southwest) on a circumnavigation of Heather Lake. Cross Heather Creek on a long, elaborate wooden bridge.

You soon reach a campsite. Camping is very poor at Heather Lake. The sites are less than level, there are no views, and the forest is damp, even in summer. However, plenty of opportunities exist for getting down to the lake, and there are a plethora of fine lunch spots.

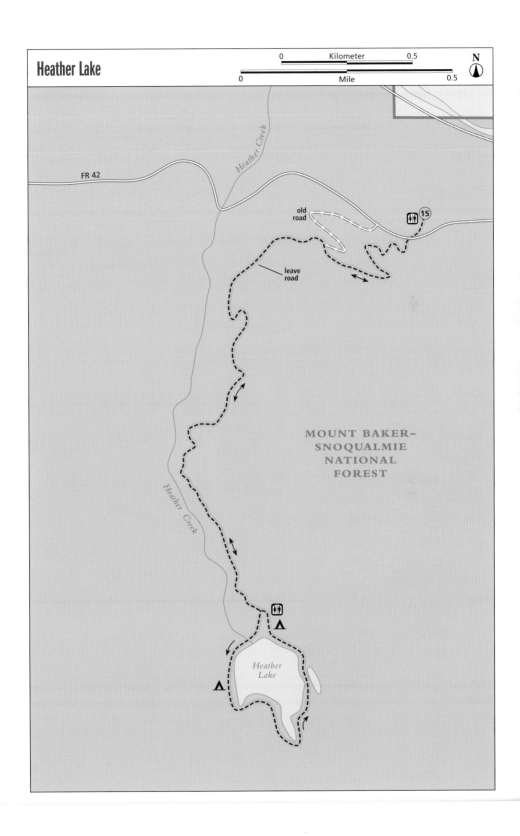

# Heather Lake

0        Kilometer        0.5

0             Mile           0.5

N

*Heather Creek*

FR 42

old road

15

leave road

MOUNT BAKER–
SNOQUALMIE
NATIONAL
FOREST

*Heather Creek*

*Heather
Lake*

# VEGETATION ON THE WEST SLOPE CASCADE MOUNTAINS

The first Europeans to reach our shores were gobsmacked by the size and age of the conifers they found and the paucity of impressive arboreal angiosperms. Relatively nutrient-rich soils along with ample rainfall, an absence of catastrophic fire, and extended drought were the main reasons for this. Our dry summers and our topography (leading to cold and snowy winters, especially in the mountains) also precluded the vast deciduous forests of eastern North America and of Europe.

In the early twentieth century, when the science of ecology was young, it was believed that plant communities developed in orderly steps much like the historic succession of kings and queens or presidents and prime ministers. "Succession" is convenient when thinking of community development as predictable, but reality doesn't work that way. One set of species isn't replaced by another set in anything resembling predictability. Today we realize that a number of outcomes, or "seres," are possible depending on factors such as type, size, and duration of disturbance acting upon species composition and community.

The vegetation type of the Cascade Mountains' western slope is lowland coniferous forest. Up to 2,000 feet in elevation, the dominant woody vegetation is Douglas fir transitioning to western hemlock / western red cedar. Red alder is common in disturbed areas. Above 2,000 feet you will find Pacific silver fir, with mountain hemlock and western red cedar. "Old-growth" is not a vegetation type. It denotes a forest where trees have reached their biological maturity after a long period with no major natural or human disturbance.

*Nothing like a walk in the woods with friends!*

Below Mount Pilchuck, multiple long ribbons of water dive into a jumble of talus before working their way to Heather Lake. Wildflowers are normally plentiful in this area. Scattered small copses of yellow cedar grow along the lakeshore, but most of the trees are mountain hemlock.

Finishing the trail around the lake, come to another campsite and the toilet. Find the trail back down to the trailhead and retrace your steps.

# Miles and Directions

**0.0** Trailhead on Pilchuck Road (FR 42)

**0.5** Old road

**0.7** Leave road

**1.0** Creek crossing

**2.0** Heather Lake

**2.4** Campsite

**3.0** Campsite

**3.1** Toilet

**6.1** Arrive back at trailhead

# Hike Information

The stunning peak that overlooks Heather Lake is Mount Pilchuck—most likely among the "long ridge of snowy mountains" sighted by Captain George Vancouver during the Englishman's 1792 voyage to western North America and through Puget Sound. There is a challenging 5.4-mile round-trip trail to the summit, gaining 2,200 feet. To get to the trailhead, drive 1 mile beyond the Verlot Public Service Center and turn right onto graveled FR 42 immediately after crossing the "Blue Bridge." Drive 7 miles to the trailhead at the end of the road.

From 1957 to 1980, Washington State Parks administered a ski area on the slopes of Mount Pilchuck, but it was closed due to poor annual snow accumulations. Atop the peak's 5,324-foot summit is a Forest Service lookout, managed and maintained by the Everett Mountaineers. The lookout, built in 1918, is available to the public for overnight trips on a first-come, first-served basis. *Pilchuck* is a Native American word meaning "red water," possibly for a creek in the area. But, who *really* knows?

# 16 Lake Twenty-two

Lake Twenty-two has a well-justified reputation for being the most popular trail in the Stillaguamish Valley. It's loved by all kinds of hikers, from families with small children through mountaineers, because of its accessibility. Because of this heavy use, the trail shows constant evidence of being upgraded with new switchbacks, water bars, and boardwalks—especially around the lake perimeter. Clearly, what makes this hike exciting is the nice forest, high quality of boardwalks, and the ability to walk all the way around Lake Twenty-two and stare up the steep walls comprising the basin.

**Start:** Trailhead along WA 92, Mountain Loop Highway

**Distance:** 5.4 miles out and back, with optional 1.3-mile walk around the lake

**Approximate hiking time:** 4 to 5 hours

**Trail number:** USDA Forest Service Trail 702

**Difficulty:** Moderate due to steepness of the trail

**Trail surface:** Forested path, boardwalk; rocky

**Seasons:** Summer and fall

**Other trail users:** None

**Canine compatibility:** Leashed dogs permitted

**Land status:** USDAFS Darrington Ranger District

**Nearest town:** Granite Falls

**Services:** Gas, restaurants, groceries; unisex vault toilet at trailhead; camping at three close-by Forest Service campgrounds: Turlo, Verlot, and Gold Basin

**Northwest Forest Pass:** Yes

**Discover Pass:** No

**Maps:** Green Trails No. 109; Granite Falls and No. 110; Silverton; USGS Verlot; USDAFS Mount Baker–Snoqualmie National Forest, Alpine Lakes Wilderness

**Trail contacts:** Mount Baker–Snoqualmie National Forest, Darrington Ranger District

**Special hazards:** No potable water at trailhead or on trail

**Finding the trailhead:** From Seattle, take I-5 north through Everett to exit 194 east (US 2). At the eastern end of the Hewlett Avenue trestle, follow signs directing you to WA 204 and Lake Stevens.

Where WA 204 meets WA 9, turn left (north). At WA 92 turn right (east) and proceed to Granite Falls. Follow E Stanley Street through downtown Granite Falls to S Alder Avenue. Turn left (north). Pass Granite Falls Junior and Senior High Schools. At the stop sign, S Alder becomes the Mountain Loop Highway (WA 92). Pass Granite Falls (the waterfall, not the town) in 1.4 miles; cross the South Fork Stillaguamish and continue upstream. Eleven miles east from the town of Granite Falls, reach the USDA Forest Service Verlot Public Service Center on the north side of WA 92. In another 2 miles reach the trailhead for Lake Twenty-two; look for the trailhead sign on the highway at exactly where you have to turn. Turn right (south), and proceed 0.1 mile to the trailhead parking lot. On heavy-use days you will see cars parked on both sides of this short access road and also along WA 92. GPS: N48 04.610' / W121 44.747'

## The Hike

Find the trailhead 50 feet west of the toilet. Walk 100 feet and come to a trail register kiosk and, 20 feet after that, a sign announcing the Lake Twenty-two Research Natural Area (RNA), established January 14, 1947. The big trees you see along the way predate any legal, scientific, or educational RNA protection.

This first part of the trail is perfect for parents with very small children. The little kiddies will enjoy an easy gravel path accompanied by a gurgling creek. The Mountain Loop Highway is close and all but invisible through a deep and shady forest.

Choosing to go on, you will soon cross a creek on a new bridge. The trail starts to climb on switchbacks that won't end until you reach the lake. There was a time when Lake Twenty-two epitomized a place overused and loved to death. The trail was beaten down and eroded. Several years of labor have cured most of that past misuse. Help to minimize your impact in this beautiful forest by resisting the temptation to cut switchbacks or step off any boardwalks that span damp ground.

*The boardwalk along Lake Twenty-two's shoreline*

*Dramatic scenery above Lake Twenty-two*

Throughout its climb to Lake Twenty-two, the trail crosses many places where moisture is weeping out of the rocks. In season, these are perfect places to find wildflowers, and the soil remains moist throughout the summer.

In 0.8 mile take the opportunity to admire a large waterfall on Twenty-two Creek. Reach a talus slope and leave the forest behind. On hot and sunny summer days, this section of trail has hikers yearning for shade. Nevertheless, it's excellent habitat for wildflowers, pikas, and birds, so keep your eyes open! Views up or across the Stillaguamish Valley to jagged mountain peaks are impressive.

Ducking back into the forest, the trail begins its final climb in shade to Lake Twenty-two. You know you're almost there when the trail drops alongside the outflow creek. Views upward toward the lake reveal massive cliffs leading to Mount Pilchuck's summit. At the lake you will be greeted by a long bridge spanning Twenty-two Creek and an even longer boardwalk. It's possible to circumnavigate the lake in either direction—your choice.

## GREEN TIP:
Go out of your way to avoid birds and animals that
are mating or taking care of their young.

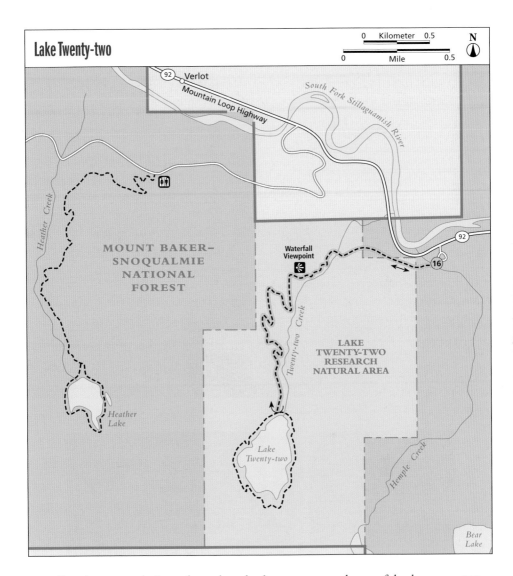

Lunch spots and views abound, as do damp areas—so be careful where you step and sit. Camping and open fires are prohibited at the lake. Due to its popularity, Lake Twenty-two is a perfect place to remember your outdoor manners. Pick up after yourself and leave no trash—including lunch leftovers. The food is not only bad for the critters and birds, but also presents an unsightly mess for the next person who chooses to eat lunch in the same spot.

## Miles and Directions

**0.0**   Trailhead along WA 92
**0.8**   Waterfall view

**2.7** Lake Twenty-two

**5.4** Arrive back at trailhead

**Options:** Four miles east of Verlot, turn right (south) onto FR 4020. In 2.5 miles turn right (west) onto FR 4021 for another 3 miles to reach the trailhead for a short, easy walk to Bear Lake. Continue 2 miles farther on the trail to Pinnacle Lake.

# Hike Information

The Lake Twenty-two Trail passes through a research natural area (RNA), public land established primarily for scientific and educational purposes under the Organic Administration Act of 1897. Principally located within national forests, RNAs exemplify typical or unique vegetation, geological or aquatic features, and preserve representative samples of ecological communities. There is speculation that the lake's unusual moniker came about by the practice of nineteenth century railroad cartographers identifying local creeks, and therefore any unnamed lake associated with that creek, in numerical order. Though they may exist, I have not seen any maps from that era to support the naming claim. As of late 2020 there is a slide at mile 1.7 that makes the way difficult for hikers to traverse.

*"Walking is man's best medicine."*

—Hippocrates

*Left: Red alder male flowers are in pendent clusters called "catkins."*
*Right: Red alder female flowers develop into superficially pinecone-like dry fruits.*

# "Issaquah Alps" & Snoqualmie River Valley Lowlands

Tiger, Cougar, Squak, and Rattlesnake Mountains and the Snoqualmie Valley Lowlands are some of the most popular places and provide some of the best Seattle hiking trails because they are so accessible. If the term "Issaquah Alps" for this region (which

*The view from Rattlesnake Ledge of the Cedar Butte (#22) and the Cedar River watershed*

*Mount Si and Little Si (#27 and #26)*

includes the Tiger Mountain Natural Resources Conservation Area) sounds pretentious at first blush, consider that appearances are often 100 percent of the reason that legislators pass laws to set aside parklands and support wilderness. There are no high, glacially sculpted peaks, alpine fell fields, and deep, azure lakes in these alps. Still, the Issaquah Alps are impressive.

▶ **Proximity to a vast urban area makes places like Tiger Mountain a glorious, and convenient, escape into wildness.**

The Tiger Mountain NRCA encompasses 4,430 acres that range in elevation from 470 feet above sea level at Tradition Plateau to 2,948 feet at the summit of West Tiger Peak 1, the highest of three peaks within the natural area. Cougar Mountain features many diverse habitats, such as mature second-growth forests, streams and wetlands, and cliffs, talus, and caves. Best of all, if you're looking for solitude without having to drive to the North Cascades or Mount Rainier, the Issaquah Alps are basically empty and unused during the week and throughout the winter.

# 17 Sky Country History Circuit

If experiencing history up close and personal is your cup of tea, this is a great hike for you. The route passes through the site of a decommissioned "Cold War" Nike Project antiaircraft missile base, around many dangerous and collapsed and flooded mine shafts, as well as past an inactive open pit where clay was mined for the bricks that helped build Seattle. All this plus a view to the north that takes in Lake Sammamish all the way to Mount Baker. Nice!

**Start:** Sky Country trailhead at Cougar Mountain Regional Park

**Distance:** 5.2-mile loop

**Approximate hiking time:** 4 hours

**Difficulty:** Moderate, with lots of dipsy-doodle ups and downs

**Trail surface:** Forested path

**Seasons:** Spring, summer, fall, and winter

**Other trail users:** Runners, dogs, horses (in some areas)

**Canine compatibility:** Leashed dogs permitted

**Land status:** Cougar Mountain Regional Park (King County)

**Nearest town:** Lakemont (Bellevue)

**Services:** Gas, groceries, Starbucks

**Northwest Forest Pass:** No

**Discover Pass:** No

**Maps:** Greentrails #203S and King County Parks and Recreation map

**Trail contact:** King County Parks and Recreation

**Special hazards:** There are many sunken, collapsed, and/or flooded mine shafts along the route. Most, but not all, are fenced and marked. Do not venture off the trails to travel cross-country. Rainstorms have been known in the past to open up new holes in the area. There is no potable water at trailhead or on the trail. Hikers have spotted bears and mountain lions (cougars) in the area. Because of the plethora of trails in this area, it is highly recommended that you always carry a topographic trail map with you.

**Finding the trailhead:** From Seattle, proceed east on I-90 and take exit 13 for West Lake Sammamish / Lakemont Boulevard SE / SE Newport Way. At the stop sign, turn right (south) and drive south on Lakemont Boulevard SE for 2.5 miles. Turn left at the signal onto SE Cougar Mountain Way and drive up the hill for 0.5 mile to 166th Way SE, and turn right. Follow 166th Way SE for 0.7 mile, passing through the entrance gate for Cougar Mountain Regional Wildland Park. This road ends at the paved parking area for the trailhead. If the gate is not yet unlocked, you can park on the street and walk 0.2 mile to the trailhead. GPS: N47 31.974' / W122 06.806'

## The Hike

There are several trail entrances here, but the main route begins on the south side of the parking area at the picnic benches and kiosk. Here you will find photos and text covering the coal-mining and Cold War military history of this area. There is also a sign with extensive warnings about getting anywhere near the many open or collapsed mine shafts. Take the opportunity to read it. Excellent small-scale topographic

*Trail sign art at the Harvey Manning (formerly Anti-Aircraft Peak) trailhead parking lot*

maps, provided by King County Parks and Recreation, are usually available at the kiosk; take one, and start hiking!

The trail quickly passes by an old structure made of cinder blocks that looks like an outhouse. A sign says you can read about the Nike base history, but don't believe it. This blockhouse is an old paint locker, that's all. Immediately before you is an open and grassy field. This is where the Nike missiles would have been staged before firing.

Between 1953 and 1963, this area was part of the US Army air defenses against a nuclear strike by the USSR. There were many such defensive Nike missile bases along the Pacific Coast during the Cold War. Nike missiles were antiaircraft weapons with explosive warheads designed to destroy any incoming missiles or airplanes. They were stored underground, not in silos, and the system to fire them required that they be carried out into the open via elevators. It could take as long as twenty minutes from the moment of alert to firing one.

After passing the defunct paint locker, look for the sign announcing Old Man's Trail. This trail drops on a gentle grade and crosses an old cyclone fence line which was designed to keep the curious from investigating the Nike base during its prime. Soon you'll encounter the first of many old, collapsed, and flooded mine shafts from the area's nineteenth-century coal-mining days. Obey the signs and stay on your side of the fence. Soon after you will come to a trail junction between the Old Man's Trail and the Cave Hole Trail. Turn right (south) and follow this wide trail for 0.1 mile to another junction, the Bypass Trail, and turn left (east) toward Fred's Railroad Trail.

When you reach Fred's Railroad Trail in 0.2 mile, turn right (south). To your left (north) is the Clay Pit Road. You will encounter another section of it later. The trail here is wide and suitable for walking two or three abreast. Reaching the much narrower East Fork Trail, hang a left (east) and reach for the nirvana of quietness. Large portions of this trail are seasonally muddy or bathed in water, but all of this has been obviated by long elevated sections, or "causeways," built above the fray to keep your footsies dry.

At this point it's worth remembering that Cougar Mountain, along with its friends Tiger and Squak, are three of the most popular hiking areas near Seattle. Yet, the Sky Country Trailhead on Cougar Mountain is a quiet gem and is lightly used, especially if you eschew weekend trips. Leaving the wider, more-trod-upon trails like Fred's Railroad Trail almost guarantees you long moments of peaceful solitude. If only there was a comfortable bench to rest your weary bones.

The East Fork Trail makes a big southeasterly loop and then morphs into the Mine Shaft Trail. Soon you will come to "#4 Air Shaft to the Primrose Mine," where you will find that comfortable bench, along with an interpretive display. Both bench and display are the result of Boy Scouts of America Eagle Scout badge projects from

## TRAIL HAZARDS 2

The animals in our region are more afraid of us than we are of them and most often cause problems when their habitat gets in the way of our development or recreation. They don't cause much trouble, but American black bears (*Ursus americanus*) and mountain lions (*Puma concolor*) garner a lot of concern among hikers. Generally speaking, there's nothing to worry about from either.

Black bears are omnivorous, shy, and retiring. They like to eat insects, fruits and berries, the occasional root or two, and carrion if it's available. Bears get into trouble because people in the suburbs leave pet food outside or don't secure their garbage cans. If they weren't looking for a free meal, bears would never be seen.

Once hunted nearly to extinction, mountain lion populations are rebounding through-out the West. Mountain lions have been known to attack people, and ten fatal attacks in the United States between 1890 and 1998 have been documented. Pets normally have more to worry about than people, but it's still important to be aware of any lion sightings in your area when going for a hike. This is not to say the danger of being attacked is nonexistent. In May of 2018, two mountain bike riders were attacked in the North Bend area by a mountain lion. One of the bikers was killed.

*Black bears are omnivorous, shy, and retiring . . . though hardly sixty-five!*

*Pay attention to warning signs and keep your distance from collapsed mine shafts.*

Troop 709. Eagle Scouts Sam Hendrickson and Connor Lee are to be congratulated for their contributions to both educating us and providing us with a spot to rest.

That huge hole in the ground in front of you, covered by quarter-inch rebar to restrict the curious among us from certain disaster, is 1,200 feet deep. It was dug not to mine coal, but rather to provide fresh air to the coal miners toiling deep below. The Primrose Mine entrance was actually 850 feet below this site and west of Lakemont Boulevard! The rising costs of mining closed the Primrose in 1923.

Leaving the #4, the trail meets the Clay Pit Road. Turn right (east) and walk 100 yards to a bench overlooking the Clay Pit and the lovely conifer-clad, occasionally snowcapped, Cascade Mountains in the background. There is a historic display here well worth your attention. For fifty years the Mutual Materials Company dug clay in this area and fired it into brick at their Newcastle facility. (An example: All of the bricks in Red Square at the University of Washington came from here. As they say, "Shop local.")

Once you've tired of history and the view, retrace your steps on the Clay Pit Road 100 feet and pick up the tread on the right (north) marked as the Tibbetts Marsh Trail. Don't forget to notice the historic bricks embedded in the ground to show you the way.

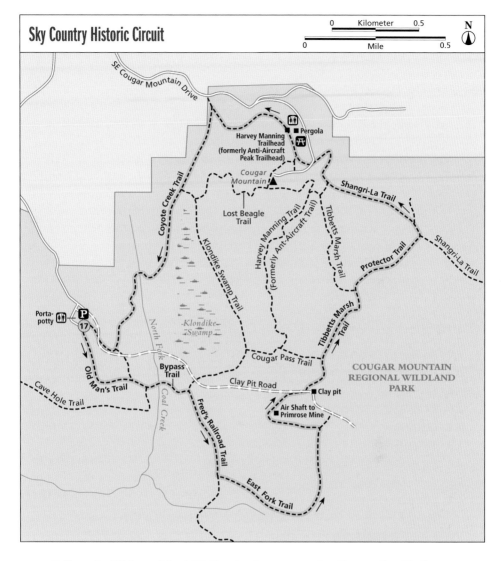

Follow the Tibbetts Marsh Trail as it plunges past the Cougar Pass Trail on your left (west), the actual Tibbetts Marsh also on your left (west), and the West Tibbetts Creek Trail on your right (east), until encountering the Protector Trail. Hopefully by this point you have your map of the region out of your pocket, because all of these trail junctions and similar-sounding names can be quite confusing. In fact, somebody gets lost yearly on these trails and requires rescuing. Please, don't let it be you.

The Protector Trail will take you to the Shangri-La Trail, left (northwest), which is another wide path encouraging groups of hikers to spread out and walk abreast. Soon, you will see a sign directing you to the Pergola, a lightly covered picnic table in a grassy field a shout and a whisper from the Harvey Manning (formerly Anti-Aircraft Peak) Trailhead (see below for trailhead directions).

People are fond of the Pergola for weddings and family events and parties. To reserve the space or either of the two picnic shelters nearby, call (206) 477-6510. There is a dynamite view to the north of Lake Sammamish and Mount Baker from the Pergola.

From the Harvey Manning (formerly Anti-Aircraft Peak) Trailhead parking lot, use the porta-potty if necessary, then stop and amuse yourself at the trail sign artwork displayed beside the King County maintenance shed. There is a picnic shelter and a seasonally open/closed flush toilet here as well.

Why does Harvey Manning deserve to be remembered with a trailhead? Well, as history tells us, what we now refer to as the Issaquah Alps (Tiger, Squak, and Cougar Mountains) would not be available to the public for recreation if not for the political and lobbying efforts of people like Manning, Ira Spring, and other activists.

Cross the open and grassy field to the nearby picnic shelter. Directly behind it find a short volunteer path to the Shangri-La Trail. Turn left (northwest) and walk for a short time until reaching the Coyote Creek Trail, where you turn left (south). From here it is slightly over 1 mile to rejoin the Clay Pit Road, which will take you back to Sky Country Trailhead.

## Miles and Directions

**0.0**  Sky Country Trailhead

**0.6**  Fred's Railroad Trail

**1.0**  East Fork Trail

**1.9**  #4 Air Shaft to Primrose Mine

**2.1**  Clay Pit view

**2.9**  Shangri-La Trail

**3.5**  Harvey Manning (formerly Anti-Aircraft Peak) Trailhead

**4.1**  Coyote Creek Trail

**5.2**  Return to Sky Country Trailhead

**Options:** The Sky Country History Circuit loop intersects many other trails and allows hikers limitless opportunities to shorten or extend their excursion at Cougar Mountain Regional Wildland Park. For this, you will need an area-wide map (see above). Non–history buffs who like waterfalls can create their own 8-mile loop to see Doughty Falls, Coal Creek Falls, and Far Country Falls. As well, with a car shuttle hikers can end their trip at the Harvey Manning Trailhead. To reach this trailhead, after passing the turnoff on 166th Way SE to Sky Country Trailhead, continue east on SE Cougar Mountain Drive / 168th Place SE for 1.7 miles to the end of the road.

# 18  Cougar Mountain

What a beautiful place—and so close to town! So unbelievably quiet, too. Administered by Metro-King County, Cougar Mountain Regional Wildland Park has 35 miles of wooded trails. There are lots of turns on this excursion, so keep your topo map and these instructions handy. It's not easy to get lost, even though the trails on this part of Cougar Mountain seem to go in every direction. If you're confused, simply turn around and head back the way you came and start over. Every walk here is a great walk, even if you end up seeing it from both directions. Be aware that several of the trails on this route have very similar sounding names.

**Start:** Bear Ridge trailhead on Renton-Issaquah Road SE (WA 900)
**Distance:** 6.2-mile lollipop
**Approximate hiking time:** 4 hours
**Trail numbers:** Cougar Mountain Regional Wildland Park Trails E3 (Bear Ridge Trail), E1 (Shangri-La Trail), E2 (Surprise Creek Trail), N7 (Harvey Manning Trail, formerly Anti-Aircraft Ridge Trail), N8 (Cougar Pass Trail), N9 (Tibbetts Marsh Trail), and E10 (West Tibbetts Creek Trail)
**Difficulty:** Moderate due to constant map reading and ease of getting confused or lost
**Trail surface:** Forested path
**Seasons:** Year-round
**Other trail users:** Horses (on some sections), runners
**Canine compatibility:** Leashed dogs permitted

**Land status:** Cougar Mountain Regional Park (King County); private
**Nearest town:** Issaquah
**Services:** Gas, restaurants, groceries, lodging; no toilet at Bear Ridge trailhead; portable toilet at Anti-Aircraft Peak trailhead
**Northwest Forest Pass:** No
**Discover Pass:** No
**Maps:** Green Trails No. 203S: Cougar Mountain–Squak Mountain; USGS Issaquah; USDAFS Mount Baker-Snoqualmie National Forest; King County–Metro Cougar Mountain Regional Wildland Park
**Trail contacts:** King County Parks and Recreation
**Special hazards:** Stinging nettle, devil's club; no potable water at trailhead or on trail

**Finding the trailhead:** Drive east from Seattle on I-90 to exit 15. Turn right (south) at the signal, and cross NW Gilman Boulevard. Proceed on Renton-Issaquah Road SE (WA 900) for 1.5 miles, passing the Talus subdivision. The parking lot is on your right (west); it's tiny (space for three or four cars) and easily missed. Signal your turn well in advance! Look for SE 83rd Place, a private road, opposite the parking area. Don't be intimidated by people behind you flashing their lights, honking their horns, and gunning their engines. There can also be a huge amount of truck traffic on this highway. Be careful!

If you should miss the parking area, don't jam on your brakes; instead, continue up the road a few miles to the traffic signal at SE May Valley Road, turn around, return to NW Gilman Boulevard, make a U-turn, and try again.

This parking area is prone to car clouts, and judging by the amount of broken glass in the parking lot, it is wise to pay attention to the warning signs at the trailhead. Take all valuables with you on the trail. GPS: N47 31.627' / W122 03.831'

# The Hike

Begin on the Bear Ridge Trail (E3), which gently ascends from the parking area through a section of the Cougar Mountain–Squak Mountain Corridor. Pass a trail sign for Bear Ridge Trail. After 0.8 mile enter Cougar Mountain Regional Wildland Park. Stop and read the rules—all four are very reasonable. The noise of the highway is far behind you; all you will hear are twittering birds, the gurgle of West Fork Tibbetts Creek, and breezes through the trees.

In another 100 feet come to the famous "Fantastic Erratic" glacier boulder. Huge swaths of ground lying under our feet in the Puget Sound region were pushed here long ago by the continental glacier moving south out of Canada. In fact, it's possible to see where the terminus of that glacier was when driving through Olympia on I-5. And when the Cascades were deeply covered by frozen water, this boulder was transported from some place far away. It came to rest here, to be covered by ferns and moss and cause curious hikers to stop and appreciate its beauty. Because the rock type of the boulder is different from the bedrock it rests upon, it's called a "glacial erratic." There are views down Tibbetts Creek drainage from the boulder's summit.

Reach a junction with Tibbetts Creek Trail (E10) and turn right (north). This junction is unmarked on older Green Trails maps. Continue along the Bear Ridge Trail for 0.2 mile to another trail junction. Turn right (east) onto the Shangri-La Trail (E1).

The E1 trail begins to drop and circles around the east side of Cougar Mountain, temporarily leaving the park and crossing private property above the Talus subdivision. There are views into the subdivision as well as north to the Sammamish Plateau development, Mount Si and Mount Baker, and east to the western flank of Tiger Mountain, Stevens Pass, and Snoqualmie Pass. Lake Sammamish lies below.

The trail begins to climb again, regaining all its lost elevation; it passes an unmarked waytrail; reenters the park; and 0.5 mile after the viewpoint reaches a junction with the Surprise Creek (E2) and No Name (E8) Trails. Go straight (west) for 0.3 mile. At the next junction turn left (west), continuing on E2 toward Anti-Aircraft Peak, ignoring the Goodes Corner Trail (E7) to Issaquah Reservoir. Reach another junction after a scant 0.1 mile, and turn right (west) back onto the Shangri-La Trail (E1). Confused yet? Pay attention—and don't put away that map!

The trail here is very wide and enters a lovely copse of red alder. After 0.5 mile you will reach yet another junction—this one with the Tibbetts Marsh Trail (N9). Remain on E1, straight ahead (northwest). Reach the Harvey Manning (formerly Anti-Aircraft Peak) trailhead in 0.1 mile and intersect with Hike #17, Sky Country History Circuit. The building you see belongs to the Cougar Mountain maintenance office.

Turn to your right (north), ignoring the road that goes down to the west, and walk past the portable toilet to reach a couple of picnic benches and the Pergola. There is a view of Lake Sammamish and points north.

*Our most famous and recognizable landmark can be seen from many trails in* Best Hikes Seattle.

Retrace your steps to the E1-N9 trail junction, and turn right (southwest) onto the Tibbetts Marsh Trail (N9). Very quickly come to the junction with the Harvey Manning (formerly Anti-Aircraft Ridge) Trail (N7) and turn right (west). In 100 yards come to the Lost Beagle Trail (N6); turn left (south) to remain on N7.

The trail meanders through a maturing forest with an extensive and impressive grove of understory sword ferns along with big patches of Oregon grape and red huckleberry. Stop and appreciate how big these ferns are! This forest is an excellent example of the differences between an overstory of red alder and one of western hemlock and Douglas fir.

After 0.7 mile reach yet another trail junction, the Cougar Pass Trail (N8), and turn left (southeast). N8, in turn, meets up again with the Tibbetts Marsh Trail (N9) in 0.2 mile for a left (northeast) turn. Cross Tibbetts Creek on a boardwalk and fallen log. After 0.2 mile N9 reaches the junction with the upper end of West Tibbetts Creek Trail (E10), where the turn is to the right (east). Descend 0.5 mile along Tibbetts Creek to the Bear Ridge Trail (E3); turn right (southeast) and follow the trail back to the parking lot in 1.1 miles.

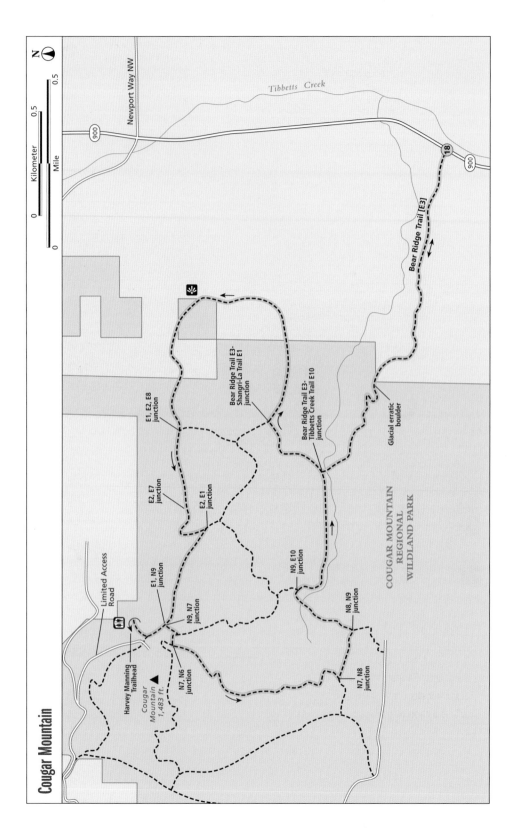

# Cougar Mountain

N

Kilometer

0   0.5

0   0.5

Mile

900

Newport Way NW

*Tibbetts Creek*

900

18

Bear Ridge Trail [E3]

Bear Ridge Trail E3-
Shangri-La Trail E1
junction

Bear Ridge Trail E3-
Tibbetts Creek Trail E10
junction

Glacial erratic
boulder

COUGAR MOUNTAIN
REGIONAL
WILDLAND PARK

E1, E2, E8
junction

E2, E7
junction

E2, E1
junction

E1, N9
junction

N9, N7
junction

N9, E10
junction

N8, N9
junction

N7, N6
junction

N7, N8
junction

Limited Access
Road

Harvey Manning
Trailhead

Cougar
Mountain
1,483 ft.

*Use walking sticks to help reduce impact to legs, knees, ankles, and feet.*

## Miles and Directions

**0.0** Bear Ridge trailhead (E3)

**0.8** Enter Cougar Mountain Regional Wildland Park

**1.1** Tibbetts Creek Trail (E10), 117'

**1.3** Junction with Shangri-La Trail (E1)

**2.4** Junction with Surprise Creek (E2) and No Name (E8) Trails

**2.7** Junction with Surprise Creek (E2) and Shangri-La (E1) Trails

**3.0** Junction with Shangri-La (E1) and Tibbetts Marsh (N9) Trails

**3.1** Harvey Manning Trailhead, toilet, picnic tables, and Pergola

**3.2** Junction with Harvey Manning (N7) and Lost Beagle (N6) Trails

**3.9** Junction with Harvey Manning (N7) and Cougar Pass (N8) Trails

**4.1** Junction with Cougar Pass (N8) and Tibbetts Marsh (N9) Trails

**4.4** Junction with Tibbetts Marsh (N9) and West Tibbetts Creek (E10) Trails

**4.9** Junction with West Tibbetts Creek (E10) and Bear Ridge (E3) Trails

**6.2** Arrive back at Bear Ridge trailhead (E3)

## Hike Information

The Talus subdivision of Issaquah is a master-planned community designed to creatively incorporate a mix of housing configurations and densities with the topography and open space of Cougar Mountain. It comprises 626 acres, with 387 acres dedicated to open space. Talus contains twelve communities consisting of single-family homes, condominium townhouses, rental apartments, and a retirement community with parks, open spaces, and walking trails.

In the 1950s and early 1960s, two active Nike missile sites were located within the park's current boundaries, in order to protect the Puget Sound region from potential air attacks (see Hike #17). Eventually these sites were decommissioned, and in the late 1960s King County took over ownership of the land that would later become Cougar Mountain Regional Wildland Park.

The Harvey Manning Trailhead was formerly called the Anti-Aircraft Peak Trailhead and the Harvey Manning Trail was formerly called the Anti-Aircraft Ridge Trail. Adding to the confusion with the trails for this hike is the gradual removal of trail numbers on the trail signs. To avoid getting lost or confused, keep your map with you at all times!

# 19 Jim Whittaker Wilderness Peak

There is no view from the summit of Wilderness Peak, though it is the highest point in King County's Cougar Mountain Regional Wildland Park. The trail up and back is still very nice. Even better, the trail is less than 20 miles from Seattle. That makes it a perfect after-work hike year-round. The mixed forest of maturing Douglas fir, red alder, western hemlock, western red cedar, and big leaf maples form a rich mosaic of vegetation. The interplay of sky and sunshine filtering through the many shades of green is immensely pleasing to the eye. For these reasons it's easy to comprehend why the trails of Cougar Mountain are so popular. But as popular as this hike is, the small size of the parking lot will always limit the number of people you see until reaching Shy Bear Pass. From there, access to a large complex of Cougar Mountain trails is possible.

**Start:** Jim Whittaker Wilderness Creek trailhead along WA 900

**Distance:** 5.7-mile lollipop (including the way-trail on summit); 3.7-mile loop without waytrail

**Approximate hiking time:** 2 to 3 hours

**Trail numbers:** Cougar Mountain Regional Wildland Park Trails E6 (Wilderness Creek Trail), E5 (Wilderness Cliffs Trail), and E4 (Wilderness Peak Trail)

**Difficulty:** Moderate, with long, steep sections

**Trail surface:** Forested path

**Seasons:** Year-round

**Other trail users:** Runners

**Canine compatibility:** Leashed dogs permitted

**Land status:** Cougar Mountain Regional Park (Metro–King County)

**Nearest town:** Issaquah

**Services:** Gas, restaurants, groceries, lodging; portable toilet at trailhead

**Northwest Forest Pass:** No

**Discover Pass:** No

**Maps:** Green Trails No. 203S: Cougar Mountain–Squak Mountain; USGS Issaquah, Renton, Maple Valley

**Trail contacts:** King County Parks and Recreation

**Special hazards:** Stinging nettle, devil's club; car break-ins; no potable water at trailhead or on trail; confusing trail nomenclature

**Finding the trailhead:** Drive east from Seattle on I-90 to exit 15. Turn right (south) at the signal, and cross NW Gilman Boulevard. Proceed on Renton-Issaquah Road SE (WA 900 west) for 3.2 miles. The turnoff for the trailhead is on your right. There is plenty of truck and commuter traffic on this highway. Be patient. Don't speed, and signal your turn well in advance.

The parking area is small and paved, and it's possible to miss both the entrance and the exit. If this should happen, don't jam on your brakes. Drive another 0.9 mile to the traffic signal at SE May Valley Road, where you can turn around safely. Return to NW Gilman Boulevard and make a U-turn. Once again, signal your turn well in advance, and try again.

This small (room for about ten cars) parking area is prone to car clouts (note the sign) and is subject to video surveillance (note the sign). Be wise—take all valuables with you on the trail. GPS: N47 30.603' / W122 05.228'

# The Hike

Pass the small information kiosk welcoming hikers to King County Parks, and begin ascending the steep E6 trail along Wilderness Creek. Cross the creek on a sturdy bridge in 100 feet. Occasionally it's possible to pick up photocopied maps of Cougar Mountain Regional Wildland Park either here or at the information kiosk.

Except for the most egregious sounds intruding on the solitude of the trail, you quickly leave behind the highway noise. Science has discovered a reliable way of measuring how much air pollution a forest can remove; it would be interesting to develop a technique for doing the same with noise. If that sort of information was known, there might be greater respect for trees.

In 0.5 mile turn right (east) toward Wilderness Peak on the Gombu Wilderness Cliffs Trail (E5). In 400 feet turn left (north), continuing on E5 and bypassing the Squak Mountain Connector Trail (E11). Note the stumps of very large trees. This maturing second-growth forest still has a long way to go.

*Here's a place to rest your weary bones and aching feet after the steep climb to Wilderness Peak.*

After a heart-thumping mile, the trail relents briefly, dropping into the basin of an ephemeral stream before resuming its upward climb. After 1.7 miles, reach the intersection with the Wilderness Peak Trail (E4). Turn right (east) and reach the summit of Wilderness Peak in 0.1 mile.

Don't expect a view from the summit—there are too many trees! Now is a good time to catch your breath, contemplate your sweat equity, and decide what to do. Begin by having a seat. The old log bench at the summit was replaced in 2009 by a log-and-plank bench donated by Mitsuo and Kimiko Mukai, with the couple's best wishes that all hikers "find inner peace, tranquility, and safety on the trails" by following the "path of bushido." A trail register is bolted to a post beside the bench. Sign it or not, but do read the amusing things previous hikers have written.

At the summit find a narrow waytrail, unmarked on maps, that drops steeply for a 1-mile shortcut to meet the Gombu Wilderness Cliffs (E5) Trail. If you choose this route, turn left (southeast) to return to the trailhead.

Cougar Mountain's many crisscrossing trails—most junctions marked, some not always—guarantee that every year or so an inattentive hiker or jogger gets lost. Don't laugh. If you do, it's an indication that you are one of those inattentive types. Keep your eye on your map, and read every trail junction closely to make sure you've chosen the right one.

If you're not using the shortcut, retrace your steps to the E5–E4 junction and continue straight ahead (west) for 0.3 mile to Shy Bear Pass. Several choices are presented. From here it is possible to reach both the Harvey Manning (formerly Anti-Aircraft Peak) and Sky Country Trailheads (#17). To the right (west), Trail S2 leads to Far Country Viewpoint or Anti-Aircraft Peak. To the left (east), Trail S4 leads to Long View Peak. Also to the left (south) is the Wilderness Creek Trail (E6) and the way home, completing this loop.

Drop steeply, cross a wet area on split logs, and soon meet the E6–E5 junction. Bear right (southeast) and cross the creek on a stout bridge. The noise of the highway soon signals the impending end of the trail and return from the wilderness to civilization.

## Miles and Directions

**0.0** Jim Whittaker Wilderness Creek trailhead along WA 900

**0.7** E5-E11, Squak Mountain Connector Trail

**1.7** E5-E4 trail junction

**1.8** Wilderness Peak

**3.1** Waytrail intersection with E5

**4.2** Shy Bear Pass

**5.7** Arrive back at trailhead

> **Option:** The Squak Mountain Connector Trail (E11) leads back down to WA 900, crossing the highway and connecting with the West Access Trail (W1) in Squak Mountain State Park. It leaves the Wilderness Cliffs Trail (E5) about 400 feet after the E5-E6 junction.

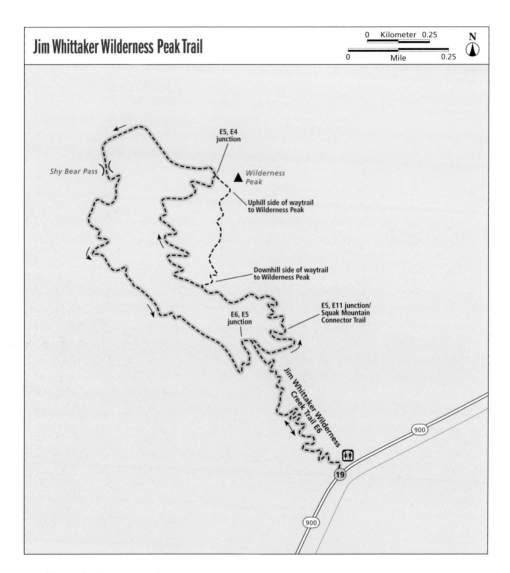

E5, E4 junction

Shy Bear Pass

▲ Wilderness Peak

Uphill side of waytrail to Wilderness Peak

Downhill side of waytrail to Wilderness Peak

E5, E11 junction/ Squak Mountain Connector Trail

E6, E5 junction

Jim Whittaker Wilderness Creek Trail E6

900

19

900

## Hike Information

Cougar Mountain Zoological Park is dedicated to increasing the understanding and appreciation of the Earth's wildlife and the role of humanity in nature through education, research, captive breeding, conservation, exhibition, and recreation. To visit, returning from Wilderness Peak on WA 900, turn left (west) onto Newport Way just prior to reaching I-90. Turn left (south) up the hill on SE 54th Street at the Zoo Landmark sign. The Zoological Park is located approximately 0.25 mile up SE 54th Street. For more information, visit cougarmountainzoo.org.

This trail memorializes Jim Whittaker, a Seattle-born mountaineer and guide and Nawang Gombu. On May 1, 1963, Whittaker became the first citizen of the United

*Cross this creek at the beginning of the trail to Wilderness Peak.*

States to attain the summit of Mount Everest, accompanied by the Sherpa Nawang Gombu (nephew of Tenzing Norgay). Whittaker was a member of the American Mount Everest Expedition led by Norman Dyhrenfurth. In the mid-1950s, Whittaker became the first full-time employee of Recreational Equipment Incorporated (REI) and later served as REI's CEO during the 1960s. At the trail's dedication to Whittaker and Gombu in 2013, Whittaker said, "Let's create a beautiful world," and, "Let's leave no child inside."

Trails in this area can be confusing. Adding to the confusion for this hike is the gradual removal of trail numbers on the trail signs. To avoid getting lost or confused, please keep your map with you at all times and refer to it at all trail junctions!

# 20 Tiger Mountain–East Summit

The opportunity for reaching two pretty dramatic viewpoints makes this hike more interesting than it otherwise might be. That's on the plus side. On the negative side is that the amount of time earning those views requires you to walk on a gravel road. This is a popular mountain bike area and new trails are continually being built.

**Start:** Tiger Summit Trailhead
**Distance:** 9.5-mile lollipop
**Approximate hiking time:** 6 hours
**Difficulty:** Moderate to difficult with steep sections of trail and with elevation gain
**Trail surface:** Gravel road, forested path
**Seasons:** Spring, summer, fall, winter (snow on the summit possible)
**Other trail users:** Runners, bicycles, service vehicles
**Canine compatibility:** Leashed dogs permitted

**Land status:** Tiger Mountain State Forest
**Nearest town:** Issaquah
**Services:** Gas, groceries, food, lodging
**Northwest Forest Pass:** No
**Discover Pass:** Yes
**Maps:** Greentrails #204S Tiger Mountain and Taylor Mountain
**Trail contact:** Washington Department of Natural Resources
**Special hazards:** Service vehicles

**Finding the trailhead:** From Seattle, proceed east on I-90 to exit 25, WA 18W. At the end of the off-ramp, turn right and drive south for 4.5 miles. Watch for the Tiger Mountain State Forest sign and make a right turn into a large gravel turnout / parking lot. Drive a further 0.3 mile on a good gravel road to the large trailhead parking area surrounding a vault toilet. GPS: N47 28.086' / W121 56.164'

## The Hike

By the large reader board you are faced by three trails. They are the Connector Trail, on your right; Iverson Railroad Trail, on your left; and the Lower Predator Trail, in the middle. Take the Lower Predator Trail. Enter the forest and, watching for mountain bikers coming down the trail, immediately begin a steep ascent which reaches the Main Tiger Mountain Road in 0.5 mile. Turn left (west) onto this wide gravel road.

The Main Tiger Mountain Road (aka 4000 Road) was built in 1972 to allow access to the summit of East Tiger Mountain and construction of communications towers. It was also built to provide access for tree planting and firefighting.

In 2.6 miles reach the Off-the-Grid Road, also known as the Crossover Road, (aka 5500 Road) and bear right (east). This road was originally constructed by contract logging crews and the Division of Forestry in the late 1940s to provide access to a fire lookout on the Main Tiger Mountain. The remaining section of 5500 Road, eastward through Beaver Valley, was originally called the Carpenter Road and began in the town of Preston.

*Communication towers atop Tiger Mountain's East Summit*

*A creek, a bridge, a trail, and a forest*

In 0.4 mile reach a junction with the East Tiger Summit Road and turn left (northwest). Pass through a rusting, though still highly functioning, heavy-duty metal gate in 0.1 mile, and in a further 0.1 mile find a waytrail on the left (west) that leads to a wide area with picnic benches and dynamite views to the west, south, and east. From here it is 0.5 mile of more road walking to where the East Tiger Summit Trail crosses the road. You will return to this junction later. In the meantime, continue another 0.2 mile to East Tiger Mountain Summit.

On the summit you will find picnic tables, a reader board with a long list of rules covering trail etiquette, and several communications towers of various sizes. Views to the west and south are commanding and sweeping and justify all the road walking.

From the summit, the East Tiger Summit Trail takes off to the south. This trail is shared with mountain bikers, so keep a lookout for them. In 0.4 mile of lovely forest hiking cross the East Tiger Summit Road (you've been here before) and continue for another 1.0 mile to the Preston Railroad Grade trail. Continue straight (west) and quickly reach the Main Tiger Mountain Road. Turn left (south). In 0.3 mile pass the Crossover Road and bear right (southeast).

From here it is 2.6 miles of road walking to the Lower Predator Trail. Continue on the road for 0.6 mile to the Connector Trail and turn right (south). In another 0.2 mile of lovely forest walking, return to the trailhead.

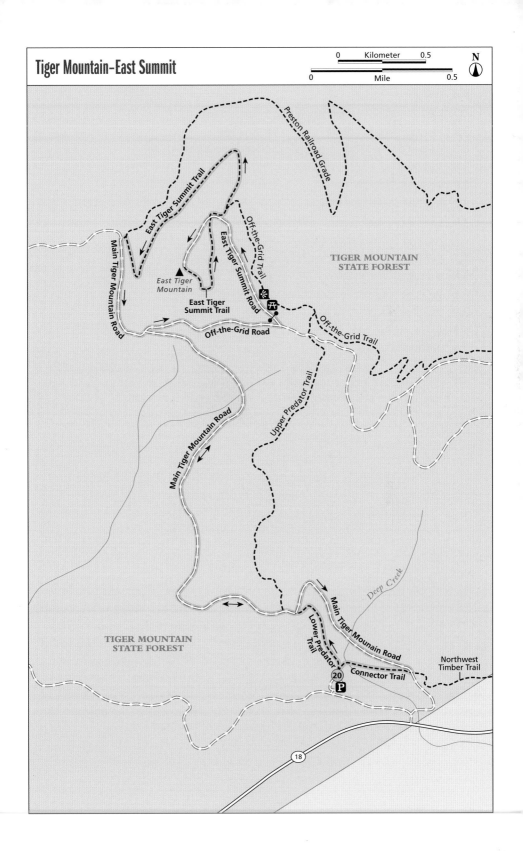

# Miles and Directions

**0.0** Trailhead

**0.5** Lower Predator Trail–Main Tiger Mountain Road junction

**3.1** Main Tiger Mountain Road–Crossover Road junction

**3.5** Off-the-Grid Road (Crossover Road)–East Tiger Summit Road junction

**3.6** Metal gate

**3.7** Viewpoint with picnic tables

**4.1** East Tiger Summit Trail

**4.3** East Tiger Summit

**4.7** East Tiger Summit Trail crosses East Tiger Summit Road

**5.7** East Tiger Summit Trail–Preston Railroad Grade trail junction

**5.8** Main Tiger Mountain Road

**6.1** Main Tiger Mountain Road–Crossover Road junction

**8.7** Lower Predator Trail

**9.3** Connector Trail

**9.5** Return to trailhead

**Options:** From the East Tiger Summit Trail, hike the Preston Railroad Grade trail to the East Tiger Trail for a 1.8 connection to Hike #21, Tiger Mountain–High Point Trail, joining it at the Paw Print Connector / Bootleg Trail. Such a route will require a car shuttle.

# Hike Information

Hungry and thirsty hikers will be interested in Issaquah's 1950s-era Triple XXX Rootbeer Drive-in (sorry, no carhops anymore) at 98 E. Gilman Boulevard in the shadow of I-90. They have huge burgers with lots of fries and their root beer floats and malted milk shakes have to be seen to be believed—then experienced. Bring your expired driver's license or student ID to add to the wall art. Drop a coin into the genuine mighty Wurlitzer and spin a platter or two. The Triple XXX is definitely Issaquah's most visible landmark! Visit triplexrootbeer.com.

*WEATHER LORE:*
*Red sky at morning, sailor take warning.*
*Red sky at night, sailor's delight.*
*If the moon rises haloed round,*
*Soon you'll tread on deluged ground.*

# 21 Tiger Mountain–High Point Trail

This forest ramble is a good rainy-day trip when Tiger Mountain is shrouded in clouds. There is an amazing ethereal quality to walking through the forest here. And since you're going to get wet anyway, you won't be bothered by wet vegetation along the overgrown sections of trail. It's a wonderful summer hike as well because it stays away from the more-popular places in an already very popular place. That, and the shady forest, is most welcome during the two or so weeks of high summer temperatures (you know ... when it gets into the 80s!) we get around Puget Sound. Be advised, though: There are several very steep sections of trail!

**Start:** High Point trailhead at West Tiger Mountain Natural Resources Conservation Area, Issaquah

**Distance:** 6.3-mile lollipop

**Approximate hiking time:** 4 to 5 hours

**Difficulty:** Moderate to difficult, with faint trails and overgrown vegetation sometimes obscuring the trail. Some trails have two names as shown on maps of the area.

**Trail surface:** Forested path; rocky, wet, muddy

**Seasons:** Year-round

**Other trail users:** Runners

**Canine compatibility:** Leashed dogs permitted

**Land status:** Washington State Department of Natural Resources

**Nearest town:** Issaquah

**Services:** Gas, restaurants, groceries, lodging; no toilet at trailhead

**Northwest Forest Pass:** No

**Discover Pass:** Yes (none needed if you park along SE 79th)

**Maps:** Green Trails No. 204S: Tiger Mountain; USGS Fall City, Hobart; USDAFS Mount Baker-Snoqualmie National Forest

**Trail contacts:** Issaquah Alps Trails, Washington Department of Natural Resources

**Special hazards:** Stinging nettle, devil's club; confusing trail junctions; some trail sign names are different from the names given on Green Trails maps; no potable water at trailhead or on trail

**Finding the trailhead:** From Seattle, drive east on I-90 to exit 20, High Point Way. At the end of the off-ramp, bear right onto 270th Avenue SE, and then immediately turn right (west) onto SE 79th Street and park. There are usually many cars already parallel-parked along the street, so join them! Do not drive all the way in to the main paved parking lot for Tiger Mountain trails unless you have a Discover Pass and wish to add nearly a mile to your hike. GPS: N47 31.933' / W121 58.542'

## The Hike

From the street parking along SE 79th Street, walk east, crossing 270th Avenue SE, to a heavy-duty metal gate blocking the street. Walk around the gate and continue along the asphalt road for 0.2 mile to the High Point trailhead. Start walking northeasterly to avoid High Point Pond, and then curve right (south), beginning a steep 0.3-mile ascent to some power lines.

*Watch for this painted tree; it marks your turn onto a faint trail.*

The High Point Trail passes under power lines to a junction with the Lingering Trail. Do not hesitate here but continue straight ahead (south), passing two defunct high-voltage switching boxes; they give an indication of how this area was not always geared toward recreation. Climb 0.4 mile to the Dwight's Way Trail, turning left (east) and continuing up. In 0.1 mile meet the Lingering Trail again; remain straight (east) on Dwight's Way. The trail levels out (more or less) and meanders through the forest. Upon reaching the Preston Trail (aka West Tiger No. 1 Trail), turn right (south).

Begin a steep climb; after 0.5 mile meet the Bootleg Trail (aka Lower Bootleg Trail) and bear left (southwest), leaving the West Tiger No. 1 Trail. This section of trail is narrow and faint in many places—keep a sharp eye! Cross the lovely East Fork Issaquah Creek (which can be seasonally high) and traverse around the south end of the drainage. Start a sharp ascent of the east side of Tiger Mountain. As you huff and puff up the hill, note the ample evidence of past logging practices.

Reach an easily missed and faintly delimited trail junction in 2.7 miles, with homemade signs marking this as the way to East Tiger on the North Railroad grade. The route is narrow, faint, and heavily overgrown and is not marked on any map.

Continue up on the Bootleg Trail, cross a creek, and notice the witness post (T23N R7E S6) marking the NRCA (Natural Resources Conservation Area) boundary. A hundred yards later, the Bootleg Trail (aka Middle Bootleg Trail) meets up with the

Paw Print Connector. Turn right (west). The Bootleg Trail (now, aka Upper Bootleg Trail) is faint through here as it maintains its long climb. Keep a sharp lookout for a faint, unsigned, trail junction. This junction is marked by two large trees with blue arrows painted on them. Heading straight (south) brings you to a view of transmission towers on West Tiger No. 1 and an unnamed summit. Instead, turn right (west) and continue on a sometimes-hard-to-see trail.

Cross through a clear-cut with excellent views toward the previously mentioned unnamed peak and the transmission towers on West Tiger No. 1. Meet again with the Preston Trail (aka West Tiger No. 1 Trail) in 0.8 mile. A turn to the left (west) leads to Hiker's Hut Viewpoint in 0.5 mile. Turn right (east). Drop down for 0.5 mile and turn left (west) onto the West Tiger Railroad grade. After 0.4 mile of wide and level trail, turn right (north) onto the Tiger Mountain Trail.

Cross a branch of High Point Creek on a wooden bridge. Keep your eyes sharp to spot three old power-line poles, still with their ceramic insulators. Cross the creek on a plank bridge. An amateur sign marks this spot as Ruth's Cove. The Tiger Mountain Trail meets with the Lingering Trail after 0.9 mile. Turn left (west) for 0.1 mile and reach the junction between Tiger Mountain Trail and High Point Trail, turning right (north). Follow this wide trail for 0.2 mile until it hits the Dwight's Way Trail. Turn left (northwest) and in 0.4 mile reach the trailhead. Walk the asphalt road back to SE 79th Street.

## Miles and Directions

**0.0** Trailhead on SE 79th Street

**0.3** Power lines and junction with Lingering Trail

**0.7** High Point Trail junction with Dwight's Way Trail

**0.8** Dwight's Way Trail junction with Lingering Trail

**1.5** Dwight's Way Trail junction with Preston Trail

**2.0** Dwight's Way Trail junction with Bootleg Trail

**2.7** North Railroad grade to East Tiger

**3.0** Witness post

**3.1** Bootleg Trail junction with Paw Print Connector

**3.8** Bootleg Trail junction with Preston Trail

**4.3** Preston Trail junction with West Tiger Railroad grade

**4.7** West Tiger Railroad grade junction with Tiger Mountain Trail

**5.0** Ruth's Cove

**5.5** Tiger Mountain Trail junction with Lingering Trail

**5.6** Tiger Mountain Trail junction with High Point Trail

**6.3** Arrive back at trailhead

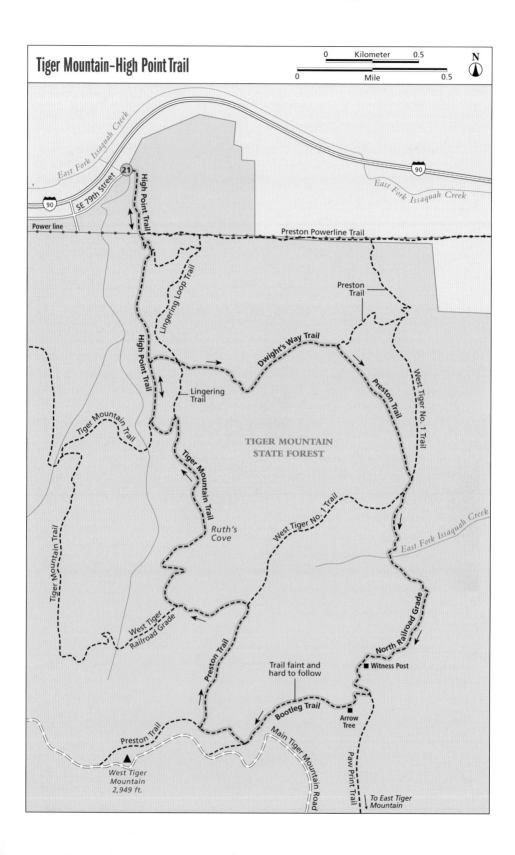

# Tiger Mountain–High Point Trail

Kilometer 0 0.5

Mile 0 0.5

N

East Fork Issaquah Creek

90

21

SE 79th Street

High Point Trail

90

Power line

Preston Powerline Trail

East Fork Issaquah Creek

Lingering Loop Trail

High Point Trail

Preston Trail

Dwight's Way Trail

Preston Trail

West Tiger No. 1 Trail

Lingering Trail

Tiger Mountain Trail

Tiger Mountain Trail

TIGER MOUNTAIN STATE FOREST

Ruth's Cove

Tiger Mountain Trail

West Tiger No. 1 Trail

East Fork Issaquah Creek

West Tiger Railroad Grade

North Railroad Grade

Preston Trail

Trail faint and hard to follow

Witness Post

Bootleg Trail

Arrow Tree

Preston Trail

Main Tiger Mountain Road

Paw Print Trail

West Tiger Mountain 2,949 ft.

To East Tiger Mountain

*Watch for this trail sign so you don't get lost.*

## Hike Information

Note that many of the names found on trail signs and marked on the Green Trails map are in conflict.

# 22 Cedar Butte

An easy-to-moderate half-day walk along the old Milwaukee Railroad grade, which ends with a beautiful view up the Middle Fork Snoqualmie River Valley. The trail is a combination of old railroad grade and forest path. The mix of deep Douglas fir and western hemlock forest with sun breaks and red alder thickets creates good opportunities for birdwatching. This great early- or off-season hike is almost always accessible, even when snow covers every other trail in the area.

**Start:** Cedar Falls trailhead, John Wayne Pioneer Trail in Iron Horse State Park

**Distance:** 3.7-mile lollipop

**Approximate hiking time:** 2 hours

**Difficulty:** Moderate

**Trail surface:** Forested path, old railroad bed

**Seasons:** Year-round

**Other trail users:** Bikes, horses, runners

**Canine compatibility:** Leashed dogs permitted

**Land status:** Iron Horse State Park; City of Seattle Cedar River Municipal Watershed Ecological Preserve

**Nearest town:** North Bend

**Services:** Gas, restaurants, groceries, lodging; vault toilets at trailhead

**Northwest Forest Pass:** No

**Discover Pass:** Yes and No (keep an eye on which parking lot you use)

**Maps:** Green Trails No. 205S: Rattlesnake Mountain; USGS North Bend; USDAFS Mount Baker-Snoqualmie National Forest

**Trail contacts:** Seattle Public Utilities, Cedar River Watershed, Iron Horse State Park, Milwaukee Road Historical Association.

**Special hazards:** No potable water

**Finding the trailhead:** Drive from Seattle on I-90 east to North Bend. Take exit 32 (436th Avenue SE) for Iron Horse State Park and the John Wayne Pioneer Trail. Turn right (south) at the stop sign. Pass the Cascade Golf Course, where 436th Avenue SE becomes Cedar Falls Road. In 2.7 miles reach the Rattlesnake Lake Recreation Area boundary, administered by Seattle Public Utilities in cooperation with Washington State Parks and King County Parks. In 0.1 mile is a small parking lot for Rattlesnake Ledge. Pass this lot. Continue to the wye in the road, and bear right to park in the free City of Seattle gravel lot. Or, bear left and follow the paved road to the paved lot at Iron Horse State Park (Discover Pass required). GPS: N47 25.886' / W121 45.897'

## The Hike

At the Cedar Falls trailhead are two clean, well-maintained, wheelchair-accessible vault toilets in bright orange buildings; many picnic tables; a hitching post; and an overbuilt reader board with brief descriptions covering the history of the old Milwaukee Railroad grade that forms the first mile of the Cedar Butte Trail. Take a moment to read what little is posted. This first section of trail is but a whisper in the long line that once stretched across the country as the Chicago, Milwaukee, St. Paul & Pacific Railroad. Afterward, easily locate a wide gravel path, immediately crossing an abandoned paved road that once went to the town of Cedar Falls.

*Cedar Butte (#22) and Mount McClellan (#33) from Rattlesnake Ledge (#23)*

In 0.3 mile reach the John Wayne Pioneer Trail; turn left (east), passing a trail sign to Snoqualmie Tunnel (18 miles) and Twin Falls (4.5 miles #25), McClellan Butte (9.5 miles #33), and Annette Lake (16.5 miles #35) trailheads. This old railroad grade is a popular year-round mountain bike route, but most traffic is confined to weekends. Directly before you is a Keep Out sign prohibiting access to the Cedar River Watershed—part of Seattle's domestic water supply.

In 1 mile pass a waytrail on the left (north) and cross Boxley Creek on an old trestle. Below, on the right (south), is a USGS stream gauge. In another 100 feet come to the Cedar Butte Trail on your right (south). In most years there is a sign nailed to a tree here. The forest path climbs steeply in a maturing second-growth forest with a well-developed understory of salal, gooseberry, blackberry, sword fern, mahonia, huckleberry, and buttercup. The trail junction you reach leads to the "Blowout" on the right. There sometimes is, and sometimes isn't, a trail sign here. However, bear left here.

Climb some more and enter a dark forest where the understory thins out. After one last steep push, reach Saddle Junction and a trail sign bolted to a Douglas fir. This spot marks the official end to where horses and bikes are allowed on the trail. The trail splits in three. To the right (west) is the top end of the Blowout Trail. Straight ahead the sign directs hikers to the South Side Trail. Do not take this route. After dropping into the drainage, the trail narrows, grows fainter, and then runs up a tree and disappears into a knothole.

To the left is the summit route. Switchbacks climb steeply, with an occasional view across the watershed to Rattlesnake Mountain. From the summit of Cedar Butte are gorgeous views up the Middle Fork Snoqualmie River to Mount Si, Mount Tenerife, Mailbox Peak, and others. Below the butte are glimpses of a few McMansions tucked into the trees along with I-90.

Once finished with the view, retrace your steps back to Saddle Junction.

Rather than turning right (west) and continuing down the main trail, walk straight ahead (south) on the Blowout Trail. Snake around without losing much elevation. The Blowout is marked by a small Overlook sign bolted to a tree. There isn't anything to see here anymore except a thick forest of spindly trees, but on December 23, 1918, a lot was happening. A break in the north bank of the Masonry Dam upstream of Rattlesnake Lake caused water from Cedar Lake (now Chester Morse Reservoir) to flood the small valley leading to Boxley Creek. Within minutes the little stream turned into a 150-foot-wide river that washed away the town of Edgewick, 2 miles downstream. Amazingly, none of the sixty or so residents of Edgewick were harmed, due to the fast thinking of a night watchman from the local sawmill. The city eventually paid more than $300,000 in damages.

Continue downhill until reaching the main Cedar Butte Trail. Turn left (west) and finally reach the John Wayne Trail again. Turn left (west), cross Boxley Creek again, and return to the trailhead.

## Miles and Directions

**0.0**  Cedar Falls trailhead
**0.3**  John Wayne Pioneer Trail junction
**1.0**  Boxley Creek
**1.1**  Cedar Butte–Blowout Trail junction
**1.4**  Cedar Butte–Saddle Junction
**1.6**  Cedar Butte
**1.8**  Saddle Junction
**2.3**  Blowout Overlook
**2.6**  Blowout Trail junction
**3.0**  Boxley Creek
**3.7**  Arrive back at trailhead

## Hike Information

Overnight backcountry camping fees for Iron Horse State Park are paid at the trailhead (for vehicles) and the campsite (for bike riders) so don't forget your wallet if you plan an overnight visit.

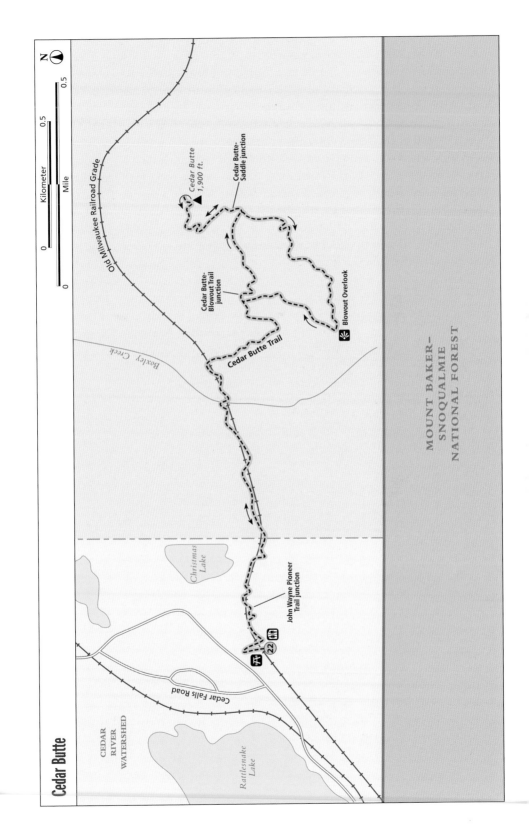

# Cedar Butte

CEDAR RIVER WATERSHED

*Rattlesnake Lake*

Cedar Falls Road

*Christmas Lake*

John Wayne Pioneer Trail Junction

*Boxley Creek*

Old Milwaukee Railroad Grade

Cedar Butte Trail

Cedar Butte-Blowout Trail junction

Cedar Butte 1,900 ft.

Cedar Butte-Saddle junction

Blowout Overlook

MOUNT BAKER–
SNOQUALMIE
NATIONAL FOREST

N

Kilometer
0      0.5      0.5
Mile
0      0.5

22

The Cedar River Watershed provides 70 percent of the water for 1.5 million people living in the greater Seattle area. A side trip to the Cedar River Watershed Visitor Center is well worth the time. Managed by Seattle Public Utilities, the center has interpretive displays and historical material and sells natural history and hiking books. They are open Tuesday through Sunday from 10 a.m. to 5 p.m. During April through October, they close at 4 p.m.

A walk around the Rain Drum Court, designed by Dan Corson, is a musical and educational experience of the finest kind! A short nature walk, with identification labels for native plants, begins in the parking area. Spur trails provide access to the shore of Rattlesnake Lake. Pick up maps of Rattlesnake Lake and a bird list at the visitor center.

The complete history of the Boxley Blowout is available at www.scn.org/cedar_butte/bb-main.html. Check it out!

*"I have two doctors, my left leg and my right."*
—George M. Trevelyan, English historian

# 23 Rattlesnake Mountain–East Peak

Rattlesnake Mountain is far from any rattling reptiles, and that's okay. It's the highest and easternmost of the Issaquah Alps and presents a challenging, but not overly so, combination of trails, former logging roads, and utility access roads. The mountain's dramatically exposed views of the Snoqualmie Valley make it a popular destination on sunny weekends. Low elevation and proximity to the ameliorating influences of Puget Sound keep it practically (but never entirely) snow-free through all but the most monstrous of winter storms. The East Peak Trail passes through land managed by the City of Seattle Cedar River Municipal Watershed Ecological Preserve, King County Parks, and Washington State Department of Natural Resources Rattlesnake Mountain Scenic Area, with help from the Washington Trails Association and Mountains to Sound Greenway Trust trail crews and volunteers. Once past the famous Rattlesnake Ledge with its impressive view, public use drops off in a major way. At the summit of East Peak is a communications tower.

**Start:** Rattlesnake Ledge trailhead
**Distance:** 9.0 miles out and back
**Approximate hiking time:** 4 to 6 hours
**Difficulty:** Moderate
**Trail surface:** Forested path
**Seasons:** Year-round
**Other trail users:** Runners
**Canine compatibility:** Leashed dogs permitted
**Land status:** Rattlesnake Mountain Scenic Area; City of Seattle Cedar River Municipal Watershed Ecological Preserve; Washington State Department of Natural Resources; King County Parks
**Nearest town:** North Bend

**Services:** Gas, restaurants, groceries, lodging; wheelchair-accessible portable toilet at trailhead
**Northwest Forest Pass:** No
**Discover Pass:** Yes and No (keep an eye on which parking lot you use)
**Maps:** Green Trails No. 205S, side A: Rattlesnake Mountain; USGS North Bend; USDAFS Mount Baker–Snoqualmie National Forest
**Trail contacts:** City of Seattle, Cedar River Watershed, King County Parks, Mountains to Sound Greenway Trust
**Special hazards:** Stinging nettle, devil's club; cliffs (sometimes icy) and exposure, with danger of falling; no potable water at trailhead or on trail

**Finding the trailhead:** Drive from Seattle on I-90 east to North Bend. Take exit 32 to 436th Avenue SE to Iron Horse State Park and the John Wayne Pioneer Trail. Turn right (south) at the stop sign. Pass the Cascade Golf Course, where 436th Avenue SE becomes Cedar Falls Road. In 2.7 miles reach the Rattlesnake Lake Recreation Area boundary, administered by Seattle Public Utilities in cooperation with Washington State Parks and King County Parks. In 0.1 mile is a small parking lot—usually full—for Rattlesnake Ledge. Pass this lot and park in the City of Seattle-provided gravel lot. Parking is free and a Discover Pass is not required unless you make the mistake of parking in the paved lot at the John Wayne trailhead. GPS: N47 26.069' / W121 46.081'

# The Hike

Walk back to the road from the parking lot. Cross and find the trail sign for Rattle-snake Ledge. Walk around the closed gate on an elevated pathway past a trail sign announcing the east trailhead for the Rattlesnake Mountain Trail (RMT). Follow this access road for 0.2 mile, with Rattlesnake Lake viewable on the left (west). Expect to see families and dogs and lots of frolicking. Reach a large grassy area with porta-potties, trash and recycling receptacles, and a bike rack. Begin ascending the trail to Rattlesnake Ledge.

Dog and human interactions, both positive and negative, are common along this stretch of trail, as are positive and negative interactions between leashed and unleashed pets. The path is wide in the beginning, allowing two-way traffic walking abreast and the occasional passing lane. There are even a few turnouts. It soon becomes a narrow trail which encourages single file traffic.

*Rattlesnake Ledge from the trailhead parking lot*

In 0.4 mile encounter a trail leading up the hill. The trail is blocked by a pole fence. Older sections of trail like this are occasionally encountered, although nonuse is quickly covering them with fallen trees and other woody debris. When in doubt, stay on the main pathway. The RMT is a work in progress and has been rerouted to avoid roads, control erosion, or reduce the grade.

After 2 miles of steady uphill hiking, reach a trail junction. Turn right (northeast), and walk 100 yards to Rattlesnake Ledge. Gray jays are fairly tame here, so if you're eating lunch, keep a weather eye out for the little thieves, or you just may lose your sandwich! Space on the ledge can be crowded on busy weekends with adults, children of all ages, and frolicking dogs. All the good and safe spots can be taken. There are no handrails, and careless behavior could have disastrous results. People *have* fallen to their deaths from Rattlesnake Ledge. Keep children and dogs on a tight leash. And watch your step—especially in wintertime when the ledge is often very icy and very slippery.

After taking in the view, return to the trail junction and continue straight ahead (northwest), passing an interpretive sign. Rattlesnake Ledge is actually three separate ledges. Each enjoys dramatic vistas of the entire Snoqualmie Valley. From the lower ledge, continue higher to waytrails leading to ledges 2 and 3, taking the same safety precautions as before. The RMT stays close to the cliff rim for some time after-ward, but dense tree growth obscures all views. The RMT now changes significantly, becoming narrower and less peopled. Good-bye, crowds; hello, peace and quiet!

Since the first edition of *Best Hikes Seattle* there have been many improvements to this next section of trail. Rather than following a route that plays hide-and-seek with the old communication towers access road to the summit of East Peak, it is now possible to remain on a well-built trail all the way to the top.

Once on the summit of East Peak there is a communications tower as well as diminishing views (due to the forest becoming increasingly mature). Picnic benches provide an excellent excuse to tarry on the peak for a relaxing lunch, weather permitting.

From the summit of East Peak it's entirely possible to continue northwest on the RMT for another 6.1 miles to the west trailhead at Snoqualmie Point, with access from exit 27 on I-90. In recent years more than 40,000 hours of volunteer and trail crew labor with $650,000 from the legislature have converted heavily logged land into a trail route that connects both trailheads.

For now, double back onto the RMT and retrace your steps past the ledges and down the mountain to the parking lot.

## Miles and Directions

**0.0**   Rattlesnake Ledge trailhead
**2.5**   Rattlesnake Ledge #1
**2.7**   Rattlesnake Ledge #2

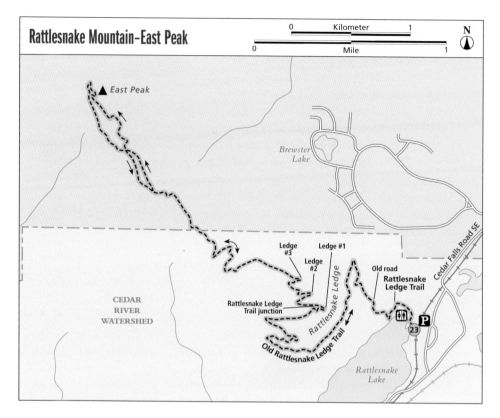

**2.9** Rattlesnake Ledge #3
**4.5** East Peak, Rattlesnake Mountain
**9.0** Arrive back at trailhead

## Hike Information

The Rattlesnake Lake Recreation Area is owned and managed by Seattle Public Utilities. Rattlesnake Lake is popular for picnicking throughout the summer. Anglers are frequent visitors as well. The lake was created by water seeping out from under 90,000-acre Chester Morse Reservoir and is also fed by runoff from Rattlesnake Mountain.

A side trip to the Cedar River Watershed Visitor Center is well worth the time. Managed by Seattle Public Utilities, the center has interpretive displays and historical material and sells natural history and hiking books. They are open Tuesday through Sunday from 10 a.m. to 5 p.m. During April through October, they close at 4 p.m.

Many areas of the western end of Rattlesnake Mountain and Ridge are owned by the Weyerhaeuser Corporation, which still conducts occasional logging operations. During field work for this third edition of *Best Hikes Seattle* the trail up Rattlesnake Mountain was closed to hikers due to its popularity and difficulty in maintaining

*The view from the top of Rattlesnake Ledge is stunning, but watch your step! There are no handrails.*

social distancing during the COVID-19 pandemic. Because of this you may encounter differences or upgrades to the trail that are not mentioned in the text.

# 24 Weeks Falls

In winter and spring, the 77-foot-tall Weeks Falls is an incredible display of cascading water. Located in Olallie State Park, on the South Fork Snoqualmie River, it is also one of the most accessible waterfalls in our region. If you're looking for an introductory hike for children, river views, fishing access, or somewhere to stretch your legs after a summer picnic, Weeks Falls is the place. Downstream of the falls is a hydro-generating facility. It's a great lesson in how electrical generation need not have a negative impact on the landscape.

**Start:** Overlook trailhead in South Fork Picnic Area, Olallie State Park
**Distance:** 1.0 mile double loop
**Approximate hiking time:** 1 hour
**Difficulty:** Easy
**Trail surface:** Forested path
**Seasons:** Year-round
**Other trail users:** None
**Canine compatibility:** Leashed dogs permitted
**Land status:** Washington State Parks
**Nearest town:** North Bend
**Services:** Gas, restaurants, groceries, lodging; no toilet at trailhead; toilets located in nearby picnic area at state park entrance

**Northwest Forest Pass:** No
**Discover Pass:** Yes
**Maps:** Green Trails No. 206S, side B: Mount Si NRCA, and No. 206: Bandera; USGS Chester Morse Lake; USDAFS Mount Baker-Snoqualmie National Forest
**Trail contact:** Olallie State Park
**Special hazards:** No potable water at trailhead or on trail; cold, swift river unsafe for swimming. Water levels in the fenced-off pool below the power plant can vary dramatically; avoid the temptation to try entering the water here.

**Finding the trailhead:** From Seattle, drive east on I-90 to exit 38 west. At the stop sign, turn right (south). The road curves to the left and becomes SE Homestead Valley Road, joining the approximate route of the Snoqualmie Pass Wagon Road (completed in 1869) and the historic Sunset Highway (old Snoqualmie Pass Highway). Pass a sign for Olallie State Park, Twin Falls State Park, and a gravel road to the Homestead Valley (east) trailhead for Twin Falls. In 0.6 mile pass a long, paved, wide spot on the left. In 0.2 mile reach a turnoff for Olallie State Park on your left (north). The intersection is not marked.

Enter the park, and drive past a large picnic area (with flush toilets; seasonally can be closed) and the ranger residence. Turn left into the parking area. The trailhead for the Weeks Falls / Overlook Trail begins in the northwest corner of the parking lot. The park is open 6:30 a.m. to dusk (summer) and 8 a.m. to dusk (winter). GPS: N47 26.192' / W121 39.250'

## The Hike

As easily seen from the size of the parking lot, this is a popular place. And no wonder! The short trail stays by the river and in deep shade all the way to Weeks Falls—which are stupendous during winter and spring and merely impressive the rest of the year.

*Weeks Falls—one of our region's most accessible waterfalls and a great hike for kids.*

Begin by the fee-collection station. The Weeks Falls Trail takes off to the right (east) on an asphalt road, which quickly becomes a forest path without losing any of its width.

Walk upstream along the river, passing frequent opportunities to stray on waytrails to river overlooks and angling sites on the river's south bank. This is also a nature trail, and there are several large interpretive signs for you to stop and read, learn, and appreciate. Occasional benches are provided to rest your weary bones and aching feet.

The trail meanders through the forest, crossing a creek on a quaint wooden bridge. When the trail splits, bear right and soon encounter an amazing sight: a huge Douglas fir. This tree is easily 30 feet in circumference at ground level and is the biggest, tallest thing around. It makes the few large western red cedars in the same grove appear puny by comparison, even though they themselves are impressive.

The trail pops out into bright sunshine, reaching a gravel access road and a unisex vault toilet. No parking is allowed here.

Immediately before you is the Weeks Falls Hydroelectric Project and beyond that, Weeks Falls. Stop for a moment to read the interpretive sign explaining the hydro project—commissioned June 5, 1987. Something that makes this hydropower plant different from many others is there isn't a dam. Upstream of the falls is a low, adjustable weir across the river. Water that pools behind the weir is withdrawn into a 600-foot-long underground tunnel, which connects to the powerhouse beside you. If water is flowing out of the concrete channel below the powerhouse, electricity is

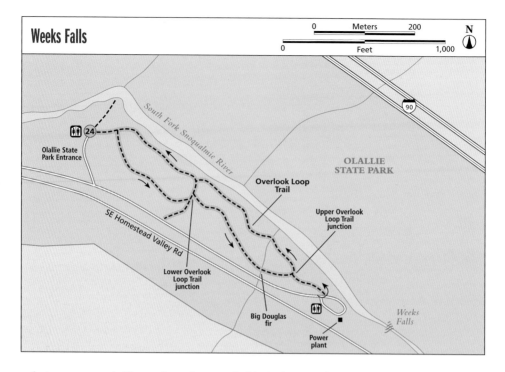

Weeks Falls

Olallie State Park Entrance

South Fork Snoqualmie River

24

SE Homestead Valley Rd

Overlook Loop Trail

Upper Overlook Loop Trail junction

OLALLIE STATE PARK

Lower Overlook Loop Trail junction

Big Douglas fir

Power plant

Weeks Falls

being generated. If not, then there probably isn't enough water in the river to both generate power and protect the fish. Within the turbine building, 5 megawatts of electricity is produced—enough power for 800 homes.

Move on 100 feet to an observation deck and Weeks Falls. Many fallen trees, along with wet and slippery rocks, make going any farther a dangerous operation. Don't forget to keep an eye on any small children.

Returning from the falls, find where the trail splits and bear right, walking close by the river. Many access points for admiring the view are available. The trail meets up with the main trail and shortly reaches the parking lot.

## Miles and Directions

**0.0**   Overlook trailhead
**0.3**   Big Douglas fir
**0.5**   Weeks Falls
**1.0**   Arrive back at trailhead

## Hike Information

Weeks Falls is the fourth of five major waterfalls along the South Fork Snoqualmie River. The Weeks Falls facility was commissioned and operates under a license from the Federal Energy Regulatory Condition (FERC Project No. 7563) that expires in 2035.

# 25 Twin Falls

A beautiful and impressive series of waterfalls along the South Fork Snoqualmie River, a high bridge over a deep gorge, and an observation deck aerie are the biggest draws for hiking the Twin Falls Trail. It's a popular route, especially from the west trailhead, but beginning from the east allows hikers to appreciate a short section of the old Milwaukee Railroad grade and views both up and down the Snoqualmie Valley. Though the trail is wide below the falls, there are no passing lanes. Solitude seekers are advised to begin at the Homestead Valley (east) trailhead, where few venture. The 135-foot-tall main Twin Falls is not the only allure to this trail. Anglers will find plenty of waytrails down to the river below the falls.

**Start:** Homestead Valley (east) trailhead in Twin Falls State Park; west trailhead for reverse hike

**Distance:** 8.0 miles out and back or 4.0-mile shuttle

**Approximate hiking time:** 5 to 6 hours

**Difficulty:** Moderate, with some steep sections

**Trail surface:** Forested path, old railroad grade

**Seasons:** Year-round

**Other trail users:** Runners, bikes (for a short while on the Milwaukee Railroad grade), anglers

**Canine compatibility:** Leashed dogs permitted

**Land status:** Washington State Parks

**Nearest town:** North Bend

**Services:** Gas, restaurants, groceries, lodging; unisex vault toilet at both east and west trailheads

**Northwest Forest Pass:** No

**Discover Pass:** Yes

**Maps:** Green Trails No. 206S, side B: Mount Si NRCA, and No. 206: Bandera; USGS Chester Morse Lake; USDAFS Mount Baker–Snoqualmie National Forest

**Trail contact:** Olallie State Park

**Special hazards:** Exposed cliff sections (protected by handrails) on lower trail; observation platforms (protected by handrails, but the platforms can be wet and slippery); no potable water at trailhead or on trail; cold and swift South Fork Snoqualmie River is dangerous for swimming

**Finding the trailhead:** For the Homestead Valley (east) trailhead, from Seattle drive east on I-90 to exit 38 west. At the stop sign, turn right (south). In 0.2 mile the road curves to the left and becomes SE Homestead Valley Road, joining the approximate route of the Snoqualmie Pass Wagon Road (completed in 1869) and the historic Sunset Highway (old Snoqualmie Pass Highway). In 0.1 mile pass a sign for Olallie State Park and Twin Falls State Park. A worn and potholed gravel road on your right (west) signals the east trailhead for Twin Falls. There is free (no Discover Pass needed) street parking available here along the roadway. Otherwise, turn right and follow the potholes. In 0.2 mile pass a pay station and gated vehicle access road to the John Wayne Pioneer Trail on your left and park. GPS: N47 26.521' / W121 40.360'

For the west trailhead, from Seattle drive east on I-90 to exit 34, 468th Avenue SE. Turn right (east) and drive 0.6 mile. Before crossing a bridge over the South Fork Snoqualmie River, turn left (east) onto SE 159th Street. After 0.3 mile pass through a small residential community (restricted parking; park here and you will be ticketed and towed) and reach the parking lot where the road ends. Park hours at the west trailhead are 6 a.m. to dusk. The lot frequently fills early, especially on weekends and sunny days. Vehicles left after park closing will be impounded. GPS: N47 27.191' / W121 42.317'

## The Hike

Begin on the south side of the east trailhead parking lot and ascend a short, narrow trail to the access road, which leaves from the parking lot. Turn right (west) and continue to the John Wayne Pioneer Trail, bearing right. This is the old Milwaukee Railroad grade, marked with a large Olallie State Park sign. Turn right (west). Even though you're walking on a wide gravel road to the sound of I-90 traffic, this is still a pleasant jaunt. A deep, dark forest is on one side and beautiful Snoqualmie Valley views are on the other.

Walk for 0.5 mile, passing the Mount Washington Trail on the left (south), and find the Twin Falls Trail. Turn right (north) and begin dropping toward the South Fork Snoqualmie River. If you continue on the John Wayne Pioneer Trail for 500 feet, you'll arrive at the Twin Falls Substation—a fine detour for those intrigued by the generation of electricity.

Returning to the Twin Falls Trail, this section is limited to foot traffic and is blocked by a gate that allows human passage only. Maybe because it sees less use than the trail below the falls, expect to see less maintenance for the next 0.5 mile. Fallen trees across the trail show evidence of many-years-old detours. This upper stretch is narrow, but not too narrow—overgrown, but not too overgrown. There are thimbleberries in season and sword ferns all the time.

Cross a culvert that keeps Washington Creek from washing away the trail. The route flattens, then drops in earnest on switchbacks to the increasing roar of falling water. Your first inkling of anything stupendous is a bench, some stairs, and then a handrail. At a sharp corner in the trail, look upstream (east) and see the upper falls.

Continue dropping lower and lower on stairs to reach, at 1.7 miles, an impressive bridge spanning the South Fork gorge. Look upstream at the lower reaches of the upper falls—a twin falls in itself. Immediately below is the lip of lower Twin Falls. The rocky reaches of the South Fork stretch below. Sharp eyes can spot the observation aerie for the lower falls on the river-right canyon wall.

Crossing the bridge, the trail climbs on stairs and crosses a creek. Don't bother with a waytrail that circumvents the river side of the handrail. It doesn't lead to any view of the falls.

**GREEN TIP:**
For rest stops, move off the trail so others won't
have to step over or around you. Find a seat on
a resilient surface without vegetation.

*The hydroelectric diversion lies above this uppermost Twin Falls.*

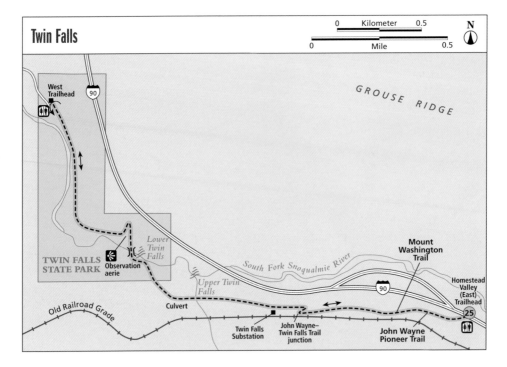

**Twin Falls**

Continue to a side trail after 2 miles—really another series of steps, which drop steeply to an observation platform that clings to the gorge like an eagle's aerie. From here a dramatic view of the lower falls fills the eye. This is no leaping fall of water; rather, the river slides and slithers down the rock, splayed into many channels, and ends in a deep pool. Standing upon the viewing platform gives observers the distinct feeling of being in a tree house. Return up the steps—all 106 of them—to the trail. You have been practicing your stair climbs, haven't you?

Once on the main trail, keep heading downhill. Leave the sound of falling water and return to the sound of highway traffic. Human traffic on the trail begins to pick up, too. After 4 miles reach the west trailhead. Along the way, you'll pass many opportunities to approach the river. Bear in mind at all times, and during all seasons, that the South Fork is swift and cold—which makes it suitable for fish, which means anglers, but unsuitable for swimming, which means you.

Use the vault toilet and pick up your shuttle vehicle, or turn around and retrace your steps uphill to the east trailhead.

## Miles and Directions

**0.0**   Homestead Valley (east) trailhead

**0.3**   John Wayne Pioneer Trail

**0.8**   Twin Falls Trail

**1.7**   Upper Twin Falls and bridge

**2.0** Lower Twin Falls view, observation aerie

**4.0** West trailhead; shuttle or turnaround point

**8.0** Arrive back at east trailhead

**Option:** A car shuttle from the east to the west trailhead is an alternative but leaves a larger "carbon footprint." The west trailhead is the more popular of the two access points to Twin Falls, and you will see a lot more people.

# Hike Information

Twin Falls is the tallest waterfall along the South Fork of the Snoqualmie River and actually represents three separate drops for a total of 230 feet, with the largest drop being 135 feet. Like nearby Weeks Falls, water from Twin Falls has been harnessed for hydroelectric production. There is an unseen diversion upstream of the falls, and water reenters the river in a large pool about 0.5 mile from the west trailhead. Due to this diversion, Twin Falls loses a lot of its impressiveness late in the summer. Like Weeks Falls, there is no impoundment of the river above Twin Falls.

# 26 Little Si

Under the shadow of its bigger brother, Little Si is so tiny, so close. Whether you need a quickie in the forest after a hard day at the office or an interesting walk with young children, Little Si is a perfect fit. Its accessibility to Seattle makes it more of an urban walk than a wilderness hike, and this popularity is reflected by a wide and beaten-down track and a thirty-car parking area with a lot of turnover—and not of the pastry kind. Nevertheless, this is still a very pretty route to take, and views from the top are just as good as from Mount Si—and require much less work!

**Start:** New trailhead parking lot along Southeast Mount Si Road

**Distance:** 3.0 miles out and back

**Approximate hiking time:** 2 hours

**Difficulty:** Easy; the trail is wide and easy to follow. There are some steep places but nothing a ten-year-old can't handle if given enough time. There are an adequate number of places to stop and rest and numerous diversions (bridges, ephemeral streams, banana slugs, rocks to climb, etc.) for children.

**Trail surface:** Forested path; rocky

**Seasons:** Year-round

**Other trail users:** Runners, rock climbers

**Canine compatibility:** Leashed dogs permitted

**Land status:** Washington Department of Natural Resources

**Nearest town:** North Bend

**Services:** Gas, restaurants, groceries, lodging; unisex vault toilet at trailhead

**Northwest Forest Pass:** No

**Discover Pass:** Yes

**Maps:** Green Trails No. 206S, side A: Mount Si NRCA; USGS North Bend; USDAFS Mount Baker–Snoqualmie National Forest

**Trail contacts:** Mount Si, Department of Natural Resources, South Puget Sound District

**Special hazards:** Exposure; no potable water at trailhead or on trail

**Finding the trailhead:** Take I-90 from Seattle to exit 32, 436th Avenue SE in North Bend. This avoids the main North Bend exit (exit 31) and traffic congestion caused by the outlet stores and other traveler services. Also, you won't have to drive through downtown North Bend.

At the stop sign at the end of the off-ramp, turn left onto 436th Avenue SE. Dead ahead is the summit of Little Si. Drive 0.6 mile, passing the flashing yellow lights, to a stop sign at Southeast North Bend Way. Note that cross-traffic does not stop. Turn left (northwest). After 0.3 mile turn right (north) onto Southeast Mount Si Road. In 0.3 mile cross the Middle Fork Snoqualmie River Bridge and pass the overflow parking lot for Little Si on the left (north) at 434th Avenue SE. The road bends to the right. In 0.2 mile find the Little Si parking lot on the left (north). GPS: N47 29.215' / W121 45.217'

## The Hike

From the parking lot the trail takes off steeply on switchbacks on a rocky slope. The view opens up to the south, exposing a fine panorama from Rattlesnake Mountain (#23) to Cedar Butte (#22) along with the Cedar River Watershed. In springtime

*This bench memorializes local climber Doug Hansen, who died in 1996 while climbing Mount Everest.*

notice the urn-shaped white flowers of salal along with their glandular, red floral receptacles. The plants are subject to a smut that causes splotches on the leaves, reducing salal's importance as a significant subsidiary forest product. Salal belongs to the same family as madrone and bearberry—plainly evident when comparing the blossoms.

Leaving the rocky slope behind, the trail tops out in 0.3 mile and enters a stand of lovely second-growth. The trail here seems perpetually damp from the deep shade of the forest; this is prime banana slug habitat. If your kids are with you put them on "slug alert!" Wetter areas have been raised above grade with occasional log causeways. Other sections are not so lucky and are becoming wider and wider as hikers step around the mud and puddles. Pass several unmarked waytrails leading off into the trees. Continue straight ahead on the doublewide Little Si Trail.

In 0.6 mile reach an unmarked and gradually disappearing trail junction on the right (northwest) for the old Mount Si Trail. Continue on the wider Little Si Trail, crossing an ephemeral stream. After 1 mile reach a split cedar fence and a DNR sign requesting that you stay on your side in order to allow plant regeneration to proceed on the other. This is an inviting spot for lunch, especially on hot hiking days: cool and moist, and with many convenient logs and rocks to sit on.

## FOXGLOVE

Foxglove (*Digitalis purpurea*) is a ubiquitous herbaceous plant found along trails and other disturbed areas. The soft, hairy leaves are toothed, ovate, and lance-shaped in a basal rosette. Its tall spikes of colorful purple, pink, rose, yellow, or white flowers entice picking fingers to return home with a blossom or two. But beware! All parts of the plant are toxic.

*Foxglove is the source of digitoxin and was a common medicinal herb during the nineteenth century.*

Because it's such a common plant, foxglove is usually assumed to be native to the Pacific Northwest. Sadly, no. It might have first been introduced to the Pacific Northwest by Dr. William Fraser Tolmie (1812–1886). Tolmie was a surgeon, trader, and, later, chief factor of the Fort Nisqually Hudson Bay Company fur post between 1833 and 1859. After leaving Washington, Tolmie settled in Victoria, British Columbia, and apparently never practiced medicine again.

A source of the heart medicine digitoxin, foxglove was a common medicinal herb in European gardens during the nineteenth century. It makes sense that it would have been in Dr. Tolmie's pharmacopoeia. Today it's a popular cultivar for vertical accents in flower gardens and is a frequent garden escapee.

Other common names for foxglove include the more colorful, and perhaps more descriptive, witches' gloves, dead man's bells, and bloody fingers.

The trail continues to climb, first gently and then steeply, in its never-ending quest to reach the summit. Pass several marked signposts for the rock-climbing area located below the summit. Come here at the right time of year and you'll hear the clink, clang, and tinkling of climbing hardware and the sounds of climbers' voices wafting dreamlike high above you through the trees.

In 1.2 miles reach a bench embedded with a brass plaque. The bench memorializes Doug Hansen, who disappeared after reaching the summit of Mount Everest on May 10, 1996—a story covered in Jon Krakauer's bestseller *Into Thin Air*.

A few steps later begin the final uphill stretch of the trail, which is steeper and longer than any previous section. The trail swings around the north nose of Little Si. Highway and other sounds rise up from North Bend, making hikers realize that it has been quiet for quite some time—due to the trail passing between Little Si and Mount Si (#27).

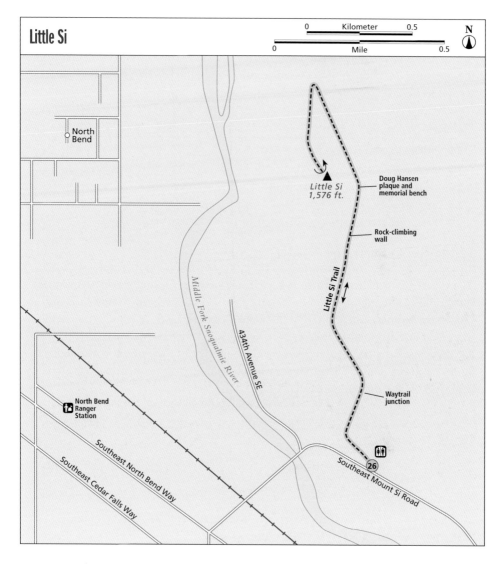

Kilometer 0.5

Mile 0.5

N

North Bend

*Little Si Trail*

Little Si
1,576 ft.

Doug Hansen
plaque and
memorial bench

Rock-climbing
wall

*Middle Fork Snoqualmie River*

434th Avenue SE

North Bend
Ranger
Station

Waytrail
junction

*Southeast North Bend Way*

*Southeast Cedar Falls Way*

*Southeast Mount Si Road*

26

Near the summit are a few openings in the trees, affording dramatic views of the south shoulder and summit of Mount Si. If you choose to step out onto the rock ledges to enjoy the views, watch your step! Especially if the rock here is wet or icy. It's a long way straight down to the bottom. A few feet below the top of Little Si are several waytrails made by impatient hikers attempting shortcuts. At 1.5 miles reach the top.

The summit views up and down the Snoqualmie River Valley are impressive. If it isn't windy and cold, have a seat. Stop and stay a while. If you're eating lunch, be aware that many others have eaten here in the past and will eat here in the future. Pick up any crumbs; refrain from the temptation to toss apple cores, orange peels, and other food waste into the trees. It's unsightly and rude and encourages begging from the local rodents and birds.

To return to the trailhead, retrace your steps. The trail always looks different from the opposing direction, so don't be in a hurry. Enjoy the reverse as much as the forward direction.

## Miles and Directions

**0.0** Trailhead along Southeast Mount Si Road

**1.0** Rock-climbing wall

**1.2** Doug Hansen plaque and memorial bench

**1.5** Summit

**3.0** Arrive back at trailhead

## Hike Information

There are two benches and two wheelchair-accessible parking spaces at the main trailhead. Pay attention to the No Parking signs along Southeast Mount Si Road—they mean business. The old trailhead, which began at 434th Avenue SE, is decommissioned and abandoned. Lots of No Parking signs there as well. Pay attention, or pay the man! If the main parking lot is full, double back to the overflow parking area as described previously. There's an access trail from the overflow parking area to the main parking lot and the trailhead.

# 27 Mount Si

Dominating the skyline over the town of North Bend like a giant stegosaurus, Mount Si is all that remains of an oceanic plate volcano. There are many classic hikes in the Seattle area, and the summit of Mount Si is the classic of classics. Without a doubt, it's one of the most popular hikes in our area. Given its popularity, it's interesting to note that within 4 miles the trail rises 3,600 feet. Hiking to the top of Mount Si is like climbing the Space Needle six times. This is not a hike for the faint of heart—or the out of shape!

**Start:** Mount Si Natural Resources Conservation Area trailhead
**Distance:** 8.3-mile circuit
**Approximate hiking time:** 6 to 8 hours
**Difficulty:** Moderate due to steepness
**Trail surface:** Forested path; rocky
**Seasons:** Year-round
**Other trail users:** Runners
**Canine compatibility:** Leashed dogs permitted
**Land status:** Washington Department of Natural Resources

**Nearest town:** North Bend
**Services:** Gas, restaurants, groceries, lodging; vault toilet at trailhead
**Northwest Forest Pass:** No
**Discover Pass:** Yes
**Maps:** Green Trails No. 206S, side A: Mount Si NRCA; USGS North Bend; USDAFS Mount Baker–Snoqualmie National Forest
**Trail contacts:** Department of Natural Resources
**Special hazards:** Loose rock, exposure

**Finding the trailhead:** From Seattle, drive east on I-90 to exit 32, 436th Avenue SE. The road signs before the exit proclaim "Iron Horse State Park–John Wayne Pioneer Trail." At the stop sign at the end of the off-ramp, turn left (north) and proceed north for 0.6 mile. Turn left (west) onto Southeast North Bend Way. In 0.3 mile turn right (north) onto Southeast Mount Si Road. After crossing the Middle Fork Snoqualmie River, the road curves right (northeast) and in 0.5 mile passes the trailhead to Little Si, arriving at the Mount Si trailhead in an additional 1.8 miles.

The gated parking lot opens at dawn and closes at dusk. It is subject to video surveillance by the King County Sheriff's Department due to the high incidence of car prowls. Lock your car and take all valuables with you. The parking lot is often full even during the week and can be overflowing on weekends or holidays. No parking is permitted along Southeast Mount Si Road. Pay attention to the signs if you don't want your car ticketed and hauled away. GPS: N47 29.305' / W121 43.385'

## The Hike

Fans of the early 1990s television show *Twin Peaks* will recognize Mount Si from a distance as the backdrop for many of the show's exterior scenes. The program was filmed primarily on soundstages in Los Angeles, although Twede's Restaurant in North Bend was used as the diner where FBI Special Agent Cooper would get a cuppa joe and enjoy some of the Northwest's famous pies. Everything about *Twin*

*Mount Si and the lower Snoqualmie River Valley from Rattlesnake Ledge*

*Peaks,* including where to visit the locations of other exterior scenes, is here: welcome totwinpeaks.com.

The trail begins north of the vault toilet, picnic tables, and water spigot and quickly passes the wheelchair-accessible 0.2-mile Creek Side Loop Trail, which is dedicated to North Bend resident Frances North. As a state legislator during the 1970s, North was instrumental in setting aside 1,100 acres of Mount Si for public use. The Mount Si Natural Resources Conservation Area now consists of 9,000 acres—once again, because of North's vision.

Cross the creek, enter deep second-growth forest, and climb steeply on a wide, rocky trail. The rocks protruding from the ground are worn shiny and smooth by the boots of the 80,000 people who yearly make use of this trail. The way to the top of Mount Si is continually a work in progress as stout bridges replace rotten logs over ephemeral stream courses, and trail rerouting eliminates the steeper sections that in some places once went straight uphill. Where the trail is too steep for switchbacks, there are tall stone steps. Way-markers are posted every 0.5 mile to assist hikers in charting their progress.

On any given day the route up Mount Si sees a number of extremes. There are Lycra-clad trail runners hauling dual bottles of water on their hips, hikers who look like they just stepped out of an REI catalog, other hikers bedecked in all sorts of glacier-climbing gear as they train to summit Mount Rainier, moms and dads with tiny tots riding in backpacks, young and old out for a forest stroll, high school students with fearless attitudes, people walking their dogs—even the occasional walker in flip-flops sans hat, pack, water, or food. Well, that's what popularity is all about. The important point is that they are all outside, enjoying their public lands.

## CAIRNS AND DUCKS

Cairns are piles of rocks used to mark a trail or locate a geographic or historic place. They can be as simple as three stones placed one atop the other or as complex as some elaborate summit cairns standing several feet high and comprising hundreds of rocks.

Cairns used for marking trails are found all over the world, predominantly in mountainous areas, but are also used in deserts. In the hardwood forests of the United States, tree blazes were historically used to mark trails. This practice is also used in our Northwest forests. An ax-cut into a tree truck is placed over a long vertical cut—almost like dotting a lowercase *i*.

The predominant builders of cairns are hikers who, skilled in the trials and tribulations of Hansel and Gretel, don't wish to leave a trail of bread crumbs behind to mark their way. Permanence, even something as transitory as a pile of rocks, is more comforting than returning from a journey only to find your trail devoured by ravenous ravens or field mice.

*Duck* is another common term for cairn. The term supposedly comes from a time when the topmost rock was used as a pointer, like a bird's beak, showing the proper direction to follow.

Following duck trails is problematic. Subsequent hikers can't be assured whether the builders knew where they were going. It's been found that ducks tend to occur where they are least needed, given that trailblazers are too occupied with finding their own way to mark it for others. It's best to rely upon yourself and your ability to read a map, use a compass, and interpret landscapes based on your own abilities and experience.

Investigate more about these piles of rock by reading *Cairns*, by David B. Williams.

*Cairns, or ducks, mark trails—but not always accurately.*

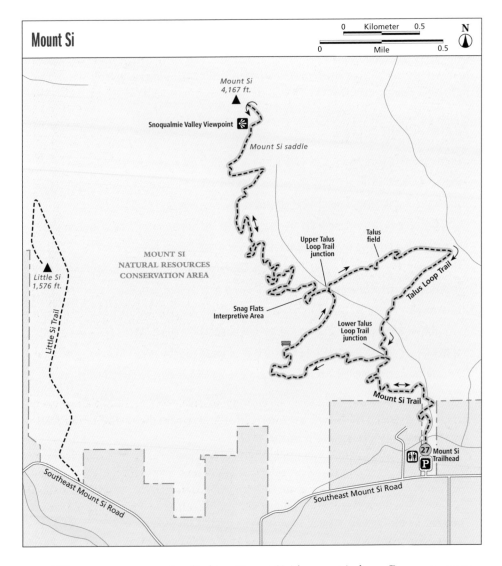

0      Kilometer    0.5    **N**

0           Mile        0.5

*Mount Si*
*4,167 ft.*

Snoqualmie Valley Viewpoint

*Mount Si saddle*

Talus
field

Upper Talus
Loop Trail
junction

MOUNT SI
NATURAL RESOURCES
CONSERVATION AREA

*Little Si*
*1,576 ft.*

Talus Loop Trail

Snag Flats
Interpretive Area

Lower Talus
Loop Trail
junction

Little Si Trail

Mount Si Trail

27 Mount Si
Trailhead

Southeast Mount Si Road

Southeast Mount Si Road

Whatever your reason for climbing Mount Si, it's a sweat inducer. Be sure to carry plenty of liquids to replace those precious bodily fluids lost to us by evaporative cooling during the ascent.

In 0.75 mile reach the bottom end of the Talus Loop Trail on the right (east). After 1.5 miles the trail levels out briefly. Three benches here give weary hikers an opportunity to rest. This is also a popular place for people to leave their toilet paper beneath softball-size rocks. Don't be one of them—even the most casual observer will notice that TP does not go away in any appreciably short period of time. Pack it in, pack it out (see "Going to the Bathroom in the Woods" sidebar on page 5).

In 1.7 miles the trail forks at a signpost. Turn left (northwest) to continue on to the summit. Turn right (east) for the Talus Loop Trail (later—see below). For the next

*The "Haystack" summit of Mount Si*

few hundred feet the trail mellows out, crossing seasonally wet areas on stout wooden bridges and reaches the Snag Flats Interpretive Area, where the role of fire in forest health is explained.

Once again the trail takes off uphill with a vengeance—this time on a series of long switchbacks. There are several older sections of trail through here, slowly returning to nature, and some (older) maps still show them. Stay on the newly constructed trail sections. This will prevent erosion and allow the forest to reclaim the older sections for itself.

At 3.7 miles pop out of the trees at a saddle in a large rocky area. There are usually many exhausted hikers lying about on the rocks and admiring the first views to the south of Mount Rainier. Keep on going, though—the top is nearby, along with better views and great lunch spots. In winter this is usually as far as snow and ice will permit hikers to safely proceed.

The trail picks its way through the rocks. Follow signs to the Snoqualmie Valley Viewpoint and Haystack Scramble. The Scramble is a Class 3, 150-foot climb to the actual summit of Mount Si. It requires hands and feet along with caution and care, and it is not advised for inexperienced climbers. People have fallen, been injured, or died here. Views of the Snoqualmie Valley are just as good from any of the vantage points below the actual summit. There are cliffs here with loose rock. Watch your step! Beware: There are people below you.

Some maps show the Mount Si Trail continuing eastward to Mount Teneriffe. This rough route is consigned only to the truly adventurous. Otherwise, retrace your steps down the Mount Si Trail to Snag Flats Interpretive Area and the Talus Loop Trail.

To extend your hike a bit, turn left (east) on the lightly used but well-established Talus Loop Trail. It's really a nice addition to your day. Soon cross an ephemeral creek and then a short talus field. Continue through thick forest for 1.3 miles until meeting up again with the Mount Si Trail at the unmarked junction mentioned earlier. Turn left (south) and reach the parking lot in 0.7 mile.

## Miles and Directions

**0.0** Trailhead at Mount Si Natural Resources Conservation Area

**0.7** Lower Talus Loop Trail junction

**1.7** Upper Talus Loop Trail junction and Snag Flats Interpretive Area

**3.7** Mount Si saddle and Snoqualmie Valley view

**4.0** Mount Si summit

**6.3** Upper Talus Loop Trail junction and Snag Flats Interpretive Area

**8.3** Arrive back at trailhead

## Hike Information

Mount Si was named for local homesteader Josiah "Uncle Si" Merritt. After the hike, if you're thirsty for the best root beer float within 100 miles, stop along the main drag in downtown North Bend at Scott's Dairy Freeze, 234 East North Bend Way. You won't be sorry. It's about as close to *American Graffiti* as you're going to find around here!

Twede's Restaurant in North Bend, at 137 North Bend Way on the corner of North Bend Way and Bendigo Boulevard, touts its fame as the diner from the early 1990s television show *Twin Peaks* with a sign proclaiming Famous Twin Peaks Pies.

A mile up the road from the Mount Si trailhead is the new Mount Teneriffe trailhead with ample paved parking and a vault toilet. From here choose the 7.4-mile route to Mount Teneriffe, a 2.3-mile connector trail to the Talus Loop Trail on Mount Si, or a strenuous 3.3-mile hike to Teneriffe Falls. Mileages are one-way and a Discover Pass is required.

# Snoqualmie River Valley Highlands

The Snoqualmie River Valley has some of the most rugged and beautiful wilderness scenery of the Central Cascade Mountains. Nearly every popular trail on the north side of I-90 leads into the 362,789-acre Alpine Lakes Wilderness. The Middle Fork

*The view southwest from Garfield Ledges, Middle Fork Snoqualmie (Photo by Carl Gronquist)*

# MIDDLE FORK ROAD (FR 56) AND THE MIDDLE FORK SNOQUALMIE PAVING PROJECT

For decades those traveling up the Middle Fork Snoqualmie River Valley suffered with a bumpy, potholed dirt road that took its toll on vehicles while spraying enormous clouds of dust on people enjoying the river corridor. Built as a road for timber extraction on the bed of an old railroad grade, the Middle Fork Road (formerly FR 56) was never designed to handle the automobile traffic it came to see. Over time, bridges held up by old timbers were rotting away, road culverts curtailed fish passage, and the annual grading of the road largely became an exercise in futility as the potholes returned within weeks.

After more than two decades of discussion and a seemingly endless cycle of meetings and public review, Western Federal Lands Highway Division awarded a $15 million construction contract in 2014 to establish a properly engineered roadbed, pave the road, formalize pullouts at key recreation sites, and replace three failing bridges and numerous culverts. The result of this work included improvements to safety, better access for law enforcement in what was once a lawless valley, benefits for fish habitat, reduced ongoing maintenance costs, and improved access for the general public.

Conservationists advocated for the final 20-foot-wide alignment to encourage lower speeds and to maintain the forested character of the corridor. Led by the efforts of the Middle Fork Outdoor Recreation Coalition (MidFORC), and with support from Mountains to Sound Greenway, the Mountaineers, the Washington Trails Association, American Whitewater, and other user groups, the new Middle Fork Road was just one element in an overall vision to enhance the recreational opportunities along the river.

Literally situated in the backyard of the town of North Bend and "freeway close" to Seattle, the valley's scenic quality and recreational potential is of unparalleled national park quality. Drawing over 100,000 visitors annually, the Middle Fork Snoqualmie River Valley is home to jagged, glacially carved peaks, immense old-growth trees, lots of hiking possibilities, and an amazing river along the road that draws anglers and whitewater kayakers. The valley of the Middle Fork Snoqualmie River is truly a wonderful and tremendous place.

Closure of the former FR 56 in 2007 at Dingford Creek and the Myrtle Lake–Hester Lake trailheads completed implementation of the 2005 Middle Fork Snoqualmie Access Travel Management Plan. According to Mount Baker–Snoqualmie National Forest, "This road-to-trail conversion is in conjunction with the recently completed Middle Fork Trail, which will provide multiple trail loop opportunities of up to 28 miles in length." Another part of this project was a new footbridge across the Middle Fork Snoqualmie River at Goldmyer Hot Springs. The effort to close FR 56 beyond Dingford Creek and convert the last 7.6 miles of road into a multiuse trail was an outgrowth of cooperative citizen planning efforts begun in the early 1990s and was supported by user groups, environmental groups, landowners, and the Forest Service. Though road closure meant the loss of vehicle access to the upper reaches of the Middle Fork Snoqualmie, it also meant that scarce maintenance funds during an era of tight budgets could be dedicated to more-critical areas of the forest. Some of these resources include enhancements for recreational users on the more heavily used sections of the Snoqualmie River, such as improved river access, sanitation facilities, vegetation restoration, and increased law enforcement presence to prevent dumping, meth labs, and other illegal activities. The project was finally completed in 2017.

Then came a heavy winter storm on December 19–20, 2019. Two sections of the Middle Fork Road were covered by slides and another section was undermined and washed away by flood runoff, 7.2 miles upriver from the Mailbox Peak trailhead. That disastrous storm dumped nearly 7 inches of rain in approximately thirty-six hours! Not until May of 2020 was the road repaired well enough to permit traffic once again.

The Middle Fork Snoqualmie River Valley is truly a treasure more precious than gold or diamonds.

*After the Middle Fork Road was opened in 2017, it was closed by a landslide in early 2019 and not reopened until the spring of 2020.*

Snoqualmie River Road (formerly FR 56, now NF 5600) deeply penetrates this national park–worthy wilderness area, which spans the Cascade Mountain crest from Snoqualmie Pass to Stevens Pass.

In 2007 FR 56 was permanently closed to automobile traffic at Dingford Creek. A new campground near the Taylor River was opened, and extensive work was done to repair and extend the Middle Fork Trail. Beginning in the summer of 2014, the long-awaited and -planned Middle Fork Road project began. Construction was completed in 2017 and the road was closed in 2019 by landslides 7.2 miles east of the Mailbox Peak trailhead (see sidebar on page 174).

▶ **Since 1998 the Forest Service has conducted studies to recommend expanding the boundaries of the spectacular Alpine Lakes Wilderness.**

Congress established the Alpine Lakes Wilderness in 1976 after previous efforts to create a national park failed. In 1998 the Forest Service began conducting studies to recommend expanding the wilderness boundaries. These studies came to fruition on December 19, 2014, when President Barack Obama signed legislation to designate 22,000 additional acres to be added to the Alpine Lakes Wilderness. Also included were Wild and Scenic designations for the Middle Fork Snoqualmie and Pratt Rivers.

# 28  Myrtle Lake

Barely within the boundaries of the Alpine Lakes Wilderness, Myrtle Lake is a popular place although the final 6.7 miles of road to the trailhead is so terrifically rugged that it's not suggested for low-clearance vehicles. Four-wheel-drive or high-clearance vehicles are recommended. Snow and high-water creek crossings make reaching Myrtle Lake a challenging prospect in spring. Best to wait until July or August, when the snow is gone and creek levels have dropped or dried up.

**Start:** Dingford Creek trailhead at gate on Middle Fork Snoqualmie Road (FR 5600)
**Distance:** 9.0 miles out and back
**Approximate hiking time:** 4 to 5 hours
**Trail numbers:** USDA Forest Service Trail 1005
**Difficulty:** Moderate to difficult depending on time of year due to a steep trail, several stream crossings, route-finding on faint trail sections, and high water and snow in early season
**Trail surface:** Forested path; rocky
**Seasons:** Summer and fall
**Other trail users:** Closed to bikes and horses
**Canine compatibility:** Leashed dogs permitted
**Land status:** Mount Baker–Snoqualmie National Forest, Alpine Lakes Wilderness Area

**Nearest town:** North Bend
**Services:** Gas, restaurants, groceries, lodging in North Bend; no toilet or trash pickup at trailhead
**Northwest Forest Pass:** Yes
**Discover Pass:** No
**Maps:** Green Trails No. 175: Skykomish; USGS Snoqualmie Lake; USDAFS Mount Baker–Snoqualmie National Forest, Alpine Lakes Wilderness
**Trail contacts:** Alpine Lakes Protection Society (ALPS), Mount Baker–Snoqualmie National Forest, Snoqualmie Ranger District
**Special hazards:** Stinging nettle, loose rock; early season high-water creek crossings

**Finding the trailhead:** Drive east from Seattle on I-90 to exit 34, North Bend. Turn left (north) onto 468th Avenue. After 0.5 mile turn right (east) onto SE Middle Fork Road. In 0.9 mile bear right at a wye onto Lake Dorothy Road. In 1.6 miles pass a pullout and parking area for the Mailbox Peak Trail. The road officially becomes FR 5600. After another 2.5 miles pass the popular Granite Creek put-in for whitewater kayakers and cross a well-built concrete bridge. A further 2.1 miles brings you to the Bessemer Mountain and Oxbow Loop Trails. Pass through the slide area that closed the road in 2019 in 2.2 miles. After 2.9 miles pass the Middle Fork trailhead and picnic area and the Middle Fork campground where the paved road ends. Soon, cross the Taylor River on a narrow bridge, enter the large parking area for the Garfield Ledges trailhead and picnic area, and turn right (east) behind the toilet, passing through the seasonally closed gate. Continue for 6.7 horrendously potholed and rough miles (four-by-four or high-clearance vehicles suggested) to the trailhead at Dingford Creek. As of June 27, 2007, the Middle Fork Road is closed permanently at this point. Park on the right (south) side of the road in a wide but rocky area overlooking the Snoqualmie River. Find the trailhead, marked by a small reader board, on the north side of the road and sign in at the register for entering the Alpine Lake Wilderness. GPS: N47 31.056' / W121 27.275'

# The Hike

From the parking area the trail climbs steadily for 0.5 mile on steep switchbacks before entering the Alpine Lakes Wilderness on a heavily eroded and rocky tread. This area is so deep in the woods that heavy logging didn't reach here until after World War II—at the same time, opening the region to recreation. Note the giant stumps, already mostly rotted away—testament to our moist environment and the action of decomposition.

Dingford Creek roars far below the trail in the early season. The rare glimpse of it through the trees, foaming over rocks and under fallen forest giants, is exhilarating.

Passing the wilderness boundary, the trail climbs at a reasonable grade, staying above Dingford Creek. Cross the outflow of Pumpkinseed Lake in 0.8 mile, stopping to appreciate the waterfall sliding down a wonderful slab of rock. The braided Goat Creek is crossed in 1.7 miles (high in early season) across rocks, and the trail (what else?) keeps on climbing.

*Snowy Myrtle Lake during an early-season excursion.*

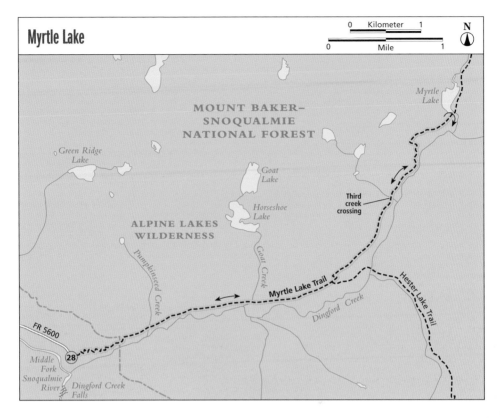

After 2.5 miles reach a trail junction. A small sign nailed to a convenient snag announces that to the right (south) is Hester Lake (Trail 1005.1). Instead, turn left (northeast). Continue climbing toward Myrtle Lake, crossing several side channels—many of which dry up later in the season. At 3.3 miles cross another braided creek (high and difficult in spring) on rocks, and begin the push toward the lake.

Trees around the shore and rocky cliffs create a pleasant setting for Myrtle Lake. Fishing is said to be fair here. A campsite is located on the other side of the outlet. A faint trail continues up the drainage toward Little Myrtle Lake, where it disappears in the upper basin.

## Miles and Directions

**0.0** Dingford Creek trailhead
**0.5** Alpine Lakes Wilderness boundary
**0.8** Pumpkinseed Creek crossing
**1.7** Goat Creek crossing
**2.5** Junction with Hester Lake Trail
**3.3** Third creek crossing

*Negotiating a difficult stretch of the Myrtle Lake trail.*

**4.5** Myrtle Lake

**9.0** Arrive back at trailhead

> **Option:** From the trail junction for Myrtle and Hester Lakes, turn right and walk up to Hester Lake. In early season this alternative to Myrtle Lake involves a dangerous ford of Dingford Creek—wide, deep, and cold with snowmelt. The remainder of the trail, faint in many places and difficult to follow, eventually reaches Hester Lake after 3 miles. There are a few campsites near the lake, and no campfires are allowed.

## GREEN TIP:

Consider product packaging before your hike and dispose of it at home. Pack out all trash and all food scraps, including nut shells, apple cores, and orange peels.

# 29 Taylor River

A walk along the Taylor River is perfect throughout spring, summer, and fall, but it's especially alluring during the two- or three-week period in summer when Seattle is suffocating in our yearly 80-degree temperatures. Tree tunnels provide ample shade, and periodic-use trails down to the river make for splashing opportunities. Water at Marten Creek and Big Creek is also available to wash off the sweat of the hike. The canyon is cool here from down-canyon drift.

The Taylor is a significant tributary of the Middle Fork Snoqualmie, and its trail (a long-abandoned logging road) follows above the river for 5 miles to the substantial bridge over Big Creek. Along the way are side trails to Marten Lake and Otter Falls. Spring brings water to many side streams that cross the trail and feed two impressive waterfalls. Some stream crossings are challenging in early season / high water.

---

**Start:** Snoqualmie Lake trailhead
**Distance:** 10.0 miles out and back
**Approximate hiking time:** 5 hours
**Trail number:** USDA Forest Service Trail 1002
**Difficulty:** Easy; wide and gentle trail
**Trail surface:** Forested path, gravel road; rocky
**Seasons:** Spring, summer, and fall
**Other trail users:** Bikes, horses, runners
**Canine compatibility:** Leashed dogs permitted
**Land status:** USDAFS Snoqualmie Ranger District
**Nearest town:** North Bend
**Services:** Gas, restaurants, groceries, lodging in North Bend; no toilet at trailhead, but there is a toilet 0.3 mile back down the road at the Garfield Ledges trailhead and picnic area
**Northwest Forest Pass:** Yes
**Discover Pass:** No
**Maps:** Green Trails No. 174: Mount Si, and No. 175: Skykomish; USGS Quad Lake Philippa and Snoqualmie Lake; USDAFS Mount Baker–Snoqualmie National Forest
**Trail contacts:** Alpine Lakes Protection Society (ALPS), Mount Baker–Snoqualmie National Forest, Snoqualmie Ranger District, North Bend Office
**Special hazards:** Loose rock; no potable water at trailhead or on trail

**Finding the trailhead:** Drive east from Seattle to North Bend on I-90 to exit 34 (468th Avenue SE / Edgewick Road). During winter closures of Snoqualmie Pass, this is as far east as you can drive. After 0.5 mile turn right (east) onto SE Middle Fork Road (FR 56). In 0.9 mile bear right at a wye onto Lake Dorothy Road. In 1.6 miles pass a pullout and parking area for the Mailbox Peak Trail. The road officially becomes FR 5600. After another 2.5 miles pass the popular Granite Creek put-in for whitewater kayakers and cross a well-built concrete bridge. A further 2.1 miles brings you to the Bessemer Mountain and Oxbow Loop Trails. Pass through the slide area that closed the road in 2019 in 2.2 miles. After 2.9 miles pass the Middle Fork trailhead and picnic area and the Middle Fork campground where the paved road ends. Soon, cross the Taylor River on a narrow bridge and enter the large parking area for the Garfield Ledges trailhead and picnic area (GPS: N47 33.350' / W121 32.146'). A rough road continues 0.3 mile to the trailhead and limited-space parking area (GPS: N47 33.634' / W121 31.937'). If parking is not available, return to the large parking area at the previously mentioned Garfield Ledges.

# The Hike

The 1921 USGS Sultan quad shows a ranger station just downstream of the conflu-
ence of the Taylor and Snoqualmie Rivers and a trail poking up the Middle Fork. The
ranger station is long gone. Leave your car at the trailhead, pass around the stout metal
gate, and cross the Taylor River on a heavy-duty highway bridge. Immediately on the
right is a short trail down to a side channel of the Taylor. It has plenty of sitting spots
for lunch and bountiful views up- and downstream. Some have even used it as an
informal camping area. The tall trunks of a mature streamside red alder forest provide
shade on hot days. To continue, return to the wide pathway, ignoring the old trail to
Quartz Creek on your left (north) that climbs alongside and above Quartz Creek.

A heavy-duty wooden bridge with impressive steel-girder underpinnings crosses
Marten Creek in 3 miles. Look left (north) before crossing the bridge for a faint path.
This is a hard-to-follow use trail up to Marten Lake. Sometimes the junction to the
lake path is marked by a cairn. Like all cairns, this one isn't always there, so keep an

*Red alders forming a bower over the Taylor River*

*One of the many side streams that flow into the Taylor River*

eye on your map and watch the topography to spot the waytrail for yourself. You'll know you passed it when you reach the Marten Creek bridge. The Taylor River Trail begins to narrow now from its earlier, wider, road-like character and crosses several streams. Two of them, including the stream exiting from Otter Falls up ahead, can be difficult to cross in early season / high water. The trail here is rough in parts but is never difficult to follow.

After 4.5 miles of hiking, another use trail left (north) beside the main trail leads to Otter Falls and a nice pond called Lipsy Lake. There may (or may not) be a hand-made sign pointing you 0.1 mile straight up to the lake and falls. Both are well worth

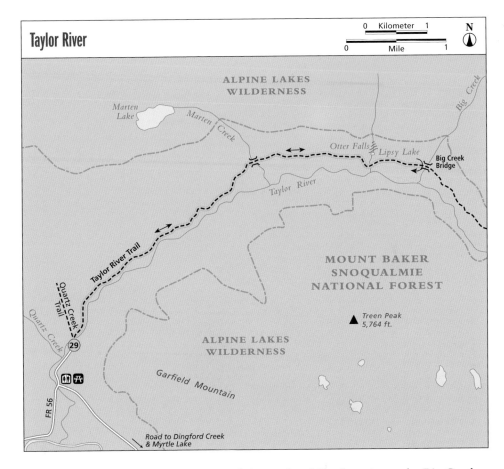

ALPINE LAKES
WILDERNESS

Marten
Lake

Marten Creek

Big Creek

Otter Falls

Lipsy Lake

Big Creek
Bridge

Taylor River

MOUNT BAKER
SNOQUALMIE
NATIONAL FOREST

▲ Treen Peak
5,764 ft.

Taylor River Trail

Quartz Creek Trail

Quartz Creek

29

ALPINE LAKES
WILDERNESS

Garfield Mountain

FR 56

Road to Dingford Creek
& Myrtle Lake

the detour! Returning to the main trail, in another 0.5 mile arrive at the Big Creek Bridge—incongruously large and overbuilt given the setting. Expect to see an amazing waterfall skittering down long slabs of rock throughout the year.

Don't feel obligated to hike the entire length of the trail; there are plenty of great places to stop and enjoy the river with lunch, a good book, or a wonderful companion. If you do make it all the way to the Big Creek Bridge, it's now time to turn around and return to your car. On the other hand, it's possible to continue on to Lake Dorothy (see #30) with a car shuttle at US 2 to lengthen your trip into an overnight backpacking excursion.

## Miles and Directions

**0.0**  Snoqualmie Lake trailhead (Taylor River Trail)

**1.0**  Quartz Creek Road

**3.0**  Marten Creek

**4.5**  Otter Falls Trail junction

*Exploring a pool below Otter Falls*

**5.0**  Big Creek Bridge

**10.0**  Arrive back at trailhead

# Hike Information

The Garfield Ledges Trail (at the alternate parking for the Taylor River hike) is a 1-mile steep route that leads to a commanding view of the Middle Fork valley. From the Middle Fork trailhead (Northwest Forest Pass required), just before crossing the Taylor River bridge, and after crossing the Middle Fork, hikers can travel downstream on the Pratt River Connector (Forest Trail 1035) to the Pratt River Trail and thence via Talapus Lake to I-90. Or, a left turn after crossing the river allows hikers to travel upstream on the Middle Fork Trail (Forest Trail 1003) to Dingford Creek and Myrtle Lake (#28), Snow Lake (#38), and Snoqualmie Pass, or Goldmyer Hot Springs. There are picnic tables and vault toilets at the Middle Fork trailhead. Enter the new Middle Fork campground, with 39 sites, across from the parking area for the Middle Fork trail.

## GREEN TIP:

Even if it says "biodegradable," don't put any soap into streams or lakes. If you need to use soap, bring the water to you.

# 30 Snoqualmie Lake–Lake Dorothy

This hike provides an opportunity for an overnight or two-night backpack trip from the Snoqualmie River to the Skykomish River, with a car shuttle to bring you back home again. This backpacking traverse across the divide combines two popular day hikes with a lightly traveled middle section. Done in reverse, the Lake Dorothy Trail is a family-worthy jaunt as far as Camp Robber Creek. Thereafter it becomes a plodding uphill trudge. A day hike to Lake Dorothy is challenging enough without walking a considerable distance. This route is from south to north, Snoqualmie Lake trailhead to Lake Dorothy trailhead, but can be hiked just as well in the opposite direction.

**Start:** Snoqualmie Lake trailhead 1002 on FR 5600

**Distance:** 17.0-mile point-to-point with car shuttle

**Approximate hiking time:** 2 to 3 days

**Trail numbers:** USDA Forest Service Trails 1002 and 1072

**Difficulty:** Moderate, with occasional steep terrain

**Trail surface:** Forested path, log bridges, gravel road; rocky

**Seasons:** Summer and fall

**Other trail users:** Runners, mountain bikes (for the first 6.5 miles from the trailhead to the Nordrum Lake Trail junction), horses (not recommended by Forest Service)

**Canine compatibility:** Leashed dogs permitted

**Land status:** Mount Baker–Snoqualmie National Forest, Alpine Lakes Wilderness Area

**Nearest towns:** North Bend, Baring, Sultan

**Services:** Gas, restaurants, groceries, lodging; pit toilet at Lake Dorothy trailhead; no toilet at Snoqualmie Lake trailhead, but there is one located 0.3 mile before the trailhead at the Garfield Ledges trailhead

**Northwest Forest Pass:** Yes

**Discover Pass:** No

**Maps:** Green Trails No. 174: Mount Si, and No. 175: Skykomish; USGS Lake Philippa and Snoqualmie Lake; USDAFS Mount Baker–Snoqualmie National Forest

**Trail contacts:** Alpine Lakes Protection Society (ALPS), Mount Baker–Snoqualmie National Forest

**Special hazards:** Loose rock; no potable water at trailhead or on trail; water filters or purification required

**Finding the trailhead:** Snoqualmie Lake trailhead: Drive east from Seattle to North Bend on I-90 to exit 34 (468th Avenue SE / Edgewick Road). During winter closures of Snoqualmie Pass, this is as far east as you can drive. After 0.5 mile turn right (east) onto SE Middle Fork Road (FR 56). In 0.9 mile bear right at a wye onto Lake Dorothy Road. In 1.6 miles pass a pullout and parking area for the Mailbox Peak Trail. The road officially becomes FR 5600. After another 2.5 miles pass the popular Granite Creek put-in for whitewater kayakers and cross a well-built concrete bridge. A further 2.1 miles brings you to the Bessemer Mountain and Oxbow Loop Trails. Pass through the slide area that closed the road in 2019 in 2.2 miles. After 2.9 miles pass the Middle Fork trailhead and picnic area and the Middle Fork campground, where the paved road ends. Soon, cross the Taylor River on a narrow bridge and enter the large parking area for the Garfield Ledges trailhead and picnic area (GPS: N47 33.350' / W121 32.146'). A rough road continues

0.3 mile to the trailhead and limited space parking area (GPS: N47 33.634' / W121 31.937').
If parking is not available, return to the large parking area at the previously mentioned Garfield
Ledges.

Lake Dorothy trailhead: Drive 4.4 miles east of Baring on US 2 and Der Baring Store to Money
Creek Road. Turn right (south) onto a paved two-lane road, immediately bridging the South Fork
Skykomish River. Drive for 1 mile, crossing railroad tracks and passing USDAFS Money Creek
Campground (on both sides of the road).

Turn right (south) onto Miller River Road (FR 6410), a good dirt road. In about 2 miles pass the
USDAFS Miller Creek group campground. After 3.7 miles reach a locked gate and bear left (east),
continuing on the main road (FR 6412). After 9 miles reach the trailhead. Park in the large lot. On
busy days, don't be surprised to see cars lining the road for 0.5 mile before the parking area. GPS:
N47 36.541' / W121 23.147'

## The Hike

Leave your car at the Snoqualmie Lake trailhead. Pass around the stout metal gate.
Immediately on the right is a short trail down to a side channel of the Taylor River. It
has plenty of sitting spots for lunch and bountiful views up- and downstream. Some
have even used it as an informal camping area. The tall trunks of a mature streamside
red alder forest provide shade on hot days. To continue, return to the wide, road-like
pathway and stroll easterly.

A heavy-duty wooden bridge crosses Marten Creek in 3 miles. The Taylor River
Trail begins to narrow now from its earlier, wider character and crosses several streams.
The trail is rough in parts but is never difficult to follow, as long as you keep a sharp
lookout for the route.

After 4.5 miles of hiking, another use trail left (north) beside the trail leads to
Otter Falls and a nice pond known as Lipsy Lake. In another 0.5 mile arrive at the Big
Creek Bridge—incongruously large and overbuilt given the setting. Expect to see an
amazing waterfall skittering down long slabs of rock throughout the year.

From the bridge across Big Creek, continue east on Trail 1002 toward Snoqualmie
Lake. There is plenty of water in Big Creek Falls throughout the summer. The route
becomes less like a road as it pushes into the forest. The roadbed continues to narrow
and deteriorate and eventually ends altogether at a trail junction 1.2 miles from Big
Creek. Bear left (east) to stay on route to Snoqualmie Lake. Right (south) goes to the
Nordrum Lake Trail. This is the limit of permissible travel for bicycles.

The sometimes rocky and heavily eroded trail begins to climb through a young
forest and enters the Alpine Lakes Wilderness, where the first thing you notice is the
increased tree size. The Taylor River thunders far below. Many small side streams are
captured and diverted by the trail. Don't be surprised at having to walk through mud
or standing and flowing water.

The trail reaches the Taylor River—no longer a horizontally raging torrent but a
tremendous series of cataracts. Walk off the trail a few feet to admire the river in all

*Taking a cooling waterfall break below Lake Dorothy at Camp Robber Creek*

its vertical glory as it drops 100 feet over a staircase of rocks. Watch your step! You don't want to slip here.

The trail climbs and finally calms down a bit 0.5 mile before reaching Snoqualmie Lake. Enter a talus field, and either plot a course through it or rely on the kindness of strangers who have ducked and/or flagged the route. Within shouting distance of the river, the trail makes one final push and reaches the heavily forested shores of Snoqualmie Lake. Log booms have been laid across the outlet and filled in with rocks to raise the level of this already large lake. Camping is limited, of unremarkable quality, and dispersed between the outlet and a marshy area 0.2 mile farther up the trail.

Backpackers unable to locate a campsite will have to trudge up switchbacks for another mile to Deer Lake. At the end of the day, this crisscrossing uphill might seem extra steep and especially hard, so it's important to trust in the map and have faith that there is indeed a lake at the top. As recompense for having to hike farther, there are nice views of Snoqualmie Lake and its basin.

Despite the nice view, an extremely poor camping area awaits the tired hiker. One campsite lies within a stone's throw of tree-lined Deer Lake and right in the middle of the trail. Less-marginal camping exists on the northeast shore. If those sites are occupied, walk another 0.8 mile to Bear Lake, where waytrails lead to three small campsites located along the lake's north shore adjacent to a babbling brook. Where they are accessible from the trail, both Deer and Bear Lakes have shallow shorelines.

If you've come this far in a day, you must be tired. Set up your tent (mosquitoes and flies love it here), eat some dinner, and rest up for tomorrow.

From Bear Lake the trail ascends 0.5 mile eastward to an unnamed pass at 3,800 feet, where all views are obscured by thick forest. Long switchbacks begin to drop down to Lake Dorothy. Peekaboo views through the trees transition to full-on vistas of Lake Dorothy when the trail finally reaches the water. Cool off in the lake and give your knees a well-deserved respite before the trail plunges back into the woods.

# Snoqualmie Lake–Lake Dorothy

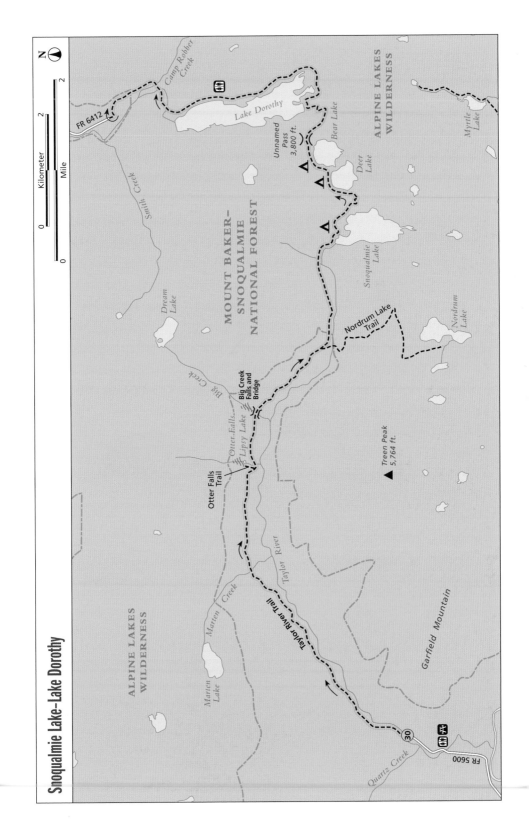

# TRAIL HAZARDS 3

The biggest trail hazards are caused by the smallest creatures: insects. They bite, they sting, and they suck. And there is precious little we can do except grin and bear it. Oh, you can complain. But what's that going to get you?

Biting flies, like the deerfly, are practiced at landing unobserved on exposed skin and causing painful bites that weep and itch for days. They are active during the day, especially around ponds, streams, and marshes. No-see-ums are small biting flies, or midges. They're extremely brutal and persistent biters active at dawn and dusk. The first aid for fly bites is to wash the bite area with soap and water and apply a bactericide and an anti-itching ointment.

Yellow jacket wasps, the bane of picnickers everywhere, can bite or sting. Yellow jackets that nest in the ground cause the biggest concern for hikers, and a misplaced foot can cause an angry nest of insects to attack. Their bite is bad; their sting is worse. Either can cause life-threatening anaphylaxis in people who are allergic. Bears, on the other hand, see yellow jackets as a huge protein source and will tear apart nests, oblivious to hordes of angry insects.

Since the introduction of West Nile virus to the United States, mosquitoes have screamed to the top of every list of concern. Only the female bites, inserting her proboscis under the skin and injecting an anticoagulant before slurping up a meal of blood. Their larvae ("wigglers") are easily found in still water. The best defense against mosquitoes is to avoid their habitat or to sparingly use repellent. Getting bitten by a mosquito is communing with nature in the most fundamental way—entering at the bottom of the food chain!

*Yellow jacket wasps bite and sting and are very aggressive around food.*

Skirt several campsites (no fires allowed), cross a wide creek coming down from Marlene and Moira Lakes, and begin a course that contours Lake Dorothy's shore. There are many fine views of the lake, with sporadic access to the water and a few campsites. The two largest camping areas have pit toilets; watch for signs.

There are many wet areas to cross on causeways. Rough wooden bridges are helpful in keeping boots and feet dry. At a junction below the lake outlet, turn left (southwest) to get closer to the lake; or turn right (east) and start plunging downhill on rock steps and inclined causeways.

Until reaching Camp Robber Creek, the trail hardly touches earth. Lake Dorothy has always been a popular hike, and the amount of money and effort directed toward minimizing human impacts is evident in the rough wooden bridges and inclined causeways throughout the next mile.

At Camp Robber Creek, cross on a strong metal bridge and admire views upstream and down. Even in late summer the amount of water coming down Camp Robber Creek is impressive as it slides and falls over rock smoothed by eons of runoff. This is a fine place for hikers in the opposite direction to stop for lunch and contemplate the upcoming steep trail! Careful people will find plenty of scenic resting areas below the bridge, along with a nice swimming hole for times when the water level is low. Be aware: The water is always cold.

Rejoining the trail, it's a simple matter to walk the remaining 0.5 mile to the Lake Dorothy trailhead where your shuttle car (or perhaps a friend?) is waiting.

## Miles and Directions

**0.0**  Snoqualmie Lake trailhead (Taylor River Trail)

**1.0**  Quartz Creek Road

**3.0**  Marten Creek

**4.5**  Otter Falls Trail junction

**5.0**  Big Creek

**6.5**  Nordrum Lake junction

**10.9**  Snoqualmie Lake

**11.9**  Deer Lake

**12.7**  Bear Lake

**13.4**  Unnamed Pass

**14.9**  Upper Lake Dorothy

**16.5**  Camp Robber Creek

**17.0**  Lake Dorothy trailhead

> **Option:** A rough, hard-to-find, and hard-to-follow 2.5-mile trail (Trail 1004) leads to Nordrum Lake from the Snoqualmie Lake Trail about 1.2 miles southeast (N47 34.471' / W121 26.673') of Big Creek. Continuing on to Nordrum Lake requires a dangerous fording of the Taylor River especially in early season. At the north end (outlet) of Nordrum Lake, the trail forks, with the main trail leading directly to the lake and the other trail continuing around the lake. Campsites can be found at the end of either route. This trail is not recommended for inexperienced hikers. Remember, fording Taylor River can be extremely dangerous during the spring runoff when the river level is high.

## Hike Information

Regulations in the Alpine Lakes Wilderness limit campfires to below 4,000 feet in elevation west of the crest of the Cascade Mountain Range and below 5,000 feet in elevation east of the crest. Campfires may be restricted below these elevations due to high use and/or lack of fuel.

# 31 Dirty Harry's Peak

This trail does nothing but go up until there is no more up to go—gaining 3,000 feet in less than 4 miles. The elevation gain and constantly walking over loose cobbles on the barest excuse for a trail make this route more challenging than similar steep trails like Mount Si or McClellan Butte. But the views in all directions from the summit of Dirty Harry's Peak are stunning, and you're unlikely to run into other people up there. Ignore any flagging you see, and stick to the defined route.

**Start:** Far Side trailhead on SE Grouse Ridge Road on the way to the Washington State Patrol Fire Training Academy
**Distance:** 8.4 miles out and back
**Approximate hiking time:** 5 to 7 hours
**Difficulty:** Difficult; rugged, steep, and rocky trail
**Trail surface:** Old rocky logging road unsuitable for man or beast!
**Seasons:** Spring, summer, and fall
**Other trail users:** None
**Canine compatibility:** Leashed dogs permitted, but it would be cruel to bring a dog on this trail
**Land status:** Washington Department of Natural Resources; Mount Baker–Snoqualmie National Forest

**Nearest town:** North Bend
**Services:** Gas, restaurants, groceries; lodging; no toilet at trailhead
**Northwest Forest Pass:** No
**Discover Pass:** Yes
**Maps:** Green Trails No. 206S: Mount Si NRCA-Snoqualmie Pass Gateway Peaks; USGS Bandera; USDAFS Mount Baker–Snoqualmie National Forest
**Trail contacts:** Alpine Lakes Protection Society (ALPS), Mount Baker–Snoqualmie National Forest Office, Washington State Patrol Fire Training Academy
**Special hazards:** Loose rock, exposure; no potable water at trailhead or on trail

**Finding the trailhead:** Take I-90 east from Seattle to exit 38, following signs to the Washington State Patrol Fire Training Academy. Turn right at the stop sign onto SE Homestead Valley Road, and pass over the South Fork Snoqualmie River. Drive past Olallie State Park and the trailheads for Twin Falls and South Fork Picnic Area. In 1.8 miles pass under I-90 and curve right onto SE Grouse Ridge Road, where the road ends in 0.1 mile at a large parking lot with a vault toilet. The road past here is no longer open to the public's vehicles. GPS: N47 25.511' / W121 37.561'

## The Hike

Find the Far Side Trail behind the reader board and walk 0.1 mile toward the creek, or pass through a yellow pole gate, which is posted as closing daily by 5:30 p.m. The trail and road soon meet. Cross over the river, and reach Dirty Harry's Trail.

The original Dirty Harry's Trail was an old logging road built by a tree cutter known by the cognomen "Dirty Harry." The name predates the Clint Eastwood movies, but enough pretend history has been written about Harry Gault to confuse

*Some of Dirty Harry's historic detritus the "Museum."*

the issue of who he really was. Additional questionable folklore has been gained over the past decades since Harry's departure from the scene, as the ort from his operations has been swallowed by a forest grown thick and tall. Since that time Harry's road devolved into a creek bed, and slippery cobbles add a touch of ankle danger to inattentive hikers.

The Department of Natural Resources and Washington Trails Association dedicated several years to rerouting and repurposing Harry's old route up the mountain. You will now climb steeply for 2 miles until reaching the junction leading to Dirty Harry's Balcony and the Ira Spring Connector Trail. This trail requires route-finding and map-reading skills in many places. It is steep and only recommended for experienced hikers. To visit Harry's Balcony, turn right (east) here for a short detour to a lunch spot with amazing views up and down Snoqualmie Valley.

Too soon for lunch? Take a load off your feet anyway, because you're not done!

When it's time to move on, continue left (northwest). Continue to climb steeply and cross the creek at a place known as Dirty Harry's Museum. Somewhere hidden in the overgrowth are rusted remnants of Harry's logging operation, including a truck. Finding the bulk of Harry's Museum entails bushwhacking through increasingly impenetrable brush.

The trail continues to climb on switchbacks. The final push to reach the summit of Dirty Harry's Peak adds yet another very steep climb of 0.5 mile across a segment

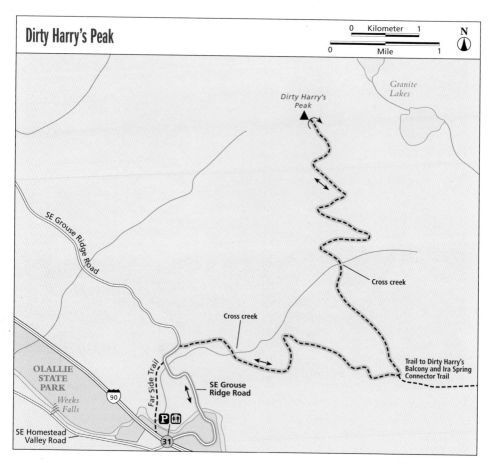

of private property. There are stunning peekaboo views in every direction, and trees on the summit conceal an equally stunning drop into Granite Lake below. Watch your step! Return to the trailhead the way you came.

## Miles and Directions

**0.0** Trailhead parking

**0.1** Trail to Dirty Harry's Peak on SE Grouse Ridge Road

**2.0** Trail junction to Dirty Harry's Balcony

**2.7** Dirty Harry's Museum

**4.2** Summit of Dirty Harry's Peak

**8.4** Arrive back at trailhead

## Hike Information

This has become a popular area for rock climbers. Defiance Ridge runs from Mailbox Peak on its northwest end to Dirty Harry's Peak on its southeast. Below its base is

*View from the summit of Dirty Harry's Peak*

flat-topped Grouse Ridge—part of the Puget Glacier's terminal moraine. The glacier descended from Canada and moved up Snoqualmie Valley.

The Fire Training Academy, located on the edge of Grouse Ridge, serves local communities, state agencies, and industry by providing live fire training to public and private fire and emergency response personnel.

> *"I had better admit right away that walking can in the end become an addiction . . . even in this final stage it remains a delectable madness, very good for sanity, and I recommend it with passion."*
>
> —Colin Fletcher, *The New Complete Walker*

# 32 Bandera Mountain

Fantastic springtime wildflower displays and distant views are the order of the day on Bandera Mountain, but hikers have to work hard for it. The steep trail gains nearly 3,000 feet in 3 miles and hopscotches over talus, never actually reaching the true summit. But views to the south of Mount Rainier and Mount Adams, west to the Olympics, and north to Mount Baker (even Vancouver Island on especially clear mornings) are stunning nonetheless and negate the noise of cars whooshing by on I-90 far below. If those drivers only knew how much they were missing! At the height of spring, vast fields of blooming bear grass (*Xerophyllum tenax*) overrun Bandera Mountain's unforested slopes.

**Start:** Trailhead parking for Ira Spring Trail (1038)

**Distance:** 6.0 miles out and back

**Approximate hiking time:** 4 hours

**Trail number:** USDA Forest Service Trail 1038

**Difficulty:** Strenuous; short, steep trail with talus

**Trail surface:** Forested path, old road; rocky

**Seasons:** Late spring, summer, and fall

**Other trail users:** None

**Canine compatibility:** Leashed dogs permitted

**Land status:** USDAFS Snoqualmie Ranger District, Alpine Lakes Wilderness Area

**Nearest town:** North Bend

**Services:** Gas, restaurants, groceries, lodging; unisex vault toilet at trailhead

**Northwest Forest Pass:** Yes

**Discover Pass:** No

**Maps:** Green Trails No. 206: Bandera; USGS Bandera; USDAFS Mount Baker–Snoqualmie National Forest, Alpine Lakes Wilderness

**Trail contacts:** Alpine Lakes Protection Society (ALPS), Mount Baker–Snoqualmie National Forest

**Special hazards:** Talus, exposure; no potable water at trailhead or on trail; no shade on second half of hike

**Finding the trailhead:** From Seattle, drive east on I-90 to exit 45 (Lookout Point Road / FR 9030 and FR 9031). Turn left (north) at the stop sign and pass under I-90. The pavement soon ends and the poorly maintained road becomes narrow hard-packed dirt with many potholes. In 0.8 mile pass the road to Talapus Lake and Trail 1039. Continue on FR 9031. After 2.0 miles pass an old logging road on the right (north). After 3.8 miles reach the large trailhead parking lot. GPS: N47 25.485' / W121 35.010'

## The Hike

Welcome to the Ira Spring Trail! At the trailhead, next to a vault toilet at the west end of the parking lot, is a picnic bench and a view southwest to I-90. Start on the trail, really an old road, and begin climbing at a good rate to reach Mason Creek after a short walk. Just beyond, signs of the former Mason Lake "trail" that once climbed straight up along Mason Creek are in evidence on the left (north).

*Bandera Mountain Trail*

The road/trail reaches a talus slope and momentarily dives out of the trees. Take this opportunity to look across the Snoqualmie Valley. The two swaths cutting east to west in the opposite slope are the John Wayne Pioneer Trail and a power line. A second talus slope means more views across the valley before the trail ducks back into the trees. The road portion soon ends in a tangle of brush, and the trail constructed in 2003 takes off up the hill.

Ascend steeply, and contemplate how much steeper the old trail must have been and how fortunate we are that the Forest Service saw fit to change things around. A third break in the forest offers more-limited views than those previous but more than makes up for it by a sidehill meadow, chock-full of wildflowers and a view up toward Bandera Mountain. Don't get your hopes up—it's still a long way to the top.

A fourth, viewless break in the forest quickly follows. Young trees are reclaiming this opening. A fifth break in the trees arrives at a switchback and affords the first good eastward view. That switchback is soon matched by another, as thinning forest segues into straggling trees. There are occasional opportunities to walk through maturing forest, but the trend is fewer trees the higher you go. This makes it possible to appreciate the scree and talus slope that marks the old route up Mason Creek. In no time the new trail reaches those rocks, missing the worst of it by swinging east.

# WILDFLOWERS

A famous paleobotanist by the name of Daniel Axelrod was dismayed at the amount of atten-tion his field-trip students paid to all the annual wildflowers encountered along a trail. He was accustomed to working with fossil plants preserved in stone and in terms of tens or hundreds of millions of years. Herbaceous plants are fairly recent arrivals—at least in terms of geologic time. Full of disdain, he addressed the class with, "I don't know why you're look-ing at that ground trash. It's going to be gone in a million years!"

It's safe to say that the only plants many people see during their perambulations around the countryside are "ground trash." In an ocean of green, the bright yellows, reds, and blues of herbaceous wildflowers are sure manifestations of spring. Bear grass (*Xerophyllum tenax*), with its basal rosette of pointy leaves and tall cluster of tiny white flowers, is found in side-hill meadows along with bistort (*Polygonum bistortoides*)—a flower that looks like somebody ran a miniature sheep up a flagpole! Some other common species include the bright orange of Indian paintbrush (*Castilleja* sp.), red columbine (*Aquilegia formosa*), and spotted leopard lily (*Lilium columbianum*). Wet meadows are home to marsh marigold (*Caltha palustris*). A shrubby white wildflower is ground dogwood (*Cornus canadensis*)—a plant best known by its bark. Another shrubby plant, salal (*Gaultheria shallon*), produces urn-shaped flowers with glandular hairs. But the true harbinger of spring is the pretty, three-petaled trillium (*Trillium ovatum*).

All wildflowers bring joy and delight to our eyes. Avoid any impulse to pluck these beau-ties from the ground. Leave them, not only for the enjoyment of others, but also for the insects, birds, and mammals that require them for food and shelter.

By this point, if it's a hot, sunny day, you're probably regretting not taking an extra liter of water, a hat, and sunscreen. If you're not prepared for more sun, it's best to consider turning back. There will be no more shade until you reach the ridge running to the summit of Bandera Mountain. A small consolation exists in fine views to the south toward Mount Rainier.

Now completely out of the trees and into talus, views keep getting better and better in all directions. Mount Defiance is the forested peak to the northwest. In 2 miles, at Bandera Junction, a sign directs hikers to Bandera Peak. Leaving the main trail, turn right (northeast) and begin climbing a trail that could use stairs and ladders. Overnight hikers can consider a trip to Mason Lake and bagging Mount Defiance (#34) by turning left here.

It's all wildflowers and rocks as the trail, such as it is, climbs straight up toward a copse of trees on the Bandera ridgeline. This is a route that underscores the importance

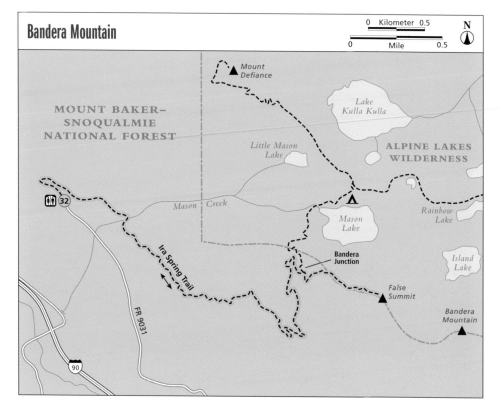

# Bandera Mountain

MOUNT BAKER–
SNOQUALMIE
NATIONAL FOREST

Mount
Defiance

Lake
Kulla Kulla

Little Mason
Lake

ALPINE LAKES
WILDERNESS

Mason   Creek

Mason
Lake

Rainbow
Lake

Ira Spring Trail

Bandera
Junction

Island
Lake

FR 9031

False
Summit

Bandera
Mountain

90

of stair-climbing as a training aid! When you're not looking at your feet, the feet of the person in front of you, or the many species of wildflowers, there are plenty of views to occupy the eye and amaze the geographer.

Once trees are reached again, the trail curves to the right (east) and, rather than going up, up, and away, traverses below the ridge and hip-hops from one small stand of trees to another. The false summit of Bandera is now revealed. If you've had it, stop here, appreciate the view, and think about going home—the views don't really get any better except for a glimpse of Mason Lake over the edge to the north.

On the other hand, if a hike isn't a hike to you without a tangible achievement (like a named peak), continue climbing along the ridge through scattered trees and talus. The trail is steep here but feels mellow compared to the first stage. There are a few more ladder-like aspects of the trail as well as a large boulder field. If you lose your way, don't be foolish by continuing on. Be wise and backtrack to your last known location. Peekaboo views open northward, with plenty of the same prodigious east, south, and west views.

Finally, dramatic views burst open to the north, where many jagged mountains push their sharp peaks and ridges into the sky. There they brush up against the bottom of the powder-puff clouds that give such beauty and dramatic backdrop to azure Cascade Mountain skies.

*Red columbine* (Aquilegia formosa)

All of a sudden the trail ends on a tiny, lightly treed promontory. Consulting their maps upon reaching the summit, many hikers are disappointed to discover they're not on the summit at all—that Bandera Mountain is another 0.25 mile farther east. The truly disappointed continue on with arduous and heinous bushwhacking to place a tick mark beside a list of peaks they've conquered. The merely happy go no farther, enjoying the same view more-motivated hikers bring with them to the wilderness, before returning back down the trail to their cars.

## Miles and Directions

- **0.0** Parking area for Ira Spring trailhead
- **2.0** Bandera Junction
- **3.0** Bandera false summit
- **6.0** Arrive back at trailhead

## Hike Information

Bandera Mountain was named by the Mountaineers Club, evidently for the Milwaukee Railroad station of Bandera 1.5 miles to the south.

Ira Spring (1918–2003) was a photographer, author, hiking advocate, and coauthor, with Harvey Manning, of the "100 Hikes" series of books published by the

Mountaineers. Spring was also cofounder, with Louise Marshall, of the Washington Trails Association (WTA). Along with many others, Ira Spring lobbied the Forest Service to close the 1958 original route up Bandera Mountain and replace it with a real trail. This effort was finally rewarded in 2003. Better late than not at all. The log bridge spanning Mason Creek was completed in 2015 thanks to the efforts of the Ira Spring Trust, the Mountains to Sound Greenway Trust, the Forest Service, and other partners.

Scott's Dairy Freeze, 234 North Bend Way, in North Bend, has the best french fries and root beer floats in the world! Especially after a long and hot hike.

*"Never ride when you can walk."*
—Bill Gale, *The Wonderful World of Walking*

# 33 McClellan Butte

Carved by glaciers, McClellan Butte is a prominent landmark along I-90 between North Bend and Snoqualmie Pass. Heading east to the pass, look south of the highway for a sharp peak that resembles an eagle about to take flight. Though the trail has seen oodles of work in recent years, it is still brutally steep in most places, and there are precious few views to reward hikers until they almost reach the top. That said, it's an excellent alternative to Mount Si, covering a nearly equal amount of miles and elevation gain, with the extra delight of significantly fewer crowds. The only real disappointment with hiking to McClellan Butte is never really getting away from the interstate noise except for a very short section on the mountain's southern flank.

**Start:** Parking area for McClellan Butte trailhead

**Distance:** 9.0 miles out and back

**Approximate hiking time:** 6 to 7 hours

**Trail numbers:** USDA Forest Service Trail 1015

**Difficulty:** Difficult; an unrelentingly long, steep trail

**Trail surface:** Forested path; rocky

**Seasons:** Summer and fall

**Other trail users:** None

**Canine compatibility:** Leashed dogs permitted

**Land status:** USDAFS Snoqualmie Ranger District

**Nearest town:** North Bend

**Services:** Gas, restaurants, groceries, lodging; unisex vault toilet at trailhead

**Northwest Forest Pass:** Yes

**Discover Pass:** No

**Maps:** Green Trails No. 206: Bandera, and No. 206S, side B: Mount Si NRCA; USGS Bandera; USDAFS Mount Baker-Snoqualmie National Forest, Alpine Lakes Wilderness

**Trail contacts:** Alpine Lakes Protection Society (ALPS), Mount Baker-Snoqualmie National Forest

**Special hazards:** Exposure (at summit); no potable water at trailhead or on trail

**Finding the trailhead:** From Seattle, drive east on I-90 to exit 42 (Tinkham Road). Turn right (south) at the stop sign, cross the South Fork Snoqualmie River, and travel 0.3 mile on FR 55, a good gravel road. Take a spur road on the right (south) marked by a handmade sign that says McClellan Butte. It is 0.2 mile on this spur road to the parking lot. Anglers enjoy challenging themselves on the South Fork Snoqualmie River, and you will see them along FR 55 if you continue driving east, past the turnoff to the McClellan Butte spur road. GPS: N47 24.729' / W121 35.358'

## The Hike

Find the trailhead at the southwestern end of the parking lot next to the toilet. Walk 100 feet and self-register at the kiosk. In 0.1 mile pass under power lines; 0.2 mile later cross an old road. In another 0.2 mile reach the Iron Horse Trail (John Wayne Pioneer Trail) and pass under another set of power lines. Turn right (north) and in 200 feet reach picnic tables, a vault toilet, and several camping pads used by bicyclists pedaling the entire Iron Horse Trail—a 100-mile rail-to-trail following the bed of the

*McClellan Butte and I-90 from the Bandera Mountain Trail (#32 and #34)*

Chicago, Milwaukee, St. Paul & Pacific Railroad. It's also known as the "Milwaukee Road." In 0.4 mile cross Alice Creek, bypassing a waytrail down to the creek, and reach the McClellan Butte Trail. Turn left (southwest).

Start climbing through thick forest. The trail angles toward but never meets Alice Creek. Cross FR 9020 in 0.5 mile and continue straight (northwest) up the hill. Don't be surprised to see lots of big trees, particularly as the trail climbs higher and higher. The way is wide and the switchbacks well graded, but this does nothing to alter how steep the trail is.

The switchbacks do, eventually, end. But the trail continues to climb by traversing upward while approaching the south side of McClellan Butte. The advantage of switchbacks becomes obvious after a minute of travel. They aren't as steep as the traverse, but by this point, everything looks vertical.

About 4 miles from the trailhead, views southward to Mount Rainier are possible along with a good glimpse below of Chester Morse Reservoir in the Seattle Municipal Watershed Reserve. Don't be discouraged by all the roads fairly close below the trail—no one but watershed employees are allowed to drive on them. The watershed is closed to all public use in order to safeguard Seattle's municipal water supply.

The trail actually loses some elevation before leaving its forest chrysalis and popping out onto the summit ridge. The trail ends not long afterward. From trail's end there is a short, extremely exposed Class 3 scramble to the actual summit of McClellan Butte.

# TREE STORIES 2

Western hemlock (*Tsuga heterophylla*, or "differently leaved hemlock") is a common associate of Douglas fir. Viewing the branches on end, western hemlock needles appear like little starbursts. The needles are of different lengths, and each one stands on a peg-like base. From a distance, western hemlock gives the impression of being tired and fatigued; the tree crown always stands limp and lazy. The dense canopy of mature western hemlock forests retards a well-developed shrub layer. Western hemlock grows faster than any other forest tree in the Northwest. Trees reach heights of 200 feet, with diameters of 3 feet. *Tsuga* is the Japanese name for hemlock native to Japan.

Western red cedar (*Thuja plicata*, or the cedar with "leaves folded into plaits") is found growing near the Pacific Coast from Alaska to Humboldt County, California, and inland to Montana. It was a popular provider of shelter, clothing, tools, and transportation to the Native Americans. The leaves of western red cedar consist of flat, overlapping scales. Trees reach heights of 200 feet, with diameters of 16 feet. Older trees are well known for possessing a tremendous

*The leaves of western red cedar consist of flat, overlapping scales. Trees reach as high as 200 feet. The bark is fibrous and rust-colored.*

buttress. A walk through a mature western red cedar forest is an olfactory enchantment verging on the divine. And yes, there is an eastern red cedar (*Juniperus virginiana*).

Whitewater kayakers look at three elements when assessing a run: How exciting and fun will it be? How difficult? And what will the penalty phase be if anything goes awry? The route from the end of the trail to the top of McClellan Butte is not hard, and the reward in terms of viewscape is pretty good. But the penalty phase is very high. One mistake, one slip, and a person could fall and tumble all the way down to the Iron Horse Trail. For that reason, many people are more than content to go no farther. The scenery at trail's end is already good enough.

To return to the parking lot, turn around and retrace your route.

## Miles and Directions

**0.0**  Trailhead on FR 55
**0.6**  Iron Horse Trail (John Wayne Pioneer Trail)
**1.5**  Cross FR 9020

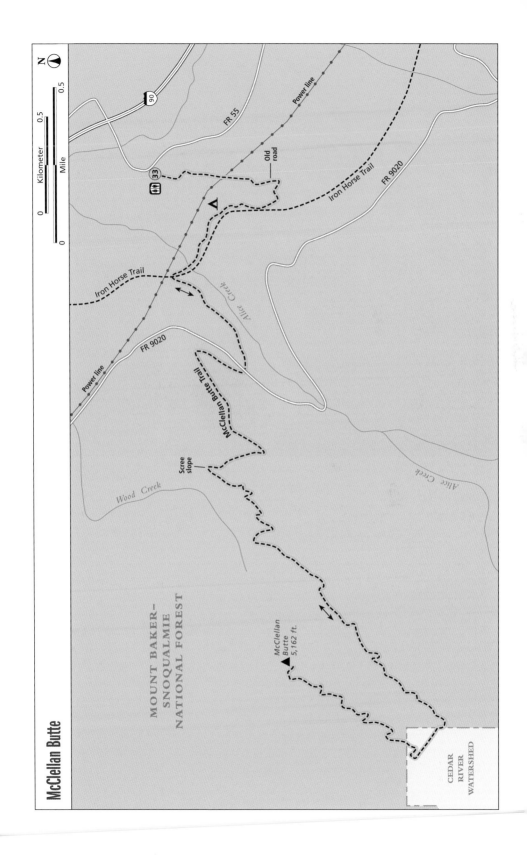

**McClellan Butte**

MOUNT BAKER–
SNOQUALMIE
NATIONAL FOREST

CEDAR RIVER
WATERSHED

McClellan Butte
5,162 ft.

Scree slope

McClellan Butte Trail

Wood Creek

Alice Creek

FR 9020

Power line

Iron Horse Trail

Old road

Iron Horse Trail

FR 9020

FR 55

Power line

90

33

N

Kilometer
0        0.5        0.5

Mile
0

*McClellan Butte, early spring*

**4.5**  McClellan Butte

**9.0**  Arrive back at trailhead

## Hike Information

McClellan Butte is named for General George B. McClellan, famous for inventing the McClellan cavalry saddle and for never quite getting his act together to successfully attack the Confederate Army of Virginia during the Civil War. Insubordinate to his commander in chief, McClellan was finally relieved of command by President Abraham Lincoln.

McClellan was also the unsuccessful 1864 Democratic presidential candidate. He was forced to repudiate his party's platform of seeking an early end to the war with a negotiated settlement with the Confederacy. He served as governor of New Jersey and spent his later years writing articles and books that defended his actions during the War Between the States. McClellan was an engineer by training and in 1853 helped survey rail routes across the Cascade Mountains. He preferred Yakima Pass, having failed to consider Stevens Pass or Snoqualmie Pass.

# 34 Mason Lake and Mount Defiance

Mount Defiance is prominently displayed to motorists heading west on I-90. They never suspect that the peak harbors vast fields of wildflowers or views that stretch south to north from Oregon to Canada and west to east from the Olympic Mountains to the crest of the Cascade Mountains. Strong hikers frequently make the round-trip journey to Mount Defiance in one day, but it's much more pleasant as an overnight excursion, with a stay at Mason Lake. There are many options to continue on as a multiday backpack trip.

**Start:** Trailhead parking for Ira Spring Trail 1038

**Distance:** 6.4 miles out and back to Mason Lake; another 4.0 miles out and back to Mount Defiance from Mason Lake

**Approximate hiking time:** 4 to 8 hours or overnight (depending on options)

**Trail number:** USDA Forest Service Trail 1038

**Difficulty:** Strenuous; short, steep trail with talus; no water; no shade on second half of hike to Mason Lake

**Trail surface:** Forested path, old road; rocky

**Seasons:** Summer and fall

**Other trail users:** None

**Canine compatibility:** Leashed dogs permitted

**Land status:** USDAFS Snoqualmie Ranger District, Alpine Lakes Wilderness Area

**Nearest town:** North Bend

**Services:** Gas, restaurants, groceries, lodging; unisex vault toilet at trailhead

**Northwest Forest Pass:** Yes

**Discover Pass:** No

**Maps:** Green Trails No. 206: Bandera; USGS Bandera; USDAFS Mount Baker–Snoqualmie National Forest, Alpine Lakes Wilderness

**Trail contacts:** Alpine Lakes Protection Society (ALPS), Mount Baker–Snoqualmie National Forest

**Special hazards:** Talus, exposure; no potable water at trailhead or on trail

**Finding the trailhead:** From Seattle, drive east on I-90 to exit 45 (Lookout Point Road / FR 9030 and FR 9031). Turn left (north) at the stop sign and pass under I-90. The pavement soon ends and the poorly maintained road becomes narrow hard-packed dirt with many potholes. In 0.8 mile pass the road to Talapus Lake and Trail 1039. Continue on FR 9031. After 2 miles pass an old logging road on the right (north). After 3.8 miles reach the large trailhead parking lot. GPS: N47 25.485' / W121 35.010'

## The Hike

The trailhead for the Ira Spring Trail is located at the western end of the parking area. Self-register for travel in the Alpine Lakes Wilderness and begin walking on an old road that ascends gently through a thick forest to Mason Creek, accompanied by traffic noise from I-90. This is a lovely and cool spot to stop and rest or eat a late lunch before proceeding up the trail.

At 2.0 miles is a sign for Bandera Junction. Turn left (northwest) and traverse a slope, bare of trees, overflowing with shrubs and herbaceous growth. To the right

*Happy hikers take a rest at Mason Lake. (Photo by Parker Lee Torres)*

(northeast) is the trail to Bandera Mountain (#32). The wildflower displays are quite impressive through here during spring and summer. The trail doesn't exactly cease its climb, but it does mellow a bit. Cross into the Alpine Lakes Wilderness, reach the ridge (with stupendous views of Mount Rainier), and follow the trail down to Mason Lake, bidding adieu to whooshing cars and I-90. The lake was named by James Tilton, territorial surveyor during the 1850s, for Charles H. Mason, first secretary of Washington Territory.

If Mason Lake is your final destination, explore the shore or make a short hike to Little Mason Lake. If camping is your objective, there are four marginal campsites on the north shore of the lake. Wooden signs bolted to trees mark each site. No campfires are allowed, and there is no toilet at the lake. Though staying at Mason Lake may not be as popular as other places in the Alpine Lakes Wilderness, it can be crowded, and late arrivals can expect to find the sites already occupied.

If Mason Lake is not your final destination and you're looking for more adventure, the trail to Mount Defiance continues northward. Climb over a short divide and descend to a junction with Trail 1009. Right (west) leads to Rainbow Lake, Island Lake, and another junction with Trail 1007 to Pratt and Olallie Lakes. Left (west) leads to Mount Defiance.

Proceeding along Trail 1009, look right (east) to occasional views through thick forest to Lake Kulla Kulla. The name is Chinook jargon and is related to the word for "bird." Word repetition suggests the bird was a big one.

Soon enough the trail resumes its upward cant, and once again hikers will be huffing and puffing. Switchbacking for about a mile through heavy forest, the trail emerges onto the south slope of Mount Defiance and another wildflower and scree

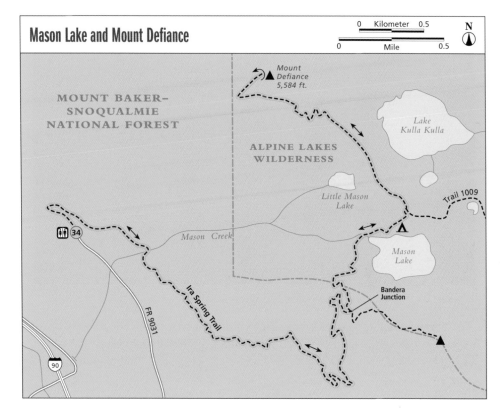

**Mason Lake and Mount Defiance**

MOUNT BAKER–
SNOQUALMIE
NATIONAL FOREST

Mount
Defiance
5,584 ft.

ALPINE LAKES
WILDERNESS

Lake
Kulla Kulla

Little Mason
Lake

Trail 1009

Mason Creek

Mason
Lake

Bandera
Junction

Ira Spring Trail

FR 9031

34

90

garden. Views southward to Mount Rainier and Mount Adams are fantastic. East is a great view of Bandera Mountain, with Mason Lake below.

Traverse west across the open slope for around 0.5 mile. Just before the trail goes around a corner to plunge back into the forest, find an unmarked narrow waytrail leading straight up the west flank of Mount Defiance. Hike to the broad, sparsely forested summit in about 0.25 mile. Views northward into the heart of the Cascades, all the way to Glacier Peak and Mount Baker, will knock your socks off. All of Puget Sound is also visible, leading right up to the Olympic Mountains.

Retrace your steps, returning to Mason Lake (if you're camping overnight) or the Ira Spring trailhead.

## Miles and Directions

**0.0**   Ira Spring trailhead
**2.0**   Bandera Junction
**3.2**   Mason Lake
**5.2**   Mount Defiance
**10.4**  Arrive back at trailhead

*Enjoying the view of Mount Rainier from the Mason Lake Trail.*

**Options:** From Mason Lake it is possible to continue on to Thompson Lake (northwest on Trail 1009) or Rainbow, Island, Pratt, Olallie, and Talapus Lakes (east on Trail 1009, Trail 1007, and Trail 1039) with car shuttle.

## Hike Information

This trail is named to memorialize photographer, author, and activist Ira Spring, who, with help from Volunteers for Outdoor Washington, urged the Forest Service to close the original trail to Mason Lake. Originally built in 1958 to enable fire crews access to the lake, the old route was badly eroded and went straight up Mason Creek, gaining 1,700 feet within a mile. The new trail was built in 2003.

*"An early morning walk is a blessing for the whole day."*

—Henry David Thoreau

**GREEN TIP:**
Hiking in a group? To avoid widening the footpath when you
come to a sensitive area like a meadow or marsh, spread out
so you don't cut a beaten path through the wet landscape.
Never create trails where there were none before.

# 35 Annette Lake

This popular and well-known trail has everything: a rushing and thundering creek, waterfalls, old-growth forest, wildflowers, views, camping, and a lake.

**Start:** Trailhead parking for Annette Lake Trail 1019 and Asahel Curtis Nature Trail
**Distance:** 7.2 miles out and back, including side trip to campsites
**Approximate hiking time:** 4 to 5 hours
**Trail number:** USDA Forest Service Trail 1019
**Difficulty:** Moderate, with several steep sections
**Trail surface:** Forested path; rocky
**Seasons:** Spring, summer, and fall
**Other trail users:** Runners
**Canine compatibility:** Leashed dogs permitted
**Land status:** USDAFS Snoqualmie Ranger District
**Nearest town:** North Bend

**Services:** Gas, restaurants, groceries, lodging; USDAFS Tinkham, Commonwealth, and Denny Creek Campgrounds nearby along I-90; unisex vault toilet at trailhead
**Northwest Forest Pass:** Yes
**Discover Pass:** No
**Maps:** Green Trails No. 207: Snoqualmie; USGS Lost Lake and Snoqualmie Pass; USDAFS Mount Baker-Snoqualmie National Forest
**Trail contact:** Mount Baker-Snoqualmie National Forest
**Special hazards:** No potable water at trailhead or on trail

**Finding the trailhead:** From Seattle, take I-90 east to exit 47 (Tinkham Road / Denny Creek-Asahel Curtis). At the stop sign turn right (south) onto Tinkham Road and cross the Snoqualmie River on a narrow two-lane bridge. At the T intersection turn left (east) onto the unmaintained gravel FR 55. Drive 0.4 mile and park in a huge paved lot. GPS: N47 23.565' / W121 28.427'

## The Hike

Find the Annette Lake Trail at the southeast end of the parking lot between the Asahel Curtis Nature Trail and a gated, wide gravel road. Begin your 1,200-foot climb to Annette Lake by ascending to the sound of I-90 on a narrow, well-trod forest path. In a hundred feet is a self-serve trail register. Cross Humpback Creek on a stout new log bridge funded in part in 2003 by the Spring Trust for Trails. The creek is an impressive cataract and would be impassable without the bridge.

Cross the old road observed at the trailhead, and continue going up the trail. Cross the road again in a few hundred feet. In 0.6 mile you will pass under a power line and then plunge back into the forest. In 0.7 mile cross the John Wayne Pioneer Trail (Old Milwaukee Railroad grade) and find the Annette Lake Trail continuing on the other side.

Cross a pretty creek on a double split-log bridge with a sturdy handrail. The higher you go, the bigger the trees. Soon enter an old-growth forest and reach a wet meadow, a short boardwalk, and an interesting bridge. Spoiler alert: In a burst of creativity, trail builders incorporated a fallen cedar log in their span, cutting steps into the trunk and adding a handrail. This sort of artistic sense is a sure sign that the trail crew saw more than just ground to be traversed. Applaud their work!

The trail steepens, and switchbacks begin. Let your gaze rise away from the ground periodically, past and through the trees—as you go higher, views across Snoqualmie Valley and down Humpback Creek begin to open up. In about 3.2 miles the trail finally flattens out as it climbs over the lip of a hanging valley and begins its last push to the lake.

Reach Annette Lake in 3.5 miles. Cross the creek to a small day-use area in and among the trees. Or find a seat with the crowds beside the outflow. A better idea is to turn left (east) and walk 0.1 mile on waytrails to the camping area. There is lake access here, as well as fine picnicking with nice views across the lake to a waterfall, Silver Peak, and Humpback Mountain. Please respect those people who have chosen to camp here by remaining outside their campsites and away from their tents. Thank you.

*Annette Lake and Silver Peak*

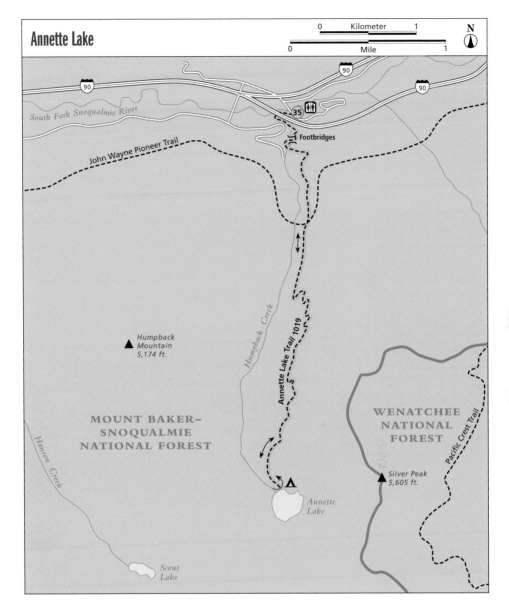

Retrace your route to reach the parking lot.

## Miles and Directions

**0.0**   Trailhead parking for Annette Lake Trail 1019

**0.2**   Bridge over Humpback Creek

**0.7**   John Wayne Pioneer Trail (Old Milwaukee Railroad grade)

**3.5**   Annette Lake

**3.6** Campsites

**7.2** Arrive back at trailhead

**Options:** The Asahel Curtis Nature Trail begins right next door to the Annette Lake Trail. The nature trail is a perfect introduction to the forest for children and newcomers to Seattle. Use caution walking on the cedar boardwalk—the planks become slippery when wet. A pamphlet for a self-guided walk on the nature trail is often available at the trailhead. Silver Peak, high above Annette Lake, was a popular climb for members of the Mountaineers during the 1930s. A route exists from the Pacific Crest Trail on the east side of the peak to the summit. People very experienced in off-trail hiking and scrambling over boulders and scree have been known to make their way up Silver Peak from Annette Lake. Hikers have also made the difficult traverse from Silver Peak to Humpback Mountain via Abiel Peak across steep slopes with loose rock, exposure, and lots of bushwhacking.

## Hike Information

Asahel Curtis, a photographer (and brother of photographer Edward Curtis) who documented the natural history and historical events of Washington, wrote: "One comes more intimately in touch with the mountains when he travels the trails. In the valleys the forests seem lower, the giant trees rise from one's side to tremendous heights, and the lower growth reaches out a friendly hand to bid you welcome; but it is on the untrodden mountain heights that the traveler receives a true reward for his toil. Here where vegetation makes its last stand amid a world of ice and snow, with the lower world stretching away to the distant horizon, nature unfolds in all her beauty." Now, how nice is that!

# 36 Melakwa Lakes

Most hikers know the Denny Creek Trail for its waterslide—admittedly a worthy goal, especially on a hot day or with small children in tow. Ah! But there is so much more to amaze and delight farther up the trail, including old-growth forest, two long waterfalls, wildflower gardens, and a subalpine lake with limited camping possibilities. This is a popular trail; don't be surprised to see large groups of people, especially on weekends.

**Start:** Denny Creek trailhead

**Distance:** 8.0 miles out and back to Melakwa Lake; 9.0 miles out and back to Upper Melakwa Lake

**Approximate hiking time:** 6 hours

**Trail number:** USDA Forest Service Trail 1014

**Difficulty:** Difficult, with steep sections and exposure at waterfall viewpoints

**Trail surface:** Forested path; rocky

**Seasons:** Summer and fall

**Other trail users:** Llamas

**Canine compatibility:** Leashed dogs permitted. The Forest Service frequently patrols this trail and issues expensive tickets to owners of unleashed dogs.

**Land status:** USDAFS Snoqualmie Ranger District, Alpine Lakes Wilderness

**Nearest town:** North Bend

**Services:** Gas, restaurants, groceries, lodging; limited services at Snoqualmie Pass; camping at USDAFS Denny Creek Campground; unisex vault toilet at trailhead

**Northwest Forest Pass:** Yes

**Discover Pass:** No

**Maps:** Green Trails No. 207: Snoqualmie Pass; USGS Snoqualmie Pass; USDAFS Mount Baker-Snoqualmie National Forest

**Trail contact:** Mount Baker-Snoqualmie National Forest

**Special hazards:** Devil's club, loose rock, exposure; no potable water at trailhead or on trail

**Finding the trailhead:** From Seattle, take I-90 east to exit 47 (Tinkham Road / Denny Creek–Asahel Curtis). Turn left (north) at the stop sign, cross over I-90, and turn right (east) at the T intersection. Pass under I-90, and after 0.2 mile reach Denny Creek Road (FR 58); turn left (north) toward Franklin Falls Trail. Cross Denny Creek on a sturdy metal bridge in 1.8 miles, continuing on the paved one-way road. After 0.3 mile reach the USDAFS Denny Creek Campground and continue on FR 58 past the campground. In 0.2 mile turn left (west) onto FR 5830, a paved road. As of summer 2020 the road is closed here due to changes in funding. However, the trailhead is still open; walk 0.3 mile to reach it. Parking is available at the nearby Franklin Falls trailhead and along only one side of the road beginning at the Denny Creek Campground. Pay attention to No Parking signs. To return to I-90, continue north on the one-way FR 5800 (SE Denny Creek Road) for 3 miles to Snoqualmie Pass where you can hop onto the interstate and make your way home. GPS: N47 24.468' / W121 26.309'

## The Hike

The trail begins on the northwest side of the now-closed parking lot, adjacent to the unisex vault toilet. Begin on a level stretch with noisy Denny Creek nearby. The trail

*Sublime subalpine scenery at Melakwa Lake*

soon climbs on a series of stairs and after about 0.1 mile reaches a bridge over Denny Creek. Rocky and log-choked, the creek loudly flows below. Look upstream and see the I-90 viaduct high above; after 0.5 mile pass under it.

The trail now begins to climb in earnest on a well-constructed and well-graded trail. Cross the Alpine Lakes Wilderness boundary in about 1 mile. Sounds from Denny Creek are still evident in places, but highway noise is completely gone. There are plenty of opportunities to step off the trail and admire Denny Creek and its cataracts.

Cross Denny Creek again after 1.1 miles to reach the famous Denny Creek waterslide. Most families stop here, and it's easy to see why. This popular place is a playground for children of all ages. Sit on the big slab of granite and soak up the rays, or dip your body in the cold, refreshing creek. Maintain a watchful eye on young children, and keep dogs on their leash. Explore upstream a few hundred feet to a small cascade. Look downstream and observe the old bridge—a sawn log.

Find the Main Trail sign, and resume the route to Melakwa Lake with significantly fewer people. They're all back at the waterslide! The trail punches out of the forest and into the open after 1.6 miles with views up-canyon. Climbing through this open slope on switchbacks, the trail reaches a viewpoint of Keekwulee Falls in another 0.2 mile.

Cross a talus field and reenter the forest. Sharp eyes will spot several waytrails through the trees and underbrush to Denny Creek and the lip of the falls. Switchbacks play hide-and-seek with talus and forest, zigzagging in and out of each. There are plenty of viewpoints down sheer cliffs to Denny Creek.

In 0.4 mile the switchbacks top out. There is no access to Snowshoe Falls. Cross Denny Creek on a sawn log, and traverse another, longer talus slope. Up the canyon is forested Hemlock Pass. Downstream are views to Snoqualmie Valley. At your feet are gardens of wildflowers, including columbine (*Aquilegia formosa*), bluebells (*Mertensia* sp.), various sedges (*Carex* sp.), marsh marigold (*Caltha leptosepala*), shooting stars (*Dodecatheon* sp.), many kinds of saxifrage (*Saxifraga* sp.), bracken fern (*Pteridium aquilinum*), yellow violets (*Viola sempervirens*), and red alder (*Alnus rubra*).

Tighter and tighter switchbacks lead to Hemlock Pass (no view), where the trail descends through thick forest to a trail junction. Turn left (west) to drop steeply in 2.9 miles and visit Tuscohatchie Lake on Trail 1011. Continue straight (north) and quickly reach Melakwa Lake after a short uphill push. Cross the outlet stream on a logjam. A small sign bolted to a tree directs hikers and campers to a privy. Camping around the outlet is limited and of poor quality. The best sites are located on the opposite shore. No fires are permitted.

Continue along the west shore of Melakwa Lake and to Upper Melakwa Lake, which affords more solitude. This tiny basin is surrounded by huge talus fields, one of which leads upward to Melakwa Pass, with Kaleetan Peak on the west and Chair Peak to the east.

Return to the trailhead by retracing your route over Hemlock Pass and down Denny Creek. Don't forget to stop and play in the waterslide at Denny Creek and cool off if it's been a hot day!

## Miles and Directions

**0.0**  Denny Creek trailhead
**0.9**  Alpine Lakes Wilderness boundary
**1.1**  Waterslide
**1.8**  Keekwulee Falls viewpoint
**3.5**  Hemlock Pass
**4.0**  Melakwa Lake
**4.5**  Upper Melakwa Lake
**9.0**  Arrive back at trailhead

## Hike Information

*Melakwa,* or *malakwa,* means "mosquito" in Chinook jargon, the pidgin language forced upon natives of the Pacific Northwest as a lingua franca by French, English, and American traders too lazy to learn the actual languages of the region. During

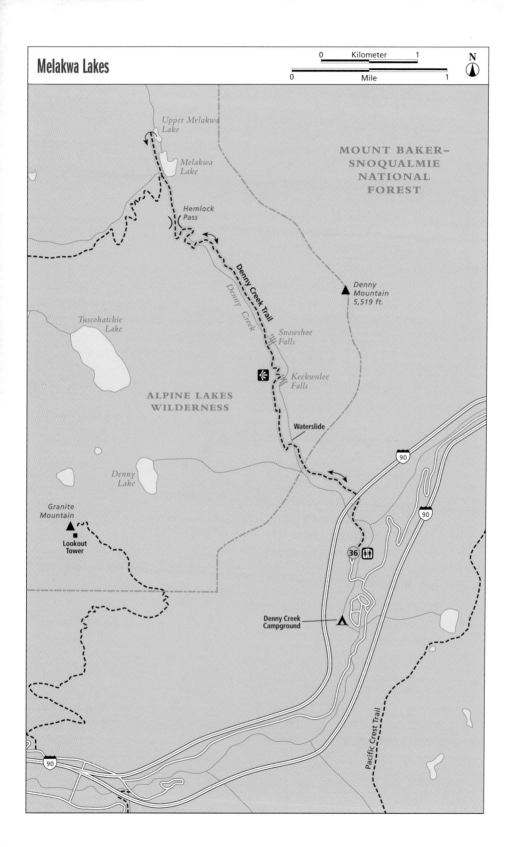

## Melakwa Lakes

Upper Melakwa Lake

Melakwa Lake

Hemlock Pass

Denny Creek Trail

Denny Creek

Tuscohatchie Lake

Snowshoe Falls

Keekwulee Falls

ALPINE LAKES WILDERNESS

Waterslide

Denny Lake

Granite Mountain

Lookout Tower

MOUNT BAKER– SNOQUALMIE NATIONAL FOREST

Denny Mountain 5,519 ft.

90

90

36

Denny Creek Campground

Pacific Crest Trail

90

Kilometer

Mile

0  1

0  1

N

*Pausing for reflection with a little lake-side time*

spring and summer, expect several different kinds of annoying flies, including mosquitos, at the lake.

Arthur A. Denny was leader of the party that founded the city of Seattle in 1852. Being first on the scene, Denny was well situated to profit from those who came later and, as one of the city fathers, encourage and finance Seattle's expansion. During the late 1860s Denny poked around the Snoqualmie Pass area, prospecting for ore and scouting a hoped-for wagon road, or even railroad, over the Cascades. Denny Creek and Denny Mountain recognize his pioneering efforts. There are many other places in King County with the Denny moniker, including a major street in Seattle. The Denny family plot in Lake View Cemetery (1554 15th Ave. E, Seattle, WA 98112) on Capitol Hill is not to be missed. It uses impressive amounts of granite, features a Teutonic eagle–topped pillar, and occupies a large swath of property.

> *"I may not have gone where I intended to go, but I think I have ended up where I intended to be."*
>
> —Douglas Adams, English humorist and novelist

# 37 Olallie Lake

There is a cost to popularity. Along with Talapus Lake, Olallie Lake has long been heavily overused and will probably continue to be so. The two lakes, beautifully situated in forested basins, are fairly close to the trailhead, relatively easy to reach, and provide both fishing and swimming opportunities. But there is also an advantage to popularity: a reworked trail including a new bridge and privies at Olallie Lake. And there are the lovely trailside streams, a rocky dell cataract, and old growth forest to admire.

**Start:** Pratt Lake trailhead
**Distance:** 7.2 miles out and back
**Approximate hiking time:** 4 hours
**Trail number:** USDA Forest Service Trail 1007
**Difficulty:** Moderate
**Trail surface:** Forested path; rocky
**Seasons:** Summer and fall
**Other trail users:** None
**Canine compatibility:** Leashed dogs permitted
**Land status:** USDAFS Snoqualmie Ranger District, Alpine Lakes Wilderness Area
**Nearest town:** North Bend

**Services:** Gas, restaurants, groceries, lodging; vault toilet at trailhead
**Northwest Forest Pass:** Yes
**Discover Pass:** No
**Maps:** Green Trails No. 207: Snoqualmie Pass, and No. 206: Bandera; USGS Snoqualmie Pass; USDAFS Mount Baker–Snoqualmie National Forest, Alpine Lakes Wilderness
**Trail contacts:** Alpine Lakes Protection Society (ALPS), Mount Baker–Snoqualmie National Forest
**Special hazards:** Devil's club; no potable water at trailhead or on trail

**Finding the trailhead:** From Seattle, drive east on I-90 to exit 47 (Tinkham Road/ Denny Creek–Asahel Curtis). At the stop sign turn left (north); cross over I-90, and in 0.1 mile turn left (west) at the intersection. Follow signs to Granite Mountain Lookout, and in 0.3 mile reach the trailhead parking. GPS: N47 23.872' / W121 29.189'

## The Hike

A wide and rocky trail to Olallie Lake begins behind the vault toilet and the Pratt Lake Trailhead information kiosk. Begin walking up the trail on a decent grade over long, loosely structured, meandering switchbacks. The sounds of I-90 filter through the thick forest of old trees. Cross numerous seasonal creeks in the first 0.5 mile. At 1.0 mile from the parking area, continue straight (west) past a trail leading east and north to Granite Mountain Lookout. Soon afterward cross two channels of an ephemeral stream that can run high in the early season during snowmelt and in the late season due to rainfall.

At 1.5 miles pass through a narrow, rocky dell below an attractive cataract. The water crosses over slabs of rock with many small waterfalls. Following a brief steep

*Rocky slopes, mountains, and old growth forest around Olallie Lake*

section, the trail starts a traverse of Granite Mountain, reaching a long, slowly disintegrating, boardwalk. At the end of the boardwalk, enter the Alpine Lakes Wilderness.

At the junction of Pratt Lake and Olallie Lake Trails, turn left (west). Hikers who continue straight (north) pass 100 feet or so above Olallie Lake, reaching a viewpoint of the lake before crossing a divide and plunging down to Pratt Lake.

In 0.15 mile cross Talapus Creek on a newly built log bridge with handrails and reach a junction, turning right (north) toward Olallie Lake. A few switchbacks and 0.2 mile later, Olallie Lake comes into view. A large bare area below the trail with excellent lake access is reserved for day-trippers.

The eleven campsites at the lake are small, scattered, and of poor quality. They can be found at the south, west, and north ends of the lake. There are two privy toilets in the forest above the west side of Olallie Lake; look for small signs attached to a tree to locate them, or keep an eye open for waytrails. No fires are allowed at Olallie Lake. There is a pretty view to the north and the head of the lake to gentle slopes, forest, and talus fields. To return home, retrace your route back down the trail.

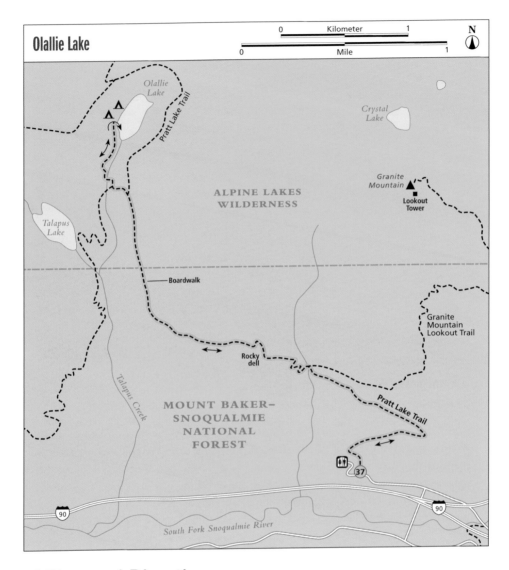

## Miles and Directions

**0.0** Pratt Lake trailhead

**1.0** Pratt Lake Trail and Granite Mountain Lookout Trail junction

**1.5** Rocky dell

**2.0** Alpine Lakes Wilderness boundary

**2.7** Pratt Lake Trail and Olallie Lake Trail junction

**2.8** Olallie Lake Trail and Talapus Lake Trail junction

**3.0** Olallie Lake

# THERE'S A FUNGUS AMONG US

Mushrooms are the most commonly seen fungus, but there are many other kinds, including athlete's foot and ringworm fungi, bread molds, and the penicillin-producing mold that grows on oranges. What we see as a mushroom is actually the fruiting body of an organism that grows below the soil surface, living off the detritus produced by plants and animals. Loosely interpreted, this makes mushrooms the equivalent of an apple or tomato with the fungal spores being equivalent to seeds.

At one time mushrooms were considered plants because they were nonmotile. But biologists now agree that plants must photosynthesize, and since fungi don't ... Also, plant-cell walls consist of cellulose and lignin. Fungal cells are made of chitin, a substance also found in the hard outer shells of insects and other arthropods.

The body of mushroom fungi consists of whitish or grayish strands called hyphae. The hyphae absorb moisture and nutrients, growing over, under, around, and through the soil, and often by growing into an object. Some fungi are involved in a mycorrhizal association with the roots of conifers. In this complex relationship, the fungus derives photosynthate from the tree. In return, the fungus provides the tree with a greater surface area to absorb water and mineral nutrition from the soil.

*Fly agaric—very pretty but deadly poisonous*

**3.6** Lake campsites

**7.2** Arrive back at trailhead

**Options:** A short trail from the parking area leads to a stoutly built picnic table at the trailhead. From the trail junction leading to Olallie Lake, turn left (south) and continue to Talapus Lake. The trail meanders and drops considerably to the lake. From the trailhead a 5.5-mile trail climbs 3,754 feet to the summit of Granite Mountain and a historic fire lookout tower. The initial lookout was built in 1916 and was one of the first on the Mount

*A beautiful fall of water along the Olallie Lake Trail*

Baker–Snoqualmie National Forest. The tower was updated in 1924 and again in 1956, and decommissioned in the 1970s as new technologies and management practices reduced the need for fire lookouts.

*"Part of the pleasure of any kind of walking for me is the very idea of going somewhere—by foot."*
—Ruth Rudner, *Forgotten Pleasures: A Guide for the Seasonal Adventurer*

# 38 Snow Lake

The popular (25,000 annual visitors) route up to Snow Lake swarms with people during summer, and finding a place to hang out along the lake's rocky beach is close to impossible on sunny weekends. Still, the lake sits within a gorgeous setting and should not be missed. An excursion in the fall to pick huckleberries is bound to feature fewer people. Such is the popularity of the lake that even a rainy day sees plenty of visitors, but at least no crowds. In spring, fields of wildflowers bloom at regular intervals along the trail—another reason for the lake's popularity. With a car shuttle, adventurous backpackers can do a one- or two-day overnight trip into the Middle Fork Snoqualmie Valley.

**Start:** Trailhead parking at Alpental Ski Area
**Distance:** 9.0 miles out and back
**Approximate hiking time:** 6 hours
**Trail number:** USDA Forest Service Trail 1013
**Difficulty:** Moderate, with steep areas
**Trail surface:** Forested path; rocky
**Seasons:** Summer and fall
**Other trail users:** Llamas and goats
**Canine compatibility:** Leashed dogs permitted
**Land status:** USDAFS Snoqualmie Ranger District, Alpine Lakes Wilderness Area
**Nearest town:** North Bend

**Services:** Gas, restaurants, lodging; unisex vault toilet at trailhead
**Northwest Forest Pass:** Yes
**Discover Pass:** No
**Maps:** Green Trails No. 207: Snoqualmie Pass; USGS Snoqualmie Pass; USDAFS Mount Baker-Snoqualmie National Forest, Alpine Lakes Wilderness
**Trail contacts:** Alpine Lakes Protection Society (ALPS), Mount Baker-Snoqualmie National Forest
**Special hazards:** Loose rock; no potable water at trailhead or on trail

**Finding the trailhead:** From Seattle, drive east on I-90 and take exit 52 (west summit to Snoqualmie Pass). Turn left (north) onto FR 9040 (unmarked) and then turn right (north) at Alpental Road, the second street. After 1.5 miles enter a large gravel parking lot used in wintertime by Alpental Ski Area. Park in the northernmost section of the lot. There is a vault toilet hidden behind some trees. GPS: N47 26.719' / W121 25.411'

## The Hike

Cross Alpental Road from the parking area (no public access is allowed past the car park) and find the marked trailhead. There is a self-registration station for the Alpine Lakes Wilderness and an information kiosk. Climb a series of stairs constructed of logs, which finally ends at a rocky trail that traverses the hillside across several avalanche chutes. The area around Snoqualmie Pass is part of the Naches Formation, volcanic rocks interlaid with sandstone that were deposited around forty-five million years ago. There are good exposures of Eocene andesite in the cliffs and rocks around these chutes.

*Cabin ruins at Snow Lake on a cold and damp day*

The trees around here are big. If hiking the Puget Sound lowlands has taken the edge off experiencing western hemlock (*Tsuga heterophylla*), enjoy these big boys—they are mountain hemlock (*Tsuga mertensiana*). The cones are much smaller than their lowland relatives, and the tree needles lack the distinctive starburst appearance of western hemlock. Both species share the characteristic tree crown, which limply bends over.

Ascend through the forest and avalanche chutes, cross talus fields, and in 2 miles reach the Source Lake Overlook Trail junction. This 1-mile round-trip spur trail takes hikers across rocky slopes to look down upon the source of South Fork Snoqualmie River.

Continuing east and north to Snow Lake, the trail begins to switchback uphill. The sometimes-rocky trail rises upslope, at times crossing the same avalanche chute visited below. The upper part of the trail is replaced in steeper areas by log steps. Cross the Alpine Lakes Wilderness boundary at 2.5 miles; cross over the lip into Snow Lake basin, and begin to descend.

The lake is visible through the trees as the trail crosses a talus field and keeps on dropping. Above the lakeshore is a sign, perhaps left by Paul Bunyan, directing hikers to campsites, the main trail, and ruins of a stone-walled cabin and cautioning everyone that no fires are allowed.

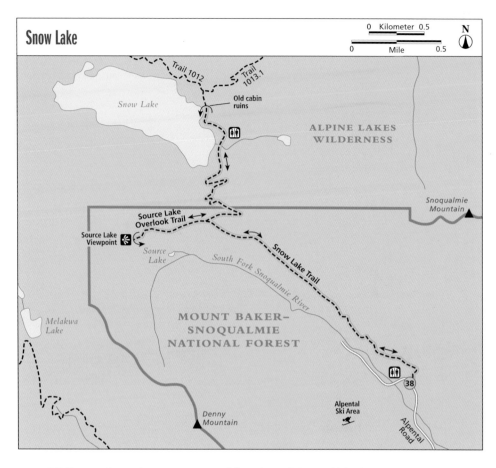

Walk past the toilet, a cute waterfall and pool, lots of blocked-off waytrails, and the vaguely delimited main trail that continues on up the valley. Reach the cabin ruins—a house, really, and a large one at that. Many of the rock walls are still standing, as is what must have been a very nice fireplace. Campsites and lake access lie below.

It's impossible to hike in the Pacific Northwest without spending some time walking in the rain. There are advantages to this! In popular places like Snow Lake, expect fewer people on the trails. Rain walking is a great opportunity to leave your stuffy house, and it beats being cooped up all day. In autumn there are huckleberries to pick and fall colors to enjoy. You're going to get wet but at the end of the day, no matter how wet you are, you can always go home and take a hot shower. Just make sure you come prepared for wet weather by bringing along the best rain gear you can afford, plenty of warm (and dry) clothes, food, and energy snacks. And keep a change of dry clothes and a towel in your car.

Campsites at Snow Lake are poor, and many of the best are now prohibited from use so that the ground can recover from generations of heavy abuse. No fires are allowed, and group size is limited to twelve; however, you'll need luck to find ample camping sites close to one another if you have a group that big.

On the return, retrace your steps down the Snow Lake Trail. At the junction with Source Lake Overlook, detour 0.5 mile to admire the cliffs and numerous creeks where the South Fork Snoqualmie River begins. Come back to the main trail and keep heading downhill to the parking lot at Alpental.

## Miles and Directions

**0.0** Trailhead at Alpental parking lot

**2.0** Source Lake Overlook Trail junction

**2.5** Alpine Lakes Wilderness boundary

**3.0** Old cabin ruins

**3.1** Snow Lake

**4.5** Source Lake view

**9.0** Arrive back at trailhead

**Options:** From Snow Lake, Trail 1012 goes on, faintly in parts, to Gem and Upper Wildcat Lakes. Or follow Trail 1013.1 to the Middle Fork Snoqualmie (car shuttle required).

# 39 Lake Lillian

Because it begins by climbing a (recovering) clear-cut hillside, this isn't as popular a route as found elsewhere around Snoqualmie Pass. But that prejudice aside, the trail soon enters an old-growth forest and leads to a beautiful lake surrounded by awesome cliffs and craggy mountains. Along the way are dynamite views across the spine of the Cascades, plus a shot at Mount Rainier. Wildflowers are abundant during summer on the clear-cut hillside and wet meadows surrounding Twin Lakes and the talus field below Lake Lillian.

**Start:** Margaret Lake trailhead
**Distance:** 9.0 miles out and back
**Approximate hiking time:** 6 to 7 hours
**Trail number:** USDA Forest Service Trail 1332
**Difficulty:** Difficult, with sections of narrow trail that are straight up and down
**Trail surface:** Forested path; rocky
**Seasons:** Summer and fall
**Other trail users:** Illegal use by mountain bikers has been a problem in the past on this hikers-only trail.
**Canine compatibility:** Dogs prohibited
**Land status:** Wenatchee National Forest, Cle Elum District; Alpine Lakes Wilderness Area

**Nearest town:** North Bend
**Services:** Gas, restaurants, lodging; no toilet at trailhead
**Northwest Forest Pass:** Yes
**Discover Pass:** No
**Maps:** Green Trails No. 207: Snoqualmie Pass; USGS Chikamin Peak; USDAFS Mount Baker-Snoqualmie National Forest, Alpine Lakes Wilderness
**Trail contacts:** Alpine Lakes Protection Society (ALPS), Okanogan-Wenatchee National Forest, Mount Baker-Snoqualmie National Forest
**Special hazards:** Loose rock; no potable water at trailhead or on trail

**Finding the trailhead:** From Seattle, take I-90 east to exit 54 (Hyak and Gold Creek). Turn left (north) at the end of the off-ramp. Proceed 0.2 mile, go under the interstate, and pass the on-ramp to I-90 westbound. Turn right (east) on Gold Creek Road (FR 4832); enter the Gold Creek Critical Wildlife Corridor Research Area and begin paralleling I-90. Soon pass the road to Gold Creek Pond on your left (north). After 2 miles the road narrows to one lane, becoming gravel at 2.4 miles. At 2.7 miles the road makes a switchback, leaving the noise of I-90 behind.

The road has numerous rough spots; consider bringing some laundry—it's heavily washboarded. Climb steadily to another switchback at 3.7 miles and then another switchback at 3.9 miles and a fork in the road. Bear left onto FR 4934 (unmarked). The road narrows, switchbacks at 4.3 miles, and switchbacks again at 4.4 miles. Continue straight ahead (northwest) into the Mount Margaret parking area. GPS: N47 21.799' / W121 21.369'

## The Hike

To find the trailhead, leave the parking lot and turn left (north), returning to FR 4934. Walk 0.2 mile up the road and take the formerly gated spur road to the left (east). Begin walking along this old road (Trail 1332) through a forest of vine maple

*Lake Lillian after an early autumnal snow*

(*Acer circinatum*), willow (*Salix* sp.), red alder (*Alnus rubra*), and maturing Douglas fir and mountain hemlock. Stay on the main road despite opportunities to turn off until reaching a junction marked by a fiberglass Forest Service stick-sign announcing a hikers-only trail. Some old-timers may recall an older metal sign bolted onto a 4-by-4-inch, 8-foot-tall post declaring that this trail is closed to motor vehicles, saddle horses, and pack stock. That sign is gone.

Turn north, then east onto a narrow trail and climb through a regenerating clear-cut. Wildflowers displays can be nice through here in early spring. As the trail climbs there are plenty of vistas east, west, and south to such familiar sights as I-90, Mount Rainier, Keechelus Lake, and the ski slopes of Snoqualmie Pass.

Keechelus Lake is also known by the sobriquet "Stump Lake" for its prevalence of tree stumps exposed in wintertime when the reservoir is low. A 128-foot-tall earth-fill structure, built in 1917 and operated by the US Bureau of Reclamation, controls the lake capacity and discharge for agriculture. Keechelus, which is supposed to mean "few fish" in the local Native American dialect, is the source of the Yakima River. Downstream is Kachess Lake, which supposedly means "more fish."

Cross an old dirt road and continue up the trail. Nearly 2 miles from the parking area, enter an old-growth forest and begin a series of nicely graded switchbacks. In 2.5 miles reach the top of a ridge and the junction to Margaret Lake on the right

## GREEN TIP:

**Stay on trails. Cutting switchbacks not only harms or destroys vegetation, it also causes unnecessary erosion and destroys trails.**

(east). Continue straight ahead (north). Pass several waytrails (northeast) that lead to views of Rampart Ridge.

The trail skirts below the summits of two peaks, including Mount Margaret, and reaches a viewpoint. More of Rampart Ridge can be seen, along with a piece of Lake Lillian, a couple of ribbon waterfalls, and Rocky Run, the stream that drains the lake. Begin descending toward Twin Lakes on a trail that sometimes could use a ladder. In 1 mile reach the lakes and cross into the Alpine Lakes Wilderness.

Twin Lakes are small and shallow and seasonally provide beautiful habitat for large hordes of mosquitoes. The first lake is the larger of the two and has a poor campsite about midway up the lake—though the scenery is nice to look at. Some people choose to camp on a small island close to shore. This is a bad idea and is discouraged, since it's impossible to get 100 feet away from water in any direction—a requirement for good campers everywhere.

Leaving the larger lake, the trail follows a creek to the smaller lake and traverses even better mosquito habitat. Climb steeply and in earnest for a short while, and then proceed to lose elevation as the trail avoids having to deal with some heinous cliffs. Cross through a wide talus field and regain all the elevation lost since passing the Margaret Lake Trail junction. A brief flat spot is reached before you ascend the remaining part of the hillside—straight up! Where's that ladder?

It's not a long climb, fortunately, before the trail reaches a lip; in 100 feet Lake Lillian pops into view, surrounded by an amphitheater of rock and jagged peaks. There is no place to go from here except for mountain goats and rock climbers.

Camping sites, located back at the lip, are paltry and far from level. Impressive views down the cliffs to Lake Laura, Rocky Run, clear-cuts, and FR 136 are nearby. Return to the trailhead by the same route.

## Miles and Directions

**0.0**  Trailhead off FR 4934

**0.5**  Junction with hikers-only trail

**1.0**  Cross dirt road

**2.0**  Enter old-growth forest

**2.5**  Lake Lillian / Margaret Lake Trail junction

**2.7**  Lake Lillian Viewpoint

**3.5**  Alpine Lakes Wilderness boundary and Twin Lakes

**3.7**  Twin Lakes

**4.0**  Talus

**4.5**  Lake Lillian

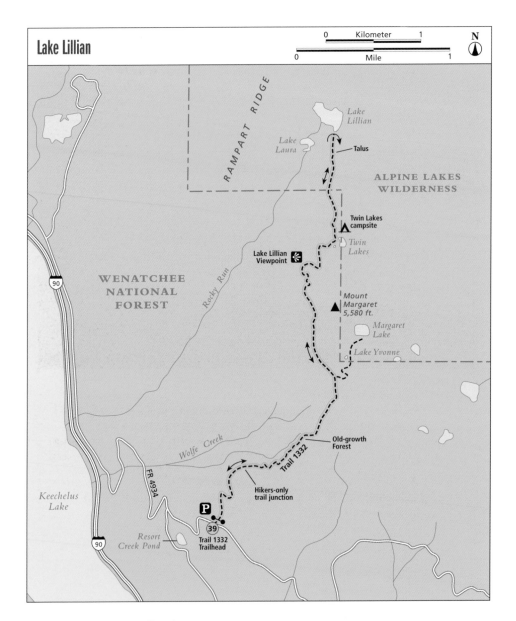

**9.0** Arrive back at trailhead

**Option:** From FR 4832, in 1 mile turn off to Gold Creek Pond and the Gold Creek trailhead. Proceed another 0.2 mile on a potholed dirt road and then turn left onto an asphalt road that quickly ends in a large paved parking lot with a vault toilet. Park and find the ADA-accessible Gold Creek Pond Trail by the reader board leading to the paved and boardwalked 1-mile circuit of Gold Creek Pond, a former gravel pit used until the early 1980s while I-90 was being constructed. With the help of the USDA Forest Service and the Washington Trails Association, the area around the pond has been reclaimed by forest,

*Corel mushroom*

meadow, and marsh—which means it's a good place for spring wildflowers and birders. There is also a large picnic area (take the left/west junction when the trail splits) with plenty of sun and shade—your choice—and a scenic view of the pond and up the drainage of Gold Creek to craggy mountains. No potable water is available at the trailhead or along the trail. A Northwest Forest Pass is required.

# 40 Margaret Lake

Reaching Margaret Lake occupies much of the same trail as getting to Lake Lillian, with the added pleasure of being a shorter hike. Another major difference between the destinations is that past the junction with Margaret Lake, the trail to Lake Lillian is steep, rough, and in many places almost straight up and down. In comparison, the entire way to Margaret Lake is along a nice and easy-to-follow route. In autumn an immense slope of huckleberries at Margaret Lake makes for good grazing.

**Start:** Margaret Lake trailhead parking
**Distance:** 7.0 miles out and back
**Approximate hiking time:** 4 to 6 hours
**Trail number:** USDA Forest Service Trail 1332
**Difficulty:** Moderate, with steep sections
**Trail surface:** Forested path; rocky
**Seasons:** Summer and fall
**Other trail users:** Illegal use by mountain bikers has been a past problem on this hikers-only trail.
**Canine compatibility:** Dogs prohibited
**Land status:** Wenatchee National Forest, Cle Elum District; Alpine Lakes Wilderness Area
**Nearest town:** North Bend; Snoqualmie Pass

**Services:** Gas, restaurants, lodging; no toilet at trailhead
**Northwest Forest Pass:** Yes
**Discover Pass:** No
**Maps:** Green Trails No. 207: Snoqualmie Pass; USGS Chikamin Peak; USDAFS Mount Baker–Snoqualmie National Forest, Alpine Lakes Wilderness
**Trail contacts:** Alpine Lakes Protection Society (ALPS), Okanogan-Wenatchee National Forest, Mount Baker–Snoqualmie National Forest
**Special hazards:** Loose rock; no potable water at trailhead or on trail; no toilet at trailhead

**Finding the trailhead:** From Seattle, take I-90 east to exit 54 (Hyak and Gold Creek). Turn left (north) at the end of the off-ramp. Proceed 0.2 mile, go under the interstate, and pass the on-ramp to I-90 westbound. Turn right (east) onto Gold Creek Road (FR 4832), enter the Gold Creek Critical Wildlife Corridor Research Area, and parallel I-90. In 2 miles the road narrows to one lane. After 2.4 miles the road turns to gravel and at 2.7 makes a switchback, leaving I-90 behind.

The road, with numerous rough spots, climbs steadily to a switchback at 3.7 miles, another switchback at 3.9 miles, and then a fork in the road. Bear left onto FR 4934 (unmarked). The road narrows, switchbacks at 4.3 miles, and at 4.4 miles switchbacks again. Continue straight ahead (northwest) into the Mount Margaret parking area at what looks like an old log-loading platform. The sounds of I-90 can be heard faintly below. GPS: N47 21.799' / W121 21.369'

## The Hike

To find the trailhead, leave the parking lot and turn left (north) onto FR 4934. After 0.2 mile take the formerly gated spur road to the left (east). Begin walking along this old road, now Trail 1332, through a forest of vine maple (*Acer circinatum*), willow (*Salix sp*), red alder (*Alnus rubra*), and maturing Douglas fir and mountain hemlock. Despite opportunities to turn off, stay on the main road until you reach a junction marked by

*Margaret Lake—the slopes above the lake are the huckleberry capital of the central Cascades!*

a fiberglass Forest Service stick-sign announcing a hikers-only trail. Hikers returning to the Margaret Lake Trail will remember from years past a metal sign bolted onto a 4-by-4-inch, 8-foot-tall post proclaiming this trail was closed to motor vehicles, saddle horses, and pack stock. No longer.

Turn north, then east onto a narrow trail and climb above Wolfe Creek through a regenerating clear-cut. Wildflower displays are quite nice through here in early season. There are copious vistas to such familiar sights as I-90, Mount Rainier, Keechelus Lake, and the ski slopes of Snoqualmie Pass as the trail climbs.

Cross an old dirt road and continue up the trail. Nearly 2 miles from the parking area, enter an old-growth forest and begin a series of nicely graded switchbacks. The preceding clear-cut walk is hot, dry, and sunny during summer and a real sweat-inducer. Of course, there is the added value of seeing more wildflowers in logged areas, but the old-growth forest shade is always welcome.

Once you're in the forest and near the top of the ridge, beware of a well-developed volunteer trail in some deadfall. It takes off southward to good views of Mount Rainier, but it is the wrong way to go.

### GREEN TIP:
Take nothing but pictures; leave nothing but footprints.

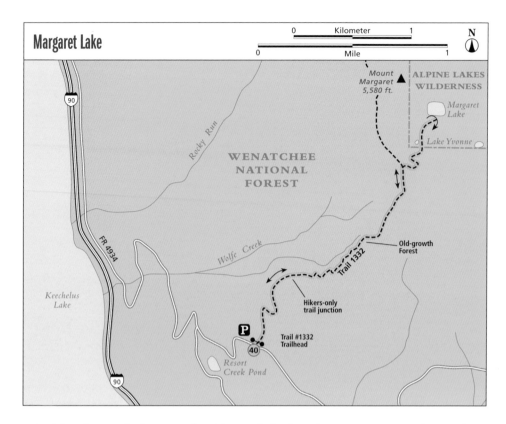

## Margaret Lake

In 2.5 miles reach the top of a ridge and the junction to Margaret Lake on the right (east). Turn right (east) here and drop precipitously on regular and nicely constructed switchbacks for 0.5 mile.

Pass into the Alpine Lakes Wilderness and notice no change except for the end of the switchbacks. After walking 0.1 mile farther, pass by the pond marked on maps as Lake Yvonne. Another 0.2 mile of flat walking reaches a lip overlooking Margaret Lake. Drop down to the lake and turn right (east) at the shore. Quickly reach a poor but heavily impacted campsite on a knoll above the lake and the end of the trail.

Margaret isn't a large lake, but she is certainly bigger than her little sister, Yvonne. On the west side of Margaret Lake is a huge talus field leading up to tree-covered Mount Margaret. Much of the talus is choked with huckleberries, which in autumn provide riotous fall colors.

## Miles and Directions

**0.0**  Trailhead off FR 4934

**0.5**  Junction with hikers-only trail

**1.0**  Cross dirt road

**2.0** Enter old-growth forest

**2.5** Lake Lillian / Margaret Lake Trail junction

**2.9** Alpine Lakes Wilderness boundary

**3.0** Lake Yvonne

**3.5** Margaret Lake

**7.0** Arrive back at trailhead

# South Puget Sound

You might think that an area overrun with highways and roads, urbanization, water diversions and dikes, office parks, farming, factories, and livestock grazing would be bereft of hiking opportunities. Fortunately, this is not the case!

*The rolling meadows and wildflowers of South Puget Sound*

*Shooting star*

South Puget Sound boasts an undisturbed mosaic of shoreline, forests, and grasslands left preserved by a scattering of state parks, DNR lands, and wildlife refugia that offer a wonderful array of hiking possibilities available year-round, no matter what the weather, be it cold and wet or dry and hot. Or anywhere in between! There are opportunities not only for hikers but for birdwatchers, wildflower enthusiasts, bike riders, anglers, whitewater and sea kayakers, or for those who just plain want to hang out and enjoy a family picnic. The following two hikes offer a sampling of everything South Puget Sound has to offer and should encourage you to explore the area further on your own.

# 41 Mima Mounds

One of the most fantastic places in South Puget Sound for springtime walking is the Mima Mounds Natural Area Preserve. Besides being a suitable excursion for all ages, the Mima Mounds have an amazing diversity of wildflowers on view. And, once summer arrives on the scene and the blooms fade away, there is still the geologic mystery of how the Mima Mounds were formed. Does it have something to do with the alternating freezing and thawing of the soil? Or were they formed by meltwater erosion during the last glacial recession? Or does pocket gopher activity have something to do with answering this conundrum? Whatever the cause of this geological bafflement, lightning-induced fires and poor soils derived from a thick mix of glacial sand and gravel have produced the botanical oddity of many treeless prairies south of Olympia. The Mima Mounds prairie is one of the most notable examples. In 1967 the Mima Mounds was designated a National Natural Landmark by the National Park Service. It wasn't until 1976 that Washington State designated this area a 637-acre Natural Area Preserve. The purpose is to protect the mima mound landforms and prairie grasslands and to provide habitat for prairie-dependent birds and butterflies.

**Start:** Trailhead at Mima Mounds Natural Area Preserve
**Distance:** 3.0-mile double lollipop
**Approximate hiking time:** 3 to 4 hours
**Difficulty:** Easy
**Trail surface:** Paved, grass, packed dirt
**Seasons:** Year-round for hiking
**Other trail users:** Parents with strollers
**Canine compatibility:** No dogs allowed
**Land status:** Department of Natural Resources
**Nearest town:** Littlerock
**Services:** Gas and limited groceries in Littlerock; camping, boating, fishing, and swimming available at Millersylvania Memorial State Park (Discover Pass required)

**Northwest Forest Pass:** No
**Discover Pass:** Yes
**Maps:** USGS Rochester
**Trail contact:** Department of Natural Resources
**Special hazards:** Gate into the preserve is locked at dusk. No potable water at trailhead. No horses or bicycles allowed. Two-seat unisex vault toilet at trailhead parking lot. Picnic area close by, accessed by short paved trail from trailhead. Private property within the preserve. Evergreen Sports (Gun) Club on west side of preserve property. Lock your car and leave no valuables behind; car prowls are expected in the area.

**Finding the trailhead:** Take exit 95 from I-5 and turn right (west) onto Highway 121 (Maytown Road) toward Littlerock. Proceed 3 miles, passing the elementary school in Littlerock to a stop sign at 128th Avenue. Bear right (west) onto 128th Avenue SW and in 0.7 mile arrive at a "T" intersection at the top of a hill. Turn right (north) onto Waddell Creek Road SW and drive a further 0.8 mile. At 127th Avenue SW, spot the sign announcing "Mima Mounds Natural Area" and turn left (west) onto a narrow paved road. In 0.3 mile pass a picnic area and small parking lot; in a further 0.1 mile the road ends at the trailhead. GPS: N46 54.313' / W123 02.851'

# The Hike

Begin your walk on the ADA Nature Trail at the west side of the parking lot. Here, you're surrounded by an immature forest of Douglas fir. At the reader board, pick up a copy of the Mima Mounds Nature Trail guide which is usually available. Pass through the fence and instantly leave the forest for the prairie.

The paved ADA Nature Trail quickly reaches a trail junction. Turn right (west), and in 100 feet come to a concrete observation deck / interpretive center. The building is meant to resemble the cut-away of a mima mound. From the top of the deck the entire preserve can be seen. Take time to read the displays covering the human, geological, and biological history of the mounds. Once done, return to the paved trail and turn right (south).

In 0.3 mile there is another observation deck. In 100 feet, at an unsigned junction, the paved ADA Nature Trail curves to the left. Bear right (south) to walk on the grassy South Loop Trail. If you're in the preserve early in the spring the carpet of

*Blue camas forms carpets of wildflowers at the Mima Mounds in early spring.*

## TREE STORIES 3

Big leaf maple (*Acer macrophylla,* or "maple with large leaves") has the largest leaves of any maple—up to 10 inches in width, and sometimes more! It's found near the Pacific Coast, from southern Alaska to southern California, and inland in the foothills of the Sierra Nevada. The fruit is a paired, winged samara resembling a helicopter rotor. The edible flowers are sweet and have been used in salads.

*Big leaf maple seeds have propeller-like wings that let them sail through the air like helicopters.*

Maples are widespread, with about 120 species worldwide. Big leaf maple is a popular street tree in the Pacific Northwest that can grow to heights of 120 feet with a diameter of over 3 feet. When grown by itself, big leaf maple produces a generous, rounded crown.

Red alder (*Alnus rubra,* or "red Alnus"—the old Latin name for the species) is the most common tree species to grow in west Cascade forests immediately after logging, fire, or other disturbance. A member of the birch family, it can grow as tall as 130 feet with diameters up to 30 inches in prime habitat. Normally, though, red alder is found in subprime habitat: poorly drained, oxygen- and nutrient-depleted soils. Fortunately a bacterium (*Frankia* sp.) growing in alder roots takes atmospheric nitrogen, which is inert, and converts it to a usable form, giving the tree a competitive advantage over other associated plants.

Red alder is deciduous and can live to the ripe old age of fifty to eighty years. The male and female flowers are separate, the latter developing into hard woody structures that resemble teeny-tiny toy pinecones. This trait makes them favorite test objects in plant identification classes. The tree is distributed from Alaska to northern California and eastward through the Rocky Mountains.

blue wildflowers you see everywhere are called blue camas (*Camassia quamash*). The plant produces an edible bulb (please don't dig them up!) that was an important food source for local Native Americans.

Weave and wind between the mounds and at 1.1 miles reach the Shortcut Trail, which peels off to the right (west). Continue on South Loop Trail. Pretty soon you'll come to a bench and a large Douglas fir tree. Here's a great spot to get out of the sun (if there is any) and contemplate the prairie. Nearly all of the preserve is being

*Mima Mounds are part of an extensive treeless prairie in South Puget Sound.*

managed to maintain the prairie. This means removing many of the larger trees; you'll see their stumps from time to time during your walk. Trees contribute leaves and branches to the ground, creating a moist layer of humus, which encourages development of a shrub layer, to the detriment of the prairie/grassland plants.

At 2.0 miles reach another bench, this one at the top of a rise. At 2.2 miles, continue straight (east) at the next trail junction, the other side of the Shortcut Trail. The old fence line you see in the near distance is a holdover from when the Mima Mounds were being farmed. In an additional 0.1 mile, turn left (north) and continue on the South Loop Trail.

You're now in familiar territory, inbound on the same section of trail you explored earlier. If you hadn't noticed it before, after 2.5 miles and on your left (west) is a third observation platform, but this one is on private property and not accessible to hikers.

After 2.7 miles the South Loop Trail ends when it runs into the paved ADA Nature Trail. Return the way you came by turning left (northwest), retracing your steps to the observation deck / interpretive center and then the parking area.

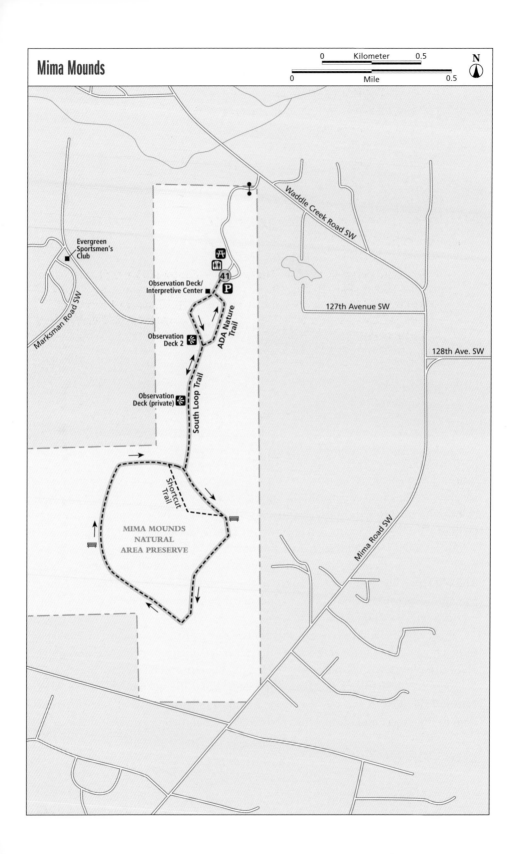

# Mima Mounds

Kilometer
0    0.5

Mile
0    0.5

N

Waddle Creek Road SW

Evergreen
Sportsmen's
Club

Marksman Road SW

Observation Deck/
Interpretive Center

41

P

ADA Nature Trail

Observation
Deck 2

Observation
Deck (private)

South Loop Trail

127th Avenue SW

128th Ave. SW

Shortcut Trail

MIMA MOUNDS
NATURAL
AREA PRESERVE

Mima Road SW

# Miles and Directions

**0.0** Trailhead at Mima Mounds Natural Area Preserve

**0.1** Trail junction toward observation deck / interpretive center

**0.12** Observation deck / interpretive center

**0.14** Return to ADA Nature Trail

**0.4** Observation deck #2

**1.1** Trail junction with the Shortcut Trail

**2.0** Bench

**2.5** Observation deck (private property) on the left (west)

**2.7** South Loop Trail ends at the paved ADA Nature Trail

**3.0** Return to the trailhead and parking lot

**Options:** East from exit 95 off I-5 on Maytown Road is Millersylvania Memorial State Park. Numerous marked trails loop through the 842-acre park. The property was originally homesteaded in 1881 by Johann Mueller, an exiled Austrian army general. The rock-and-log buildings were constructed by the Civilian Conservation Corps during the Great Depression of the 1930s.

# 42 Billy Frank Jr. Nisqually National Wildlife Refuge

The Nisqually River Delta is a special place. Why? Because it's a wetland: an area inundated or saturated by ground- or surface water that supports a unique community of plants and animals specifically adapted to life in waterlogged soil. Wetlands like the Nisqually are incredibly productive ecosystems. They're the best places in the world for birdwatchers but are also incredibly exciting for anybody intrigued by the amazing dynamic between what happens when freshwater meets salt water. The Nisqually River Delta has a long history of human intervention and impact. The wetland is now on the mend and the recovery can be measured and seen in years, not lifetimes. Restoration efforts are ongoing at the Refuge, and this, along with the interest brought about by the change in seasons, guarantees that something fascinating will always being going on there.

**Start:** Parking lot at Norm Dicks Visitor Center
**Distance:** 4.5-mile lollipop
**Approximate hiking time:** 2 to 3 hours
**Difficulty:** Easy
**Trail surface:** Boardwalk, gravel
**Seasons:** Year-round
**Other trail users:** No jogging or bicycles are allowed
**Canine compatibility:** No dogs are allowed
**Land status:** United States Fish and Wildlife Service, National Wildlife Refuge
**Nearest town:** Olympia; gas and food available in Nisqually

**Services:** Gas, food, lodging
**Northwest Forest Pass:** Yes
**Discover Pass:** No
**Division of Fish & Wildlife Pass:** Yes
**National Park Service Entrance Fee:** Yes
**Maps:** USGS 7.5 minute Nisqually
**Trail contact:** Nisqually National Wildlife Refuge
**Special hazards:** Stinging nettle; flush toilets and potable water available at the Visitor Center

**Finding the trailhead:** From I-5 take exit 114 to Nisqually and head north. Turn right (east) on Nisqually Cut-off Road and follow the signs to the Refuge. GPS: N47 04.345'/ W122 42.786'

## The Hike

Before starting your walk, take time to get oriented to the Refuge by touring the Norm Dicks Visitor Center. Afterward, amble east to the ADA-approved Twin Barns Loop Trail. The concrete walkway quickly becomes a sturdy boardwalk under a shady forest of giant trees.

In 0.2 mile come to a trail junction and turn right, toward the Riparian Forest Overlook, which is reached in another 0.1 mile. Then, double back to the Twin Barns Loop Trail and turn right (north), passing alongside a gravel Refuge access

*A perfect place to see birds and bugs!*

road. In 0.3 mile, reach the junction between the Twin Barns Loop and Brown Farm Dike trails. Continue straight for 0.1 mile to the Nisqually River Overlook. The Nisqually people once occupied forty villages along this 78-mile-long river, making their living from fishing for salmon. On the surrounding prairies they harvested blue camas (*Camassia quamash*), various berries, and hunted for deer on the lower slopes of Mount Rainier.

Rejoining the main trail with a right turn (northwest), walk for 0.3 mile, leaving the forest behind, to a junction between the Brown Farm Dike / Twin Barns Loop Trails and continue straight ahead. In 0.6 mile of walking on an old dike through open country, you will come to an observation tower. On one side of the dike you'll see lots of cattail (*Typha latifolia*) in areas where the water doesn't all drain away. On the other side of the dike, when the tide is out, is a lot of mud. That green leafy stuff you see at low tide is a green algae called sea lettuce (*Ulva lactuca*).

The boardwalk of the Nisqually Estuary Trail begins at the observation tower and leads 1.0 mile out into the Nisqually wetlands. There can be lots of waterfowl to see, and that's what the Shannon Slough Blind in 0.3 mile and the McAllister Creek Viewing Platform in 0.1 mile are there for. The last 700 feet of the boardwalk—before it dead-ends at the Puget Sound Viewing Platform—is closed during waterfowl hunting season. Most of the boardwalk follows all that remains of a 5.5-mile earthen

*Historic barn built by Alson Lennon Brown for his farm in the early twentieth century*

▶ Billy Frank Jr. was a Native American of the Nisqually Tribe. Throughout his life Frank was an environmental leader and a tireless advocate for Indian treaty rights. He was also known for his work promoting cooperative natural resources management. In November 2015, Frank was posthumously awarded the Presidential Medal of Freedom by President Barack Obama in a ceremony at the White House.

dike, which Seattle attorney Alson Lennon Brown had built beginning in 1904 using a combination of human labor and a horse-drawn scoop. Brown's dike created a huge amount of very fertile ground that was then developed for farming.

Walk back 1.5 miles to the Brown Farm Dike Trail / Twin Barns Trail junction and turn right (south) onto a wide gravel road. There are picnic tables and ADA–approved chemical toilets here. The two white barns are all that remain from Alson Lennon Brown's farm and dairy. His farm became the Nisqually National Wildlife Refuge in 1974 when the US Fish and Wildlife Service purchased the property. The refuge was renamed for Billy Frank in 2015.

From here there is an optional side trip through the forest to the Twin Barns Observation Platform (0.4-mile round-trip). Otherwise, walk along the road for 0.4 mile and return to the parking lot and visitor center.

# Billy Frank Jr. Nisqually National Wildlife Refuge

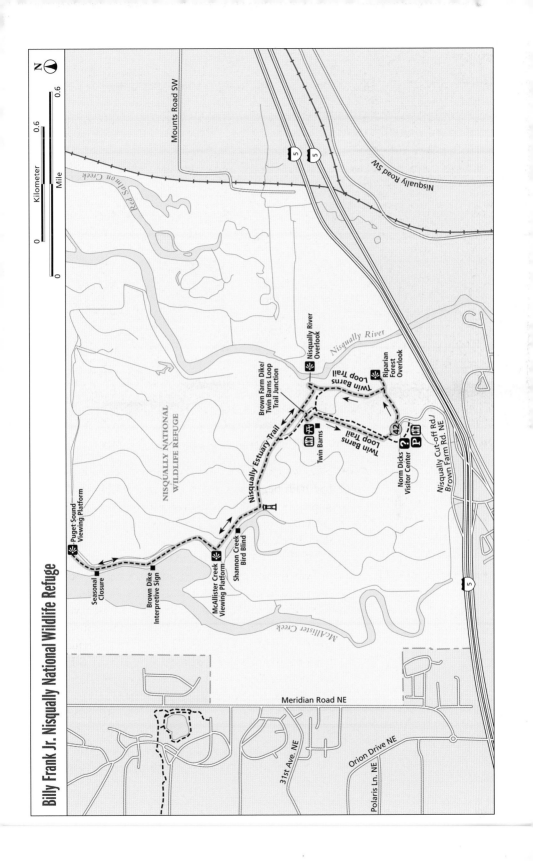

## Miles and Directions

**0.0**  Norm Dicks Visitor Center / parking lot

**0.2**  Trail junction to Riparian Forest Overlook

**0.3**  Riparian Forest Overlook

**0.6**  Twin Barns Trail / Brown Farm Dike Trail junction

**0.7**  Nisqually River Overlook

**1.1**  Brown Farm Dike Trail / Twin Barns Loop Trail junction

**1.6**  Observation Tower and Nisqually Estuary Trail

**1.9**  Shannon Slough Bird Blind

**2.0**  McAllister Creek Viewing Platform

**2.3**  Brown Dike Interpretive Sign

**2.6**  Puget Sound Viewing Platform

**4.1**  Twin Barns Observation Platform

**4.5**  Parking lot / end of trail

## Hike Information

Nisqually National Wildlife Refuge trails are open from sunrise to sunset. The Norm Dicks Visitor Center is open Wednesday through Sunday, 9 a.m. to 4 p.m., and is usually staffed by volunteers. The visitor center has displays educating the public about the Nisqually watershed and the importance of the Pacific Flyway for North American birds. It's well worth the effort to tour the center before beginning your hike. Let them know how much you appreciate their commitment and their work. The Refuge administration offices are open Monday through Friday, 7:30 a.m. to 4:30 p.m.

*"The sole criterion is to walk with the senses, with hands that feel, ears that hear, and eyes that see."*

—Robert Brown, *The Appalachian Trail: History, Humanity, and Ecology*

# Appendix A: Resources and Agency Contact Data

This list includes clubs, hiking forums, access/advocacy groups (including online groups and organizations), and land management agencies charged with administering the public lands covered in this book.

## Alltrails.com

AllTrails helps people explore the outdoors with a large collection of detailed, hand-curated trail maps, as well as trail reviews and photos crowdsourced from a community of ten million registered hikers, mountain bikers, and trail runners. There is a free version as well as a "pro" version, which charges a fee for use.

## Alpine Lakes Protection Society

www.alpinelakes.org
Give thanks to these people for their wilderness advocacy and their excellent 1:100,000 topo map that covers the Alpine Lakes Wilderness and surrounding area. ALPS led the successful campaign to designate the Alpine Lakes Wilderness, now comprising almost 400,000 acres. In more recent years, the ALPS areas of concern have broadened to protect the entire central Cascades.

## American Whitewater

PO Box 1540
Cullowhee, NC 28723
(866) BOAT-4-AW (866-262-8429)
membership@americanwhitewater.org;
www.AmericanWhitewater.org
American Whitewater restores rivers dewatered by hydropower dams, works to eliminate water degradation, improves public land management, and protects public access to rivers for responsible recreational use by boaters, hikers, anglers, and other individuals and groups.

## Billy Frank Jr. Nisqually National Wildlife Refuge

100 Brown Farm Rd.
Olympia, WA 98516
Phone: (360) 753-9467
Fax: (360) 534-9302
nisqually@fws.gov

## City of Everett, Public Works

3200 Cedar St.
Everett WA 98201
(425) 257-8800
everettpw@everettwa.gov

## Darrington Ranger District Office

1405 Emens St.
Darrington, WA 98241
(360) 436-1155

**Darrington Ranger District**
Verlot Public Service Center
33515 Mountain Loop Hwy.
Granite Falls, WA 98252
(360) 691-7791

**Daybreak Star Cultural Center, United Indians of All Tribes Foundation**
**Discovery Park**
5011 Bernie Whitebear Way
Seattle, WA 98199

PO Box 99100
Seattle, WA 98199
(206) 285-442
www.unitedindians.org/daybreak.html

**Discovery Park**
Seattle Department of Parks and Recreation
3801 Discovery Park Blvd.
Seattle, WA 98199
(206) 684-4075

**Hike Metro**
https://sites.google.com/site/seattlemetrobushiking
What? You don't have a car? Then take the bus! Here are some links to walks, hikes, and outdoor adventures in the Seattle area that you can reach by public transit. The best part of all . . . no car needed! Don't forget your ORCA Card (a contactless smart card system for public transit in the Puget Sound region of Washington)!

**Hiking Northwest**
www.kuresman.com
A compilation of thirty-plus years of trip reports from hikes throughout our region by John Kuresman. This guy gets around!

**Iron Goat Trail**
http://irongoattrail.org/
Need to know the history of this historic trail? Then, you've come to the right place.

**Iron Horse State Park**
150 Lake Eastern State Park Rd.
North Bend, WA 98045
(360) 902-8844
https://www.stateparks.com/iron_horse_wa.html

**Issaquah Alps Trails Club**
PO Box 668
Issaquah, WA 98027
(844) 392-4282
contact@issaquahalps.org
www.issaquahalps.org
The club serves as a voice for protection of our open spaces, trails, and quality of life. Their mission is to act as custodian of the trails and the lush, open, tree-covered mountaintops known as the Issaquah Alps.

**King County Parks and Recreation**
201 S. Jackson St.
KSC-NR-0700
Seattle, WA, 98104
(206) 477-4527
https://www.kingcounty.gov/services/parks-recreation/parks/parks-and-natural-lands.aspx

**Meadowdale Beach Park**
6026 156th St. SW
Edmonds, WA 98026
https://snohomishcountywa.gov/
Facilities/Facility/Details/Meadowdale
-Beach-Park-56

**Mid Fork Rocks**
http://www.midforkrocks.com/
Advocacy organization for the Middle
Fork Snoqualmie River

**Milwaukee Road Historical
Association**
PO Box 307
Antioch, IL 60002-0307
office@mrha.com
www.mrha.com

**The Mountaineers, Everett Branch**
https://www.mountaineers.org/
locations-lodges/everett-branch/about
The Pacific Northwest's largest recreation and conservation organization.

**The Mountaineers, Seattle Branch**
7700 Sand Point Way NE
Seattle, WA 98115
(206) 521-6000
info@mountaineers.org
www.mountaineers.org

**Mountains to Sound Greenway
Trust**
2701 First Ave., Ste. 240
Seattle, WA 98121
(206) 382-5565
info@mtsgreenway.org
www.mtsgreenway.org
This group is trying to reverse the trend
along I-90 to become the province of
strip malls, billboards, and spreading
urban development. They're working to
keep an accessible landscape of forests
and open spaces as outdoor recreation
for people and habitat for wildlife.

**Mount Baker–Snoqualmie National
Forest**
2930 Wetmore Ave., Ste. 3A
Everett, WA 98201
(425) 783-6000
(800) 627-0062

**Mount Si**
www.mountsi.com
Photos, maps, and everything you would
ever want to know about Mount Si.

**Northwest Hikers**
www.nwhikers.net
An online forum to talk about hiking,
hiker issues, places to hike, to buy or sell
gear, or find a hiking companion.

**Okanogan-Wenatchee National
Forest**
Cle Elum Ranger District
803 W. Second St.
Cle Elum, WA 98922
(509) 852-1100

## GREEN TIP:
Please be courteous to others. Many people visit the outdoors for peace, quiet, and solitude. Please avoid making loud noises and intruding on others' privacy. Keep your pets under control, your phone on "silent," and avoid playing loud music through your earphones.

**Olallie State Park**
51350 SE Homestead Valley Rd.
North Bend, WA 98045
(360) 902-8844
www.parks.wa.gov

**O. O. Denny Park**
City of Kirkland Parks and Recreation
12032 Holmes Point Dr. NE
Kirkland, WA 98034
(425) 587-3300
eparks@kirklandwa.gov

**Port of Seattle**
PO Box 1209
Seattle, WA 98111
(206) 728-3000
www.portseattle.org

**Seattle Audubon Society**
8050 35th Ave. NE
Seattle, WA 98115
(206) 523-4483
info@seattleaudubon.org
www.seattleaudubon.org

**Seattle City Light**
700 Fifth Ave., Ste. 3200
PO Box 34023
Seattle, WA 98124-4023
(206) 684-3000
www.seattle.gov/light

**Seattle Department of Parks and Recreation**
100 Dexter Ave. N
Seattle, WA 98109
(206) 684-4075
www.seattle.gov/parks

**Seattle Public Utilities**
Cedar River Watershed
19901 Cedar Falls Rd. SE
North Bend, WA 98045
(206) 733-9421 or (425) 831-6780
CRWPrograms@seattle.gov
http://www.seattle.gov/utilities/environment-and-conservation/our-watersheds/cedar-river-watershed/education-center

**Sierra Club, Cascade Chapter**
180 Nickerson St., Ste. 202
Seattle, WA 98109
(206) 378-0114
info@washington.sierraclub.org
https://www.sierraclub.org/washington
Environmental activists, club outings, and more.

**Skykomish Ranger District Office**
74920 NE Stevens Pass Hwy.
PO Box 305
Skykomish, WA 98288
(360) 677-2414

**Snohomish County Parks Department**
6705 Puget Park Dr.
Snohomish, WA 98296
(425) 388-6600
https://snohomishcountywa.gov/1074/
Parks

**Snoqualmie Ranger District**
North Bend Office
902 SE North Bend Way, Bldg 1
North Bend, WA 98045
(425) 888-1421

**Spring Family Trust**
5015 88th Ave. SE
Mercer Island, WA 98040
(206) 718-4441
johnespring@gmail.com
www.springtrailtrust.com
A charitable trust dedicated to enhancing hiking opportunities in Washington State with grants for trail building and maintenance projects.

**Wallace Falls State Park**
14503 Wallace Lake Rd.
Gold Bar, WA 98251
(360) 793-0420

**Washington Department of Natural Resources**
Main Office
PO Box 47000
1111 Washington St. SE
Olympia, WA 98504-7000
(360) 902-1000
www.dnr.wa.gov

**Washington Department of Natural Resources**
South Puget Sound District
950 Farman St. N
PO Box 68
Enumclaw, WA 98022-6381
(360) 825-1631
southpuget.region@dnr.wa.gov

**Washington Native Plant Society**
6310 NE 74th St., Ste. 215E
Seattle, WA 98115
(206) 527-3210
Info@wnps.org
www.wnps.org
Conservation and preservation of Washington's native flora is combined with education by exposing plant lovers to trails and unique habitats. They also conduct field trips to areas of special botanical interest.

**Washington State Patrol Fire Training Academy**
50810 SE Grouse Ridge Rd.
PO Box 1273
North Bend, WA 98045
(425) 453-3000
FireTrainingAcademy@wsp.wa.gov
https://www.wsp.wa.gov/
fire-training-academy/

**Washington Trails Association**
705 2nd Ave., Ste. 300
Seattle, WA 98104
(206) 625-1367
www.wta.org
WTA protects hiking trails and wildlands, takes thousands of volunteers out to maintain trails, and promotes hiking as a healthy, fun way to explore Washington.

**Washington Water Trails Association**
4649 Sunnyside Ave. N, #305
Seattle, WA 98103;
(206) 545-9161
www.wwta.org
wwta@wwta.org
WWTA advocates for the right of public access to and from waterways. They also steward those waterways, salt- and freshwater, and adjoining shore lands.

**Western Slope No Fee Coalition**
PO Box 135
Durango, CO 81302
(970) 259-4616
http://westernslopenofee.org
A principal voice of the many Americans who believe in public ownership and public funding of public lands, Western Slope No Fee Coalition welcomes support from people of all recreational pursuits and political persuasions.

**Wilderness Society**
Pacific Northwest Office
2003 Western Ave., Ste. 660
Seattle, WA 98121
(206) 624-6430
www.wilderness.org
Their name says it all.

*"Climb the mountains and get their good tidings. Nature's peace will flow into you as sunshine flows into trees. The winds will blow their own freshness into you, and the storms their energy, while cares will drop off like autumn leaves."*
—John Muir

# Appendix B: Further Reading

## Field Guides

Alden, Peter, and Dennis Paulson. 1998. *National Audubon Society Field Guide to the Pacific Northwest*. Knopf.

Mathews, Daniel. 1999. *Cascade-Olympic Natural History*. Raven Editions.

Peterson, Roger Tory. 1998. *A Field Guide to Western Birds*. Houghton Mifflin.

Pojar, Jim. 2004. *Plants of the Pacific Northwest Coast: Washington, Oregon, British Columbia, and Alaska*. Lone Pine Publishing.

Whitney, Stephen, and Rob Sandelin. 2004. *Field Guide to the Cascades and Olympics*. Mountaineers Books.

## Hiking Guides

Dreisbach, Bob. 2000. *Seattle Outdoors*. Entropy Conservationists.

Romano, Craig, and Alan Bauer. 2013. *Day Hiking Central Cascades*. Mountaineers Books.

Smoot, Jeff. 2003. *Hiking Washington's Alpine Lakes Wilderness*. Falcon Guides.

Stekel, Peter. 2016. *Best Wildflower Hikes Western Washington*. Falcon Guides.

Sykes, Karen. 2002. *Hidden Hikes in Western Washington*. Mountaineers Books.

Williams, David B. 2017. *Seattle Walks*. University of Washington Press.

Zilly, John. 2003. *Beyond Mount Si*. Adventure Press.

## History

Ferguson, Robert L. 1996. *Pioneers of Lake View: A Guide to Seattle's Early Settlers and Their Cemetery*. Thistle Press.

Seidel, William. 2003. *Sons of the Profits*. Nettle Creek Publishing.

Williams, David B. 2015. *Too High and Too Steep: Reshaping Seattle's Topography*. University of Washington Press.

## Natural History

Kozloff, Eugene N. 1978. *Plants and Animals of the Pacific Northwest: An Illustrated Guide to the Natural History of Western Oregon, Washington, and British Columbia*. University of Washington Press.

Kruckeberg, Arthur R. 1995. *The Natural History of Puget Sound Country*. University of Washington Press.

Renner, Jeff. 2005. *Mountain Weather: Backcountry Forecasting and Weather Safety for Hikers, Campers, Climbers, Skiers, and Snowboarders*. Mountaineers Books.

———. 1993. *Northwest Marine Weather*. Mountaineers Books.

> *"If this isn't nice, I don't know what is!"*
>
> —Kurt Vonnegut

# Hike Index

# About the Author

Peter Stekel is a professional writer and avid hiker. He is the author of *Best Wildflower Hikes Western Washington, Beneath Haunted Waters: The Tragic Tale of Two B-24s Lost in the Sierra Nevada Mountains During World War II,* and *Final Flight: The Mystery of a WWII Plane Crash and the Frozen Airmen in the High Sierra.* Peter has a BA in botany from the University of California, Davis, did graduate work in ecology at Humboldt State University, and contributed to the Idaho Wildflowers app. Visit him at www.peterstekel .com.

*Photo by Jennie Goldberg*

# THE TEN ESSENTIALS OF HIKING

**American Hiking Society**

American Hiking Society recommends you pack the "Ten Essentials" every time you head out for a hike. Whether you plan to be gone for a couple of hours or several months, make sure to pack these items. Become familiar with these items and know how to use them. Learn more at **AmericanHiking.org/hiking-resources**

 **1. Appropriate Footwear**

 **6. Safety Items** (light, fire, and a whistle)

 **2. Navigation**

 **7. First Aid Kit**

 **3. Water** (and a way to purify it)

 **8. Knife or Multi-Tool**

 **4. Food**

 **9. Sun Protection**

 **5. Rain Gear & Dry-Fast Layers**

 **10. Shelter**